SHOWING THE FLAG

SHOWING THE FLAG

**The Mounted Police
and Canadian Sovereignty
in the North,
1894 – 1925**

WILLIAM R. MORRISON

University of British Columbia Press
Vancouver, 1985

Showing the Flag: The Mounted Police and Canadian Sovereignty in the North, 1894–1925
© The University of British Columbia Press 1985

This book has been published with the help of a grant from the Canada Council.

All photographs included in this book are from the Public Archives of Canada.

Canadian Cataloguing in Publication Data

Morrison, William R. (William Robert), 1942–
    Showing the flag

Includes index.
Bibliography: p. 209
ISBN 0–7748–0245–6

1. Royal Canadian Mounted Police – History.   2. Canada,
Northern – History.   3. Canada – Politics and government
– 1896–1911.*   4. Canada – Politics and government,
1911–1921.*   5. Northwest, Canadian – History – 1870–
1905.*   I. Title.
FC3216.2.M67 1985   363.2'09719   C85–091556–2
HV8157.M67 1985

International Standard Book Number 0–7748–0245–6

Printed and bound in Canada by John Deyell Company

*To Elizabeth, Linda, Catherine,
John, Claire, and Ruth Morrison*

Contents

Illustrations

following page 108

Maps

Acknowledgements

My first thanks are due to Morris Zaslow, who kindled my interest in northern Canada at the University of Western Ontario nearly twenty years ago. Jane Fredeman of the University of British Columbia Press encouraged me with this book and performed surgery on my prose style. My colleague, Ken Coates, read the manuscript and made many useful suggestions for expanding it. My wife and children put up with me while I was writing it. The Brandon University Research Committee and Peter Hordern, Dean of Arts, provided logistical support. Jim Darlington and Ross McLachlan of Brandon University's Cartographic Laboratory drew the maps. The Historical Section at R.C.M.P. Headquarters in Ottawa generously responded to inquiries and requests for photographs. My thanks to all these people.

William R. Morrison,
Department of History,
Brandon University.

Introduction

As RECENTLY AS Canada's centennial year there was virtually nothing in print on Canada's north except narrative histories, of which Pierre Berton's *Klondike Fever* is a worthy example, and dozens of popular articles and books about "colourful" characters. Even now, most accounts published are stories of northern explorers, gold seekers, and frontiersmen issued to satisfy an apparently endless demand for thrilling tales from the high latitudes.[1] Certainly this approach to history attracts a wide audience, but it has left major questions of national and northern concern unanswered.

In the past fifteen years, however, a sizeable number of analytical studies of northern subjects have appeared. The first general history based on archival sources was Morris Zaslow's *The Opening of the Canadian North, 1870–1914*. This volume and his subsequent *Reading the Rocks: The Story of the Geological Survey of Canada* emphasize the "opening" of the north by agents of southern expansionism—the explorers, missionaries, police, civil servants, and traders who acted as harbingers of a new southern way of life. Also in this genre is Richard Diubaldo's *Stefansson and the Canadian Arctic* as is, in many ways, this volume as well.

There are also many modern works on specific northern subjects, particularly in the field of Native history. Here narrative has been replaced by analysis, and old beliefs, such as the idea that Native people were the helpless victims of fur traders, have been challenged.[2] Nonetheless, new methodologies and interpretive approaches are still almost in their infancy in the study of the north.

What is true of the historiography of the north in general is true of the police in particular, especially in regard to their northern service. After generations of narrative accounts, there has been a recent surge of historical inquiry. The pioneer in this field is R. C. Macleod, whose study of the police on the southern plains, *The N.W.M.P. and Law Enforcement, 1873–1905*, emphasizes for the first time in a work on the police their role in the metropolitan policy of the central government; it also poses important questions about the nature of authority and justice in a frontier society.

In their northern service, the police were agents of metropolitanism *par excellence*,[3] but since Ottawa had only a vague idea of what to do with the north, the police felt free to suggest what policy towards Natives, traders, wildlife, and other matters should be. Police reports regularly urged the federal government to take action of one sort or another on these matters, and sometimes the advice was adopted. In their early concern for the preservation of the musk-ox, for example, the police helped to initiate government policy, and in this sense they may be said to have shaped the history of the north.

Any study of the Mounted Police must necessarily deal with basic questions concerning law and authority, and it is gratifying to note that scholars are turning their attention to these subjects. Of particular value—because it deals explicitly with northwestern Canada—is the work of sociologist Thomas Stone, who has examined the functioning of systems of informal and legally constituted law. His assessment of the interdynamics of group organization among the miners of the Yukon and the whalers of the eastern Arctic poses the kind of analytical questions about sovereignty and law which must be asked if the role of the police is to be properly understood.[4] In "The Mounties as Vigilantes," he suggests that miners were defending the social order in the Yukon and that the Mounted Police attempted to replace it with new values of their own— the conclusion is debatable, but it helps formulate a new approach to the history of the police.

Another seminal study of the attempts of Euro-Canadian authority to impose its social and cultural standards on a Native population is Robin Fisher's *Contact and Conflict: Indian-European Relations in British Columbia, 1774–1890* (Vancouver, 1977). Fisher does not deal with the Mounted Police, but his analysis of "directed and non-directed cultural change" in British Columbia provides a marked contrast to the pattern of Native-white relations in the Yukon and Northwest Territories. In British Columbia the advance of settlement reduced the Native people to a peripheral and threatened position and led to the dominance of settler-oriented government policies which showed little concern for Native welfare, depending heavily on coercion to compel the Native peoples' acquiescence to British and Canadian law. In the north, white prejudices and the demands of southern authority were not present to the same extent because its continuing marginality convinced the federal government that there was no need to adopt harsh policies towards northern Natives.

In their relations with the Native people, the police displayed an attitude of Social Darwinism typical of their era. The police had a marked effect on the Native way of life, and, what is less well known, the Natives, especially the Inuit, made a deep impression on the police as well. They respected the Inuit because they were "successful" and self-reliant, and they denigrated the Indians because they seemed not to be. Few Canadians for many years thereafter were so free of ethnocentrism that they would have granted the Native people equality, either in theory or in fact; thus, the police held no more than the current public and official view.

Even the mythology of the police has come under analytical scrutiny. In his *Visions of Order,* Keith Walden examines the "century of popular image" through an analysis of an immense amount of writing about the police in every form from Ph.D. theses to comic books and concludes that the "mythic presence" of the Mounted Policeman, largely an innovation of popular culture, has for over a century "helped to resolve some of the puzzling and terrifying contradictions of modern life . . . [showing that] stability did not necessarily embody tyranny; law could be compatible with justice; and duty to society could be reconciled with personal desire."[5] Again, these are very modern concepts, which the older generation of police chroniclers would likely have found incomprehensible.

Most of the area to be studied here is in the Arctic and sub-Arctic regions of the country. A more precise definition would be those northern regions penetrated for the first time by the police during the three decades after 1894. This includes areas as far apart as York Factory, the mouth of the Coppermine River, Ellesmere Island, and parts of northwestern British Columbia. The years 1894 to 1925 cover the period between the first involvement of the police in the Yukon and the approximate date when they had demonstrated Canadian sovereignty over the entire inhabited north and much of the uninhabited territory as well. This, then, is a study of how, why, where, and to what extent the Mounted Police contributed to the history and development of Canada's northern frontier. As they had earlier done in the prairies and woodlands of western Canada, the police in some ways shaped the north, chiefly in directions prescribed by Ottawa. It may well be asked why Ottawa felt it was necessary to send the police rather than civil servants to the north, since except in the Yukon, there was never much actual police

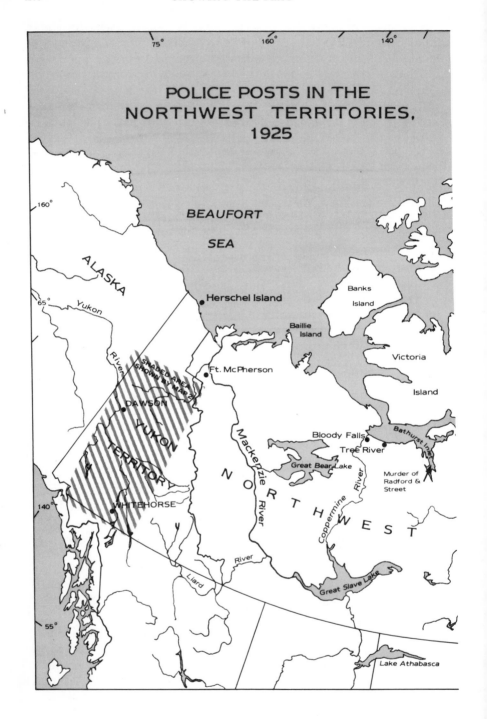

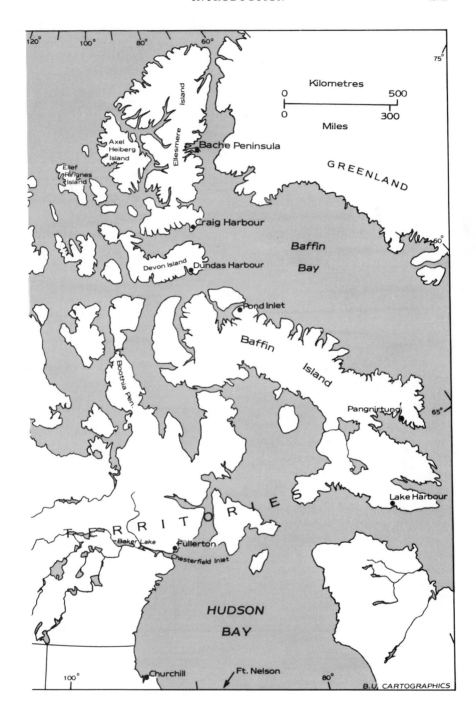

work to be done. The answer is partly that the police had proven their worth on the prairies, where a para-military force had certainly been necessary. In the north, a similar military presence was largely superfluous, but there was no equally efficient alternative.

The police were, therefore, the medium through which the central government—first by neglect, and then by design—changed the history of the Canadian north. The police, in turn, were shaped by the northern frontier, adapting their methods and their institutions to northern circumstances. Their image in the eyes of the rest of the world was largely made in the north. The police did not "develop" the northern frontier; this was done largely by missionaries, miners, and traders, who preceded them or who were their contemporaries. The police were essentially overseers of much of this development.

The work of the police in the Canadian north between 1894 and 1925 was thus crucial in its history, for the police were the main factor in bringing it into the orbit of government control. A study of the work of the police in the area reveals much of significance about the force and the effect the north had on it, about Canadian attitudes towards the north—especially official ones—and about northern development in general.

During the years at the turn of the twentieth century, the Canadian government took notice of the north almost for the first time and finally took positive action both to establish its authority and to bring to this vast region the mixed blessings of government services and control. Thus, for example, the Yukon was transformed in six years from an unsettled country into a Territory with an urban centre, laws, a post office, a telegraph system, and the other varied paraphernalia of early twentieth-century civilization. The Mounted Police brought much of this to the north, and what they did not actually control, they kept a very close watch over. So closely involved were the police with the Yukon that studying the history of the Territory without including them would give almost as distorted a picture as studying it without the miners.

In the western Arctic and Hudson Bay regions, the work of the police, though perhaps not as critical, was nonetheless highly important. The arrival of the police in these two regions in 1903 marked a turning point—the era, in our day well advanced, in which they were to become increasingly tied to Ottawa. It was the beginning of the end of the unregulated north, in which the Natives and whites alike had done much as they pleased, and the start of the contemporary era of government control. The police, the chief agents of the central government, were largely responsible for carrying out this transformation. In this far north, the Arctic coast, and the islands, this is even more true.[6]

Without the Mounted Police, the history of Canada's north would have been much different. Historical "ifs" are always hard to evaluate, but it can certainly be shown that the appearance of the police marked the establishment of effective Canadian control. One of the many services which the police performed in the Yukon, for example, was to demonstrate beyond any doubt that the goldfields would be peaceful and under the unquestioned authority of the central government. Had the police not been present, the Yukon might have sunk into semi-anarchy in the style of California fifty years earlier. It is also possible that Canada's actual title to the region might have come into serious question.

Farther to the north and east the threat to Canadian sovereignty was less acute, and the role of the police tended to be more symbolic. Had the police not penetrated the western Arctic and Hudson Bay just after the turn of the century, the result would likely have been a continuation of the power vacuum which existed there. In the high Arctic, however, an area which the police reached after 1920, Canadian sovereignty was actually in doubt, especially in the area of the Sverdrup Islands and Ellesmere Island. The presence of the police in this region, given Canada's questionable claims to it, was of the highest importance.

The police changed the north from a largely unregulated society to one which operated, in theory and increasingly in fact, under much the same rules and terms as the rest of the country. This change was effected both by enforcement of the laws and by the performance of a wide variety of other public services. This book will show to what extent the police were the agents of conscious government policy, what determined this policy, and how the police interpreted it in the performance of their duties.

1. The Mounted Police

UNDER THEIR VARIOUS NAMES,[1] the Mounted Police have played a vital and often controversial role in Canadian history, and nowhere has this been more true than in the Canadianization of this country's northern frontier. But this is more than just the history of a remarkable body of men. It is about differing concepts of authority and the role of government in new country. As such, it is an excellent example of the process of metropolitanism at work in Canada.

The story told here is not about the north from the inside, but rather an examination of the process by which the Canadian government, in roughly the first quarter of this century, sought to assert its sovereign rights over the Yukon and the Northwest Territories. The "frontier" moved steadily, separating territory in which the authority of government was actual from that in which it was only nominal—in short, it was a frontier of sovereignty.

Canada has historically had two kinds of sovereignty—"symbolic" and "developmental."[2] Symbolic sovereignty consists of actions taken to fulfil the formal requirements of sovereignty under international law. The most important of these is occupation, but they include various demonstrations designed to show, partly to the inhabitants of the territory, but particularly to the rest of the world, that the state is sovereign there. Sometimes these actions are of a practical nature: carrying the Yukon mail during the gold rush is a good example, since the administration of a postal service is an internationally accepted proof of sovereignty.[3] Sometimes they were entirely symbolic, such as the establishment of a post office at the Bache Peninsula Detachment on Ellesmere Island in

1926 when there were no Canadian citizens within hundreds of miles in any direction.

Developmental sovereignty, on the other hand, occurs when the government acts on a specific policy for a territory under its control. The Dominion Lands Survey and the treaty and reserve system of the southern prairies are early examples and go far beyond symbols. At times, as in the western Arctic, symbolic sovereignty takes place decades before developmental sovereignty; at others, as in the Yukon, the two occur almost simultaneously. In Canada the most prominent agents of both forms have been the Mounted Police. On the southern prairies, the N.W.M.P. made the symbolic "long march" across the west and then performed many of the developmental tasks of keeping the Indians on their reserves and enforcing the laws of social control which opened the land to settlement.[4] In the north the Mounted Police performed the acts of symbolic sovereignty: patrolling, confronting miners and Native people, and planting flags. Later they established developmental sovereignty—by explaining and enforcing laws, mining codes drawn up in Ottawa, customs regulations, gambling and liquor laws; and later still they were the first agents of the modern welfare system.

The role of the police will be familiar to any student of the British colonial system. The Mounted Police were, in a certain sense, the Canadian equivalent of those forces of imperialism—the British Army, the Royal Irish Constabulary, and the various colonial police forces—which brought British law and civil administration to the wild corners of the Empire. The difference in the Canadian case was that the colonial power was in Ottawa rather than in London. As agents of this central power, the police imposed on the Canadian north a system largely alien to it, a system which originated elsewhere, in a different culture, and which was designed not to express the aspirations of the north, but to regulate and control it.

Like the Royal Irish Constabulary, to which the Mounted Police were often compared, the N.W.M.P. was primarily an agent of external control, not a domestic "police force" in the ordinary sense. The Canadian government wanted to make the northern frontier become and remain "Canadian" so that Ottawa's absolute sovereignty would be unquestioned. It was frequently obvious that the federal government had little idea what to do with the north or what it might be good for; but the government was determined that, useful or not, the north should belong to no one else. Exercising police powers demonstrated that the police were agents of control, but this function was subordinate to the exercise of sovereignty. In other words, the Canadian government sent the police to bring law to the Inuit not out of a concern for their welfare or a desire to regularize their society, but rather to demonstrate that these people and their land belonged to Canada. This political nature of the force was thus of the highest importance.

Some features of the organization of the Mounted Police were of particular importance to their work on the northern frontier. The word most often used by early writers to describe the original North-West Mounted Police, established in 1873, was semi-military,[5] which suggests that the force was not designed to be an ordinary body of police. But while the N.W.M.P. developed into a unique force because of its size, functions, and organization, at its inception there existed models for it. The Royal Irish Constabulary was just as military if not more so.[6] Furthermore, the most distinguishing feature of the force was not its semi-military nature, which was really expressed in non-essentials. The N.W.M.P. was full of ex-military men, and at first it used military titles for its ranks—major, colonel, and so forth—although this system was superseded within a few years by the present nomenclature. Moreover, members of the force, like soldiers, were in theory and often in practice on duty twenty-four hours a day. It is also true that the N.W.M.P. was originally provided with field artillery, although it was not used in the north, and the police did have a Maxim gun on the Chilkoot Pass. But the quality which most distinguished the force from ordinary police—versatility—also distinguished it from the army. The whole raison d'etre of the Mounted Police was that they should be able to turn their hands to whatever tasks, however prosaic or bizarre, that the government should lay before them. Their ability to do so made them quite different from the ordinary soldier.

A better adjective for explaining the role of the police in the development of the Canadian north is "semi-political."[7] They were political in two ways. Their daily operations were influenced to a limited extent by political considerations. It was, for instance, true, as the public generally believed, that commissioned officers often owed their commissions to their political allegiance. The Canadian civil service was strongly influenced by politics at the turn of the century, and this was as true of the police as of any government agency. Hardly any application for a commission in the force before 1900 was without its letters of recommendation from judges, cabinet ministers, and other political heavyweights. Political influence was used, even by ordinary constables, to obtain favours which might have otherwise not been forthcoming, and this practice was a source of annoyance to police officials, who could not always control it. "Under strict rules of discipline," the comptroller complained, "men can be brought to time [i.e. to imprisonment] for going outside the proper channels, but as you know, we cannot enforce these regulations when a member of Parliament or a Senator or a prominent supporter of the government writes to the Minister. Their representations must be recognized."[8] The police were not political hacks, nor did they use their positions for political ends, but many of them were staunch Conservatives or Liberals and, more to the point, were known as such and were appointed partly for this reason.[9]

Supplying the police was part of the normal sphere of government patronage. The government deliberately injected a political note into daily operations of the police by requiring the force to buy its supplies only from merchants and wholesalers who were government-approved, that is, who supported it politically. Thus, for instance, in the later stages of the gold rush, funerals of indigents in Dawson had to be conducted by a strongly Liberal firm with the suggestive name of Brimston and Stewart.[10] Nor was there any furtiveness about the distribution of patronage. Lists of "friendly" local merchants were distributed to most detachments. The one for Winnipeg in 1901 covered everything from auctioneers to windmill outfitters.[11] Clifford Sifton, a master practitioner of the art of patronage, could write with no apparent hesitation to Sir Wilfrid Laurier that "the only house in Canada dealing in such goods [saddlery] whose members are friendly to the administration ... is ... Adams Bros. . . . and I should be glad if the patronage of the North West Mounted Police were given to them." That loyal firm's chief competitor was described by Sifton as "the most uncompromising and violent opponent of the Government, and perhaps the most offensive to our Liberal friends of any Conservative in the city of Winnipeg."[12]

As well, the Mounted Police, like any other branch of the civil service, tended to be drawn into political brawls more or less as innocent bystanders. The so-called "Yukon scandals" of the turn of the century were a case in point. The Conservative opposition, attempting to prove that the government was administering the Yukon in a corrupt and partisan manner, subjected the police to a fair amount of peripheral criticism, especially because the chief target of the attack, the former commissioner of the Yukon, a strong Liberal, was an ex-officer of the force.

These political considerations, however, did not loom large in the north. What really mattered was the second, larger political role of the police as the agents of government policy in regard to the unsettled parts of the Dominion. From the inception of the force throughout the entire period covered by this study, this aspect of police duty was paramount. Initially, the police served as one of the foundations of Sir John A. Macdonald's "National Policy." Macdonald desired the peaceful assimilation of the west, and the N.W.M.P. was formed to ensure that once the Wolseley expedition and the Manitoba Field Force had established

Canadian sovereignty over the prairies, there would be no further disturbances or opposition to the Canadian presence, especially from the Native people. Many books suggest that the force was formed to protect the Indians from the abuses of American whiskey-traders, noting the Cypress Hills massacre and similar incidents as the factors which impelled the government to send the Mounted Police west. Yet the truth may lie in a slightly different emphasis. One historian of the police, commenting on the Cypress Hills massacre, says, "What mattered profoundly was that at least thirty Indians . . . had been murdered on Canadian soil, with the Canadian government powerless to prevent the massacre or avenge it."[13] What alarmed Ottawa was not the death of the Indians but the demonstration of the impotence of dominion government as far as its authority over the new territories was concerned. The first care of the government was to keep the west secure and to protect white settlers; its main concern for the Indians was that they should cause no trouble.[14]

Thus, the Mounted Police were from the first agents of the high policy of the Canadian government. How real the danger to the west from the United States was is a matter for historical conjecture. In his history of the period, P. B. Waite describes American influence on the western prairies as "both innocent and sinister"; innocent because it was unconscious, and sinister because it was "the same process by which the United States had acquired both Texas and Oregon."[15] The Mounted Police were expected to curb this influence by, for instance, discouraging any "wild west" tendencies which might manifest themselves. It was this political role that was the really important distinction between the N.W.M.P. and many other police forces (in the United States, for example, the same role was played by the regular army). After 1890, the Mounted Police were chosen once more for the job of establishing Canadian control, first over the Yukon goldfields and, later, over Hudson Bay and much of the Arctic.

The work of the Mounted Police on the northern frontier was extraordinarily diverse. The means by which the police established or solidified government control—depending on the area and time under consideration—lay mainly in the performance of a variety of services. The police did do some flag-planting on remote islands and on the Yukon passes, but this was only a small part of their importance to the establishment of government authority.

Not much attempt has been made here to analyse the human aspect of the Mounted Police except where generalizations can be made about attitudes common to the police as a whole. The approach taken by the police to the problems of the Indians and Inuit on the northern frontier seems, for instance, to have been governed by a discernible *zeitgeist*, and their opinion of Americans, though it did not have the opportunity to manifest itself everywhere in the north, was similarly quite uniform.

Does this mean that the police can be characterized as a homogeneous body of men with similar social and political attitudes? The answer is both yes and no. On some questions, such as the two just mentioned, there was considerable unanimity, especially among the officers, who inevitably contributed the most to the written record. These men mostly belonged to the Anglo-Saxon elite of eastern Canada (the French-Canadians among them seemed to have held the same opinions) and thus had many attitudes in common. Men educated at the Royal Military College in Kingston or who had served in the militia or in one or both of the Riel rebellions, as so many of the officers had, were bound to have similar views on many things. Knowing the feelings of the Canadian late Victorian and Edwardian middle classes about American frontier democracy, it is possible to predict what the officers of the Mounted Police would think of Skagway and the American population of Dawson—and the prediction is borne out by the evidence. The reactions of the same officers to the presence of the French tricolour at the Mackenzie River missions is just as imaginable.

But generalizations are more dangerous in the purely philosophical realm, especially in considering the non-commissioned ranks. R. C. Macleod has drawn up a table indicating the former occupation of recruits taken into the force between the years 1873 and 1902. The four largest groups are as follows: skilled workers, 29 per cent, farmers, 27 per cent, clerks, 15.6 per cent, police or military, 10 per cent.[16] From these figures, he makes the following deduction about the character of the force:

[M]ost recruits came from occupations that were rising in the scale of social and economic importance in late Victorian times. If the nineteenth century was the great age of the middle class, the twentieth century was to be the age of the lower middle class. In the period under consideration the lower middle class was expanding to include the two groups from which a majority of the police were drawn. These were clerks and skilled workers.... The growing social and economic importance of these groups and the increased self-confidence that accompanied this growth were reflected in such developments as the extension of the franchise and the rise of the trade union movement. Much of the success of the Mounted Police and their reputation for energetic and impartial law enforcement stemmed from the awareness, subconscious perhaps, that they represented the direction in which society was moving.[17]

This seems highly speculative. Certainly, the police thought of themselves as an elite—their clashes with minor civil servants in the Yukon showed their distaste for menial or subordinate tasks. But to deduce that the police were subconsciously aware that they represented the direction in which society was moving would be difficult to support, and more prosaic conclusions are reached here.

The internal structure of the Mounted Police in this period also reflected its semi-political nature. From 1882 until 1920 the headquarters of the force was at Regina. This meant that all recruit training was done there, the commissioner was located there, and from Regina came all directives on the internal operations of the force. However, a close liaison with the government was also needed. This service was provided by the comptroller, whose offices were in Ottawa. As his title suggests, the comptroller, who was a civilian rather than a uniformed member of the force, was originally concerned with financial matters, government appropriations, and the like. However, the comptroller rapidly rose in importance, and the first holder of the position was by 1883 a deputy minister, virtually responsible for the whole force.[18] As a civilian, the comptroller was outside the police hierarchy, but he was the voice of the government to the police, and vice versa. Because all reports to the government and directives from it were sent through his office, his importance soon far exceeded his nominal position.[19]

The internal organization of the police fluctuated somewhat with changing requirements for service, but a basic pattern was maintained throughout. The largest unit of organization in the force was the division, commanded by a superintendent. In 1899 there were ten divisions, eight in the Northwest Territories[20] and two in the Yukon. Each division comprised a number of detachments, commonly about a dozen, which were sometimes grouped into sub-districts. If the detachment was in a large town, it might have twenty or thirty men and be commanded by an inspector; on the other hand, there were many detachments in small places manned by one constable or a constable and a corporal. The force also had a number of surgeons and veterinary surgeons; in 1899 there were six of the former and two of the latter. The police also hired numbers of supernumerary or "special" constables for specific duties such as driving sleds, packing, hunting for meat, and so forth; Native employees fell under this heading.

A noteworthy feature of the Mounted Police was the durability of the men who held its important offices. Only three commissioners ruled the force over a period of forty-five years: Lawrence W. Herchmer, from 1886 to 1900, A. Bowen Perry, from 1900 to 1922, and Cortlandt Starnes, from 1922 to 1931. Frederick White was made clerk in charge of the police in 1876 and comptroller in 1880, when the position was created. He held the post until 1913, by which time it had already begun to decline in importance.[21] Improved communications after World War I made it easier for the government to deal directly with Regina, and when the police headquarters were moved to Ottawa in 1920, the position was abolished. The fact that there was very little turnover in these two positions and in others, and very long terms of service for other officers and men, meant that police policy and routine were steadier and more consistent than they otherwise might have been.

Personalities were important on the government side too. The name that figures most largely in the government's dealings with the police is that of Clifford Sifton, who was minister of the interior from November 1896 to February 1905, during which time the force penetrated the Yukon, the western Arctic, and Hudson Bay. An aggressive energetic man, he left his mark on the north, especially in the Yukon. The same applied, to a lesser extent, to his successor, Frank Oliver, but it was much less true of succeeding ministers.

The chain of command in the N.W.M.P. was not completely rigid; when circumstances required, the government and the police could bend the bureaucratic structure. As an example, control over the police in the Yukon during the gold rush was taken away from the commissioner in Regina and placed directly under the government, through the comptroller and the commissioner of the Yukon. The government's intense interest in the region once the gold rush got underway was reflected in its close contact with the police. An entire level of command was thus excluded completely, and the only connection the commissioner of the Mounted Police had with the Yukon was the task of finding reinforcements to send there.

At the time the force began its service on the northern frontier, its reputation was clouded. The activities of the N.W.M.P. during the North-West Rebellion of 1885 had brought a good deal of criticism. The police were accused of making tactical blunders and of not having done their part in preventing or suppressing the trouble. After the rebellion, there had been a wholesale change of staff, including the appointment of a new commissioner. Most popular works on the police[22] have attempted to refute the charges, claiming that for most of the rebellion period the force was under the command of the British leader of the expedition, General Frederick Middleton, who did not permit it to give a proper account of itself. More recent accounts give the attacks more credence,[23] but the truth or otherwise of the charges is not the concern here. What is to be noted is that during the post-rebellion period the police were eager to prove their mettle and their value to Canada—such, at least, is the impression given by the tone of contemporary police correspondence. Service on the northern frontier was to give them the opportunity of doing so.

By the mid-1890s then, the government had at its call an organization with twenty years of experience, a well-trained force of men who were prepared to carry out its directives wherever necessary. After 1890 the police began to make tentative moves towards the north; in that year, a patrol was made from Norway House to York Factory to examine a possible land route to Hudson Bay.[24] Patrols were also made to the Athabasca and Peace River areas. But in general, during the ten years following the North-West Rebellion, the police were too busy on the prairies to extend their influence very far to the north. And when in 1894 the call to go north did come, it brought the police not to Hudson Bay, but to a remote and little-known corner of northwest Canada—the Yukon.

2. The Yukon: The Early Period

THE LAND about to challenge the police was brutal and primitive; a land of extremes—of heat and cold, of calms and storms, of beauty and desolation. Then and now largely unknown to southerners, it is possibly the oldest continuously occupied part of Canada. Human occupation may date back 100,000 years; certainly, Indians had been in the Yukon millenia before any European arrived on the St. Lawrence.[1] But although it had long been home to several thousand Indians, only the most hardy and experienced white men could hope to survive and prosper there. Men of this stamp had been trading and prospecting in the valley of the Yukon River even before the purchase of Alaska by the United States in 1867, thirty years before the great rush.[2]

Trading activity in the Yukon basin began in 1847, when the Hudson's Bay Company built Fort Youcon at the junction of the Yukon and Porcupine Rivers. The American purchase of Alaska in 1867 opened the entire northwest to competitive trade. The Hudson's Bay Company was evicted from Fort Youcon in 1869 and retreated to Rampart House in the northern Yukon. Private traders, most of them American, filled the void.[3] These commercial enterprises were concerned with the fur trade, not mining, but in 1886–87 gold was discovered on the Fortymile River, and as miners began to enter the country, the traders concentrated on them. The oldest trading company was the Alaska Commercial Company, which had been founded in 1868; the other great commercial power was the North American Trading and Transportation Company, formed in 1892. Both were owned and controlled in the United States.

As is common in a speculative, highly mobile industry such as placer gold mining, the commercial centres in the Alaska-Yukon area were peripatetic; new posts were built wherever the concentration of miners seemed to justify them. Thus, in the years immediately after 1890, posts were constructed at Circle City, Selkirk, Ogilvie, and Cudahy. Particularly after 1888, business on the river increased so much that several new steamers had to be built to handle the traffic. Heavy goods always came up the river by steamer, but the route over the coastal mountains which was later to be used by the gold-seekers was known and used quite early in the country's history. A United States Army party, headed by Lieutenant Frederick Schwatka, came over the Chilkoot pass from Dyea as early as 1883 on their way to a survey of the Yukon River,[4] and early prospectors commonly used it.

Speculative mining in the Yukon took place in a surprisingly haphazard fashion. Although the first real strike was made in 1886, it had been fairly common knowledge since the 1850s that the area was likely to be rich in gold. A minor functionary of the Hudson's Bay Company at Fort Youcon, in Alaska, wrote home in 1864 stating rather diffidently that gold could be found up-river so thick that it could be picked up with a spoon, but that he did not think he would bother to go searching for it except as a last resort.[5] Perhaps the 1860s was the wrong psychological time for a gold rush to the Yukon, for with possibilities in British Columbia, much closer to civilization, only a few men cared to risk the privations of the unknown land far to the north. There was a technological problem as well; in the 1860s the techniques necessary for mining in the climate and topography of the Yukon had not yet been developed.

Thus up to 1896 the Yukon country was explored in a slow and casual fashion. Before 1894 there were no government officials in the region at all except for an occasional surveyor. According to William Ogilvie, the Americans were first upon the scene, in the person of Captain C. W. Raymond of the United States Corps of Engineers, who took observations at Fort Youcon in August 1869 and informed the Hudson's Bay Company men there that—as they well knew—their post stood on American soil. In 1877 the Canadian government employed Joseph Hunter, a civil engineer from Victoria, to survey the point at which the international boundary crossed the Stikine River in northwestern British Columbia. This was the extent of official activity in the area prior to Ogilvie's journey in 1887 to fix the place where the Yukon River crossed the 141st meridian.[6] In the same year, G. M. Dawson and R. G. McConnell of the Geological Survey of Canada explored the Liard, Pelly, and Lewes River regions, quitting the country by way of the Chilkoot Pass.[7]

Before 1894 there was no law enforcement in the country, no collection of customs and gold duties, and, what was most inconvenient for the

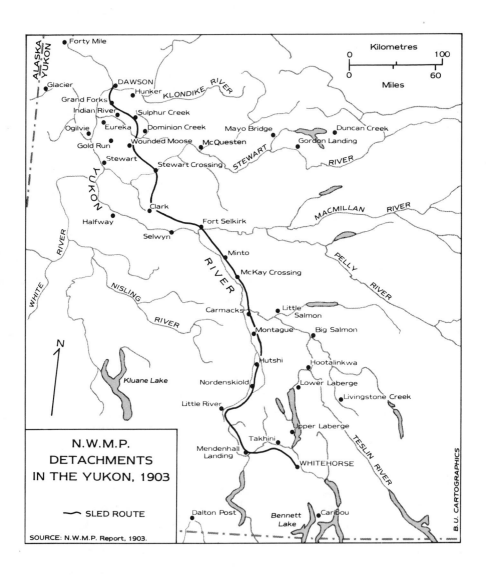

N.W.M.P.
DETACHMENTS
IN THE YUKON, 1903

SLED ROUTE

SOURCE: N.W.M.P. Report, 1903.

residents, no legal method of recording mining claims or settling disputes. There was a code of mining regulations, and a fairly workable system for settling disputes established by the miners themselves, but they were extra-legal and potentially unstable. By 1898 this situation had been almost completely transformed, largely through the efforts of the N.W.M.P.

Although the miners in the Yukon were hardly representative of Victorian middle-class society, they had a certain interest in preserving some sort of law and order in their communities. Since there was no official law, they invented their own, based on the traditions and experience of several decades of mining, chiefly in the United States. The basis of this law was a kind of direct democracy—the so-called "miners' meeting," in which any miner with a grievance could call an assembly to hear a case, discuss it, and give out a decision or sentence as required. Criminal cases were swiftly and, in the beginning, generally fairly dealt with. Civil law, especially mining law, which was the real concern of the miners' meetings, was conducted in accordance with a set of rules based on American mining law. Apparently there was considerable local variation in these codes; Ogilvie reported that in Alaska "each locality makes its own by-laws, elects its recorder, fixes the amount of the recording fee, and decides the size of the claims."[8] The usual penalty for infractions was expulsion from the community. The institution of the miners' meeting, although loosely based on U.S. legal precedents, accurately reflected the American ideal of the self-governing community which, unhampered by external controls, felt free to conduct its affairs as it saw fit. In the best tradition expounded by Frederick Jackson Turner, the miners formed a society which, in theory, produced its own democracy. Most of these men were Americans, and most were unaware of, or unconcerned by, the fact that they were living outside American territory, which did not augur well for Canadian sovereignty in the area. Forty Mile, the main community, was close to the border of Alaska, but despite Ogilvie's survey of the boundary, the prospectors searched for gold on both sides of it as if it did not exist—and for practical purposes in the early 1890s, it did not.

This American tradition of frontier self-government was bound to conflict with the Canadian system, which was based upon paternalistic control by a far-off central authority. In British countries the source of authority lies theoretically with the Crown rather than with the "people," especially with the sort of people who found their way to the Yukon at the end of the nineteenth century. Even if the miners' meetings had functioned in a fair and rational manner, they were bound in principle to be anathema to the government of Canada. In fact, they had inherent weaknesses. In an ideal world the miners' system might have worked well, but in the Yukon it suffered from the imperfections of the men who ran it. Inevitably, demagogues brought about unfair decisions, while the practice of holding meetings in saloons often turned them into carnivals. In the later period, the meetings "increasingly acquired an entertainment function at the expense of . . . government and the administration of justice."[9] Joe Ladue, a Yukon veteran, said of the meetings, "they begin by being fair, but after a while cliques are formed, which run things to suit the men who are in them, or what is just as bad, they turn the sessions into fun. Nobody can get justice from a miners' meeting, when women are on one side."[10] Many miners, libertarians or not, recognized the need for a more regularized and disinterested system of justice; soon this was to be brought from outside by the Mounted Police.

The Canadian government was not altogether ignorant of the situation in the Yukon. From William Ogilvie and others it received reports on the area. Ogilvie had sent detailed reports of his expedition of 1887, and in 1888 he had personally placed before the deputy minister of the interior, A. M. Burgess, his views of the mining prospects. The gist of his advice was that the government ought not to worry about the smuggling which was going on or about the fact that mining was generally being conducted in complete ignorance and disregard of Canadian mining law. Government intervention in the area of Forty Mile, he said, would merely drive the miners to Alaska and scotch the prospects of the Canadian goldfields. According to Ogilvie, his advice was followed: "It was decided to allow things to stand as they were for awhile, but I was directed to keep my eye on the region, and whenever I thought it time to take possession to notify the Department."[11] This he did in September 1893.

If his book of Yukon reminiscences is a guide, Ogilvie was not a particularly modest man; and it is doubtful if the government relied on his opinions and observations to quite the extent he liked to think. His suggestions were probably taken into account, for he was an intelligent man and, moreover, one who was relatively disinterested. But Ottawa had other sources of information. The government was increasingly becoming the target of advice, both solicited and unsolicited, from businessmen and clergy living in the Yukon. After 1890, complaints began to trickle down to Ottawa to the effect that the Yukon was suffering for want of government supervision. Those elements of society which stood to benefit the most from government intervention began to clamour for it. The traders, who comprised a small but disproportionately influential class, were concerned about possible disorder. Since most of them were Americans, representing American companies, they were aware of the chaos of the California gold rush. In the event, the situation in the Yukon in the early 1890s was not to be analogous to California in 1849 because the Yukon was slower to develop and because by the time the rush occurred, the N.W.M.P. were in place. The merchants could not, however, have foreseen this, and their nervousness is quite understandable.

What the traders particularly wanted was some sort of regulation of Yukon society. It was not then violent, but there was potential for violence, which might be bad for business. The large trading companies had considerable capital invested in trade goods, debts, and storage and transportation facilities. Anything which guaranteed social and economic stability would thus be to their advantage. Even if the advent of Canadian authority were to mean imposition of customs duties, they would have to be paid by all and might fall more heavily on the independent trader. The Indians also made the traders nervous; along with the clergy and some of the more perceptive miners, they were uneasy about the effect that the large amount of liquor being brought into the country might have on the Native population.

The liquor traffic, which seems to have been the thing that more than anything else alarmed the missionaries, was evidently extensive well before the actual gold "strike." As early as 1893, the local Anglican bishop, W. C. Bompas,[12] had written two letters to the superintendent general of Indian affairs, pleading for some regulation of the unchecked liquor traffic, which, he said, was causing his Indian charges to spend "nights of debauch," endangering the relations between the two races.[13] In the following year Inspector Charles Constantine,[14] on his initial mission to the area, took, if anything, a stronger view. He found that the country was controlled by what he called a "whiskey ring," which sold liquor to the miners at fifty cents a drink, reaping large profits. The Indians contented themselves with a home-brew called "hoo-chin-oo," made of molasses, sugar, and dried fruit, which made them violent and sometimes poisoned them. He suggested a strong force to control this traffic.[15] No one, not even the bishop, suggested that liquor be banned; public demand could not be denied to that extent. But it seemed only sensible to control the flow, obtain tax revenue, exclude the criminal element from a share in the profits, and protect the Indians as much as possible.

In his letters to the government, Bishop Bompas suggested that the Yukon needed a police force; ten men would be sufficient, he said, since there were only about two hundred miners in his immediate vicinity. The assistant manager of the North American Trading and Transportation Company wrote Ottawa in the same vein, warning of the danger

from the Indians. He brandished a carrot as well as a stick, suggesting
that the customs revenue from the area would more than pay the expenses of a police force since "the outlook for gold . . . is very encouraging." He predicted that if customs officers went in, the trading companies would buy their goods in Canada, whereas at present, because of
the smuggling, they were forced to buy in the United States.[16] It is
significant that the impetus for government intervention came as much
from the north as from Ottawa. Moreover, although it came chiefly from
the commercial sector, it was also the wish, according to Constantine's
later report, of a good many of the miners themselves. The law-abiding
elements seem to have been unusually apprehensive, for there was very
little crime; it was the possibility of future trouble which unnerved them.
In the United States such appeal for "law and order" often fell on deaf
ears; hence the necessity for miners' meetings and vigilante committees.
In Canada they did not.

Why was the government so quick, relatively speaking, to act on the
complaints and requests it received from the Yukon? One reason was
that this was the sort of situation that the government was equipped by
experience to manage by the mid-1890s. The nineteenth-century territorial quarrels between Canada and the United States, and especially the
Oregon crisis of 1846, stood as examples to apprehensive Canadians of
what could happen if Americans were permitted to occupy a disputed
area unchallenged. The purchase of Alaska in 1867 showed that Americans were not uninterested in the northwest corner of the continent.
There had been controversy over the Alaska-British Columbia boundary
as early as the 1870s.[17] The example of California, and to a lesser extent
British Columbia, showed what could happen if public order were neglected during a gold rush. The North-West Rebellion of 1885 had also,
perhaps, taught the government the dangers of procrastination. It is
little wonder then that Ottawa moved with alacrity to ensure that this
most distant of her inhabited possessions remained securely in the
Dominion.

The Canadian government had in the Mounted Police a body of men
whose flexibility and adaptability had been proved for over twenty years
on the Canadian prairies. And those who were concerned that its reputation had been, if not stained, at least called into question by its forced
inactivity during the rebellion of 1885 and by an investigation held in
1892 into the alleged tyranny of Commissioner Herchmer[18] thus welcomed the suggestion at the beginning of 1894 that the N.W.M.P. would
be the logical body to bring Canadian sovereignty to the Yukon. The
minister of the interior was responsible for the North-West Territories, so
it was from his office that the idea properly came. The original sugges-

tion was to send an officer and five men north, but Frederick White,[19] comptroller of the police, suggested that such a small body might not be met "in the right spirit by between three and four hundred miners who hitherto have respected no laws but those of their own making."[20] Rather, he thought, a police officer, styled "Agent of the Dominion Government," should be sent north to carry out a reconnaissance; one man, or two, would be sufficient to spy out the situation without unduly alarming the miners. This course was adopted later in the same year.

The decision came at a fortunate time for the police, for it gave them a new lease on life at a time when their numbers were being reduced from the thousand-man strength they had been given in 1885 and when there was some talk of abolishing them altogether since their original mission had been served. This idea was one of the pawns in the ferociously partisan federal politics of the era. For example, in 1894, one opposition Liberal member of Parliament, James McMullen, attacked the N.W.M.P. as the tool of the government's unjust tariff policy:

The only ground upon which you can advocate a continuance of the mounted police force [is] that it may be used as a preventative force against smuggling. . . . The result of our high tariff is: that under the excuse of keeping the Indians and the half-breeds in the North-west from murdering the population there, we are keeping a mounted police force to prevent smuggling . . . 800 men riding around from place to place, having an enjoyable time, living like lords, and doing little or nothing except in the way of preventative duty along the frontier at a cost of $700,000 a year.[21]

The next year the Liberal party took a different tack and used the rumoured reduction in the strength of the force to draw a horrifying picture of prairie dwellers, deserted by the police, falling prey to murderous savages—all because of false economies on the part of the government.[22] Others accused the government of weakening the police by making its commissioned ranks "a dumping-ground for the scions of political favourites," a charge which as has been shown was not entirely unfounded.[23] Commissioner Herchmer was compelled to explain that although the force was being reduced by a hundred and fifty men, only the dead-wood was being lopped off, and the police were not being rendered less effective.[24] The communities of the North-West Territories howled that any diminution of the police force would leave them defenceless against the Indians,[25] nevertheless, it seemed that with the civilizing of the prairies proceeding at a rapid rate, the attrition of the N.W.M.P. would continue and that they would eventually be replaced with a more domestic, less military force. In fact, however, the settlement of the prairies brought the police more work rather than less, expanding to meet the changed requirements of a more settled community. But the police had been set up, and still thought of themselves, as a force of pioneers. Perhaps they could find a new frontier to pacify.

In the face of this shrinking process, the men in command of the police naturally looked with favour on an opportunity to prove their worth anew. It was with considerable dispatch and enthusiasm that the commissioner responded to a resolution of the Privy Council, approved by the governor-general on 26 May 1894, to send a police officer into the Yukon. That resolution read in part as follows:

in reference to ... a letter from Mr. C. H. Hamilton, Secretary and Assistant Manager of the North American Trading and Transportation Company, and also two letters ... from the Rt. Rev. Dr. Bompas, Bishop of Selkirk. ... The Minister desires to state that in the interests of the peace and good government of that portion of Canada, in the interests also of the public revenue, it is highly desireable that immediate provision be made for the regulation and control of the traffic in intoxicating liquor, for the administration of lands containing the precious metals, for the collection of customs duties upon the extensive imports being made into that section of Canada from the United States with the view of supplying the miners, for the protection of the Indians, and for the administration of justice generally.[26]

This resolution sums up neatly all the reasons for sending the police to the Yukon. Commissioner Herchmer suggested that an officer and a non-commissioned officer be sent north as soon as possible to "take possession of the territory."[27] This officer was to have as many titles as Pooh-Bah, for he was to act for all branches of the government which had any interest in the area. The government's uncertainty about the reception which the miners might give its emissaries is reflected in the instructions, which bade the officer exercise "discreetly ... without risk of complications, the powers conferred upon him by his several commissions."[28]

The man selected to make this reconnaissance trip was Inspector Charles Constantine; he was accompanied by Staff-Sergeant Charles Brown. Constantine left his post at Moosomin, N.W.T. (he was then in command of the Moosomin sub-division, or sub-district) on 20 May 1894 and travelled to Ottawa, where Frederick White put him up at his club and took him around to meet the various ministers who were interested in the Yukon, particularly the minister of the interior.[29] Then, after winding up his affairs at Moosomin, he travelled to Victoria and left with Brown for Juneau on 22 June, arriving four days later. Rather than waste time on the long voyage up the Yukon River, Constantine determined to go into the interior by the shortest route, the Chilkoot Pass. He

travelled from Juneau to Dyea (which he spelled Dia-Yah), a practice
which was becoming increasingly popular among the newer crop of
miners, and prepared to cross the pass. There he found to his dismay
that the local Indians who served as packers had not been so debauched
by the white man that they had lost all sense of the profit motive. They
had, he wrote, "but one idea, and that is how much they can get out of
you, and being at their mercy as to packing, I had, as a rule, to submit to
their extortion."[30]

This irritation was understandable, but it was not entirely fair. The
Indians felt that they owned the pass and had a right to charge tolls on its
users. Since it was presumably unthinkable that a police officer should
carry his own baggage, and since at any rate the two men had eight
hundred pounds between them, they were forced to pay fifteen cents a
pound for getting their equipment over the pass. In fact, the charge
some years earlier was only half what Constantine paid, but during the
rush it rose considerably higher. Constantine rather exaggerated the
hardships of his trip. It was not really difficult to go over the pass
empty-handed; it was the repeated trips in winter, loaded with supplies,
that made it torture for the prospectors of 1897–98.

The arrival of the two policemen at Lake Lindeman marked the end
of the difficult part of the journey, and after an easy trip down the
Yukon River, they arrived at the mining community of Forty Mile. Since
this first mission was for reconnaissance, Constantine took pains to secure opinions from every section of the community (the white community, that is), and in this he was careful not to neglect the most numerous
segment, the miners. These men were professionals and knew what they
were talking about.

The miners were of two minds. They all thought, as miners will, that
although the country was not yet prosperous, it offered great
possibilities—that a little more exploring and prospecting could bring
handsome rewards. But some wanted the country opened up more fully
for exploration, to facilitate this discovery; this could best be done, they
said, by improving navigation on the Yukon River.[31] Others wanted to
keep the society closed, lest thieves, gamblers, and rival miners come
flooding in. The professional nature of these men is further indicated by
the fact that Constantine reported surprisingly little drunkenness among
them. "Many of the miners do not drink at all," he wrote, "and but few to
excess. . . . When they come in from the mines for winter they have a
general carouse. . . . [then] the camp settles down . . . and is . . . quiet."[32]
He found that the difficulties of transporting supplies into the country
tended to restrict the incoming flow of miners, partly because of
rumours of hardship and scarcity of food. Oddly enough, it was the
opinion of many miners that there were no really large concentrations of

gold in the country and that what there was was spread evenly enough so
that a modest profit might be made almost anywhere. Few men had to
that time made more than a small sum from mining.[33]

It cannot be determined exactly how Constantine found out what the
miners were thinking. If the sentiments he voiced were those of the
"respectable miners"[34] who wanted schools to be opened so that they
could bring in their families, they were probably not those of the majority, who were hardly "respectable" to that extent.

In his report, Constantine advised the government on a wide variety
of matters, in many of which, such as liquor, mail, mining, Indians, and
Americans, may be seen the beginnings of tasks which were to occupy
the police over the following six or seven years. As to liquor, though he
confirmed the complaint of Bishop Bompas that it was flowing unchecked into the country, Constantine did not support the bishop's
alarms about unbridled drunkenness. On the subject of Indians, Constantine delivered a severe opinion—they were "a lazy, shiftless lot and
are content to hang about the mining camps. They suffer much from
chest trouble, and die young."[35] Constantine's view is not untypical of
that of the police generally; as a rule, they did not hide their contempt
for the Yukon Indians, who seemed to them to spend most of their time
begging for food and whiskey. What Constantine did not realize, and
perhaps did not care to discover, was that the Indians he saw were not
typical of the Native population. In 1894, and for the next half-century,
the majority of Yukon Indians successfully pursued a nomadic way of
life, coming to the settlements only to trade. The Indians Constantine
complained of were a minority, most of whom had been incapacitated by
disease.[36] Tubercular Indians did not travel much. Constantine estimated their numbers at five thousand, which, owing to the diseases
which had raged among them since the coming of the miners was probably twice the actual total; a census taken several years later showed an
Indian population of fifteen hundred.[37] In August 1894, Bishop Bompas
arranged a meeting between Constantine and local Indians and acted as
the interpreter. Constantine was relieved to find that the Indians were
friendly towards the Canadians because the Hudson's Bay Company had
always treated them more fairly (or less dishonestly) than had the
Americans.[38] His main worry seems to have been to ensure that the
Indians would cause no trouble; if he was satisfied that there was no
danger from them, he did not care what happened to them. Constantine
was a policeman first and thought of himself primarily as a keeper of the
peace and enforcer of the laws. That he had been made an Indian agent
for this trip did not concern him much, particularly since the Indian
Department had, while asking him to take any action he could in the

Indians' interest, warned him to keep his expenses at an absolute minimum.[39]

The central point of Constantine's report was that the Yukon was quiet and peaceful enough that a fairly small force could be relied upon to do the job of policing. The only source of conflict would lie in the attempt to enforce laws with which the miners were not familiar, especially the customs laws. Constantine reported that the miners were "very jealous of what they consider their rights"[40] and would have to be dealt with firmly in the introduction of dominion law to the area. He believed that a sufficient force would be two officers, a surgeon, three senior NCOs, three corporals, and thirty-five or forty constables, together with the proper equipment and supplies. As was the common result of such requests from civil servants, he was to get half this number, which was likely what he really wanted.

Having satisfied himself about the state of local affairs, Constantine returned south at the end of October 1894, leaving Brown to winter in the Yukon. Before departing, he extracted the sum of $3,248.82 in customs duties from the miners. He found this duty "distasteful," probably because the miners grumbled a good deal. Constantine reported that there was a possibility of trouble arising over the matter, but that "better counsels ... prevailed" and that money was collected without open resistance.[41] This was an important first demonstration of sovereignty.

The winter of 1894–95 was spent in preparation for the expedition of the next summer. The government apparently had some reservations and second thoughts, for as late as May 1895, Frederick White was writing of "a good deal of hesitation on the part of the Government about sending any police to the Yukon District."[42] Probably this was on the grounds of the expense involved. In the same letter, however, White admitted that the move, once made, would almost certainly be permanent and that the government would have to take the long view of the whole matter, especially in the question of arranging to supply the detachment.

From the vantage point of ninety years, it is clear that the decision to extend the police service to the Yukon was not as well thought out as it might have been. Lack of real knowledge of conditions in the Yukon, Constantine's report to the contrary notwithstanding, led the police hierarchy into some errors of judgment. The lines of demarcation as to who was going to do what, as far as civil service functions went, was never made clear, and when the growth of population exceeded everyone's original expectations, the discrepancies between vague guidelines and harsh realities became glaringly apparent.

A good example of how the acorns of good intention became great oaks of discord can be found in the mail service. Before the arrival of the police, what mail service there was in the Yukon was provided by the trading companies on a private basis. It was realized on all sides that the police would need a more regular service, so in May 1895, Frederick White suggested that until the population of the Yukon increased to the point where a regular mail service was deemed necessary, the police could be authorized to carry one mail in and one out during the winter of 1895–96, across country from Fort Cudahy to Juneau.[43] The police thus undertook a duty which soon meant a tremendous amount of work and which they were to spend a good deal of effort in the next few years trying to escape. Much the same was true of the customs service; the police cheerfully offered to collect customs and then found, as the work increased, that they had incurred an obligation which was not easy to throw off. Many such tasks seem to have been taken up by the police from lack of appreciation as to what was likely to be involved; on the other hand, a good part of such work was incurred simply because there was no one else to do it.

After a winter of planning, Constantine and a party of eighteen left Regina on 1 June 1895, and travelling via St. Michael's they reached Fort Cudahy on 24 July.[44] They spent the greater part of that year erecting a police post, Fort Constantine, near Fort Cudahy. The building of this post gives an idea of the purely physical difficulties under which the police were forced to operate. Since there was no timber in the area suitable for building, Constantine sent his second-in-command, Inspector D'Arcy Strickland, with a work party nearly thirty miles up the river to get logs. At the end of three weeks' hard work in a muggy Yukon summer, they brought four hundred logs downstream; another two hundred and fifty were later required. Foundations proved a problem. Spongy moss two feet thick was laboriously removed from the ground so that the sun could melt the ice and they could lay mud-sills. The work was finished by early October, and by January 1896 Constantine could proudly say that he was making his annual report from "the most northerly military or semi-military post in the British Empire."[45] And in Seattle there were editorial murmurings about British fortifications in the far north.

As soon as they had established themselves in their new post, the police set about making their authority felt in the district. The word "district" is of special significance, for on 26 July 1895, Ottawa had created a new District of Yukon.[46] The setting apart of the Yukon as a separate district shows that as early as 1895 the government had recognized its special character. Constantine was made land agent and collector of customs, which meant he not only had to enforce the laws, but to interpret and administer them as well. He was in fact to be for the present judge, jury, and executioner in these fields as well as in others. For several years his successors found themselves in the same position, and the substitution of police common sense for orthodox legal knowledge and procedure was to become an important aspect of law enforcement in the Yukon.

It was in his capacity of land agent that Constantine encountered his first real challenge. This opposition came from the miners on Glacier Creek in the summer of 1896, and it marked, as nothing else could have done, the passing of the old free way of life in the Yukon and the replacement of the older system of justice by the new. The facts of the incident were briefly as follows: two owners of a claim at Glacier Creek leased it to a third man, who defaulted on the payments to his labourers and left the country. A meeting was then called, and the miners seized the claim in lieu of wages and sold it to a fourth man. Thereupon, the original owners appealed to the police for redress. When the new owner appeared at the police office, which was also the recording office, and was refused registration of his purchase, he left "breathing defiance." Constantine realized "that this was the turning-point, and should I give them their way or recognize them in any manner, trouble would never cease." He immediately sent Strickland to the disputed claim with ten men, telling him to act circumspectly but firmly, and sent a note to the miners' leaders warning them to desist, which they did. The claim was handed back to its original owners, and the most serious challenge to police authority in the Yukon ever presented by an organized group vanished.[47] The denouement of the affair was described by M. H. E. Hayne, one of the police NCOs who took part in it:

Thereupon a party of twelve of us, armed with Lee-Metfords and prepared for all possible contingencies (for no one could foretell how the matter would end, or in what spirit we should be received), went up Forty Mile river in boats and marched across country from Forty Mile to Glacier. I suppose we presented a formidable appearance with our rank and file and our magazine rifles, or perhaps the wrong-doers were beginning to realize that their action had been unjustifiable, for we experienced no resistance of any kind. We warned those in possession off the claim under penalty, and formally handed it to the original owner. We had not to make a single arrest, and after informing every one at the creek that such a proceeding was not legal and must not occur again, we simply marched back to head-quarters, and thus the whole business, which might easily have grown to alarming proportions, closed peacefully and satisfactorily. . . . No ill-will was born us for our share in the proceedings, and I think that every one was in his heart

*glad to feel that there was a force in the land that would protect his individual
rights and those of others.* [48]

This was exactly the sort of matter on which miners' meetings traditionally ruled—one where the law seemed unfair (under Canadian "justice"
the miners were never paid). The old order had passed in the Yukon,
and American-style frontier democracy had been replaced by British
paternalism.

In the absence of testimony from the miners concerned, it is not easy
to ascertain why their defence of their much-vaunted liberties should
have been so feeble. The police had relatively few men, and the whole
affair made Constantine sufficiently uneasy that he privately appealed
for a larger detachment. [49] M. H. E. Hayne suggests that the miners were
overawed by the display of military force, since the police descended
upon them carrying Lee-Metford rifles. Probably the miners' desire for
order outweighed their desire for self-government, and they were not as
solidly organized as might be supposed. Those who were already "well-
disposed" doubtless had an influence on their fellows. In fact, the police
did not impose unwanted controls upon the miners, despite the totally
different approaches to justice of the two groups. Most of the miners
wanted public order, and they thus welcomed the "public affirmation of
a particular set of class norms and values in the face of a perceived threat
to the supremacy of these norms within the community." [50]

Although the police were successful in this encounter, their position in
the Yukon was not yet clear-cut. Indeed, there was considerable uncertainty even at the highest government levels about exactly what role they
were expected to play. George M. Dawson, the director of the Geological
Survey and an experienced observer of Yukon affairs, [51] warned the
deputy minister of the interior, A. M. Burgess, in April 1896, that opposition to the police was likely to increase with the fresh advent of "rough
characters" and that the force should be increased. Burgess was non-
committal in reply, giving the opinion that he thought twenty police
were enough. Commenting on the exchange of letters, White lamented
the fact that the federal election had prevented any decision being made
as to a formal system of government for the Yukon, in the absence of
which, he said, he was forced to tell Constantine to stand pat and keep
most of his men near Fort Constantine, even though that meant the loss
of a season's progress and a good deal of customs revenue. [52]

Thus for lack of specific instructions, the police were compelled to
adopt an unaggressive attitude as far as extending government authority
was concerned. In their primary role of law enforcement, the police had
little to do, for although more miners were entering the country, there

was still little crime. The Judicial Return of the Yukon Detachment from August 1895 to May 1896 shows only four cases tried, all minor, of which two were dismissed.[53] The police did not provide a government for the Yukon—they could not; what they did was serve notice that there was a government that intended to make its force felt and that in the meantime the laws must be obeyed.

A general view of the situation of the police in the Yukon on the eve of the gold rush is provided by a letter from Constantine to Commissioner Herchmer, dated Fort Constantine, 5 January 1896, which touches on all the important themes of the police service at that time and place—Indians, personnel problems, Bishop Bompas, Americans, climate and terrain—and is worth quoting extensively.

Dear Mr. Commissioner: I wrote you in Oct. last. You may or may not have received it. I have sent by this mail my report so that I need not touch on matters connected with the building in this letter except in a general way. Taking all in all we are very comfortable. Our chief trouble and work is in procuring fuel. We burn about 2 cords of wood a day in the severe weather, all of which has to be cut and hauled by the men a distance of 1/3 of a mile. The wood is nearly all green. I have been obliged to buy some dry wood, as a reserve, at a cost of $8 per cord delivered at the foot of the bank opposite the Barrack gate. The men there haul it up and cut and distribute it to the offices &c. The [illeg.] stove "Hazlewood" does the work required of it well. It heats a room 60 x 22 and the men do not complain in the least of cold. For the past 10 days the thermometer has registered from 45 to 65 below zero [F] and the Lord only knows how low it will go tonight, as it now appears to be colder than any previous night.

Ogilvie has spent the Xmas tide with us amusing himself by putting up a sun dial in the square which will be of great use to us when the sun appears, as time in the past has been guesswork.... I am anxious that either yourself or Mr. White will come in next summer. Unless one or the other do so you will not be able to realize the nature of the country, the difficulties of travelling and what we have had to contend with, you will also be able to judge for yourself your wants and necessities.... Since I wrote you last Sergt. Brown has taken his discharge.... Brown took his discharge of his own free will. He has acted very badly, and had things come to my knowledge while he was in the Force he would not have left it a staff Sergt. I send you statements of parties here made voluntarily and brought about by his conduct official and private since his discharge.... He has made himself obnoxious to all he has had to do with in his official capacity as customs officer and has made enemies for the gov't & Dept where he might have made friends for them. I am afraid it might go further.... It would seem as if from the first that he & S/S Hayne had a compact to work into each other's hands in the Customs work. Brown should not be allowed to return here in any official capacity *whatever. . . . The facts are these—the U.S. Meteorological station at San Francisco sent some weather instruments for scientific purposes to Mr. Harper, a respectable trader at Fort Selkirk 240 miles above here. Along with the instruments came two official letters, one from the Supt. or other person in authority, the other from the British Vice Consul there stating they were for scientific purposes and on loan for that purpose. . . . The official letters were addressed to me as Customs officer here. I handed them over to Brown, who had a commission as Customs officer, to file in the office. He seized the instruments refusing any reason to the parties for so doing although they offered $100 as security or duty if collectible. He refused to do anything and now has them in his possession. . . .I told him his conduct was harsh tyrannical & unjustifiable. This was all done in order to get even in a private matter. I could tell you many other things but will not take up yr time or my own in doing so. Ogilvie is afraid it may work against us in the settlement of the Boundary dispute, as the Americans are very touchy about matters of this sort. The authorities in Washington have been most kind to him giving all facilities for going through their territory with his men goods & instruments. . . . I am bitterly disappointed in Brown. His good fortune has so puffed him up with a sense of his own importance that he cannot be ordinarily civil to anyone. He has done the force much harm here.*

Bishop Bompas is a disturbing element. He has no use for any person unless he is an Indian. Has the utmost contempt for the whites generally and myself in particular because I would not give an order to the Dr. to attend Indians, in fact to go over a couple of times in the week to see if they were all right. The Indians are chiefly American ones, a lazy shiftless lot, living on the miners through the prostitution of the squaws. There is a comfortable living for them if they would work which they will not do, preferring to take what they can get so long as they do not starve. During the fish and game season they could procure sufficient of both to keep them comfortably during the winter, but no, they must have a feast and gorge themselves so long as any food lasts. There has been no crime here, my action of sending a couple of hard cases down the river last fall, was a warning to many of the same kind, who went on their own acct., and the few left have behaved themselves. . . .

I have had a lot of worry and anxiety since I arrived here, anxiety for the winter and the comfort of all hands, want of confidence in some who should have, if not lessened the burden, not have added to it—I look for your support in what I have done or may have to do.[54]

On the eve of the great discovery of gold, the challenge faced by the police in the Yukon had been uncomplicated, certainly in comparison to what was soon to come. Up to 1896 the police had had fairly clear sailing in the Yukon, in large part because of the swiftness of Ottawa's response to the situation and because the obstacles they had to overcome were the traditional ones: physical difficulties and small-scale opposition to their authority. In overcoming them they did well; the post was built and the miners outfaced. These were much the same duties as the police had been accustomed to performing on the prairies. Hardships and the antipathy of local groups were challenges the police could easily meet; it remained to be seen whether their performance would suffer when after 1896 they were faced with a set of considerably more complex problems.

3. The Police and the Gold Rush

THE GOVERNMENT, however, was not to be given much time to develop a plan for governing the new district. In August 1896 the discovery of gold at Bonanza Creek gave to the whole matter an entirely new sense of urgency. The story of the immediate stampede of nearly all the men in the Yukon to the Klondike area, which has the rare distinction in Canadian history of being both melodramatic and true, needs no repetition.[1] But it greatly affected the operations of the police.

When the rush to the Dawson area occurred, the police naturally moved with the miners and transferred the centre of their operation to the new town.[2] This involved a good deal of confusion and the labour of building a post all over again. Fortunately, there was no immediate rush from the "outside"; because of the extreme slowness of communications the new discoveries did not become common knowledge until the early summer of 1897. Had the flood of gold-seekers managed to get to the Yukon in early 1897, the police, with their tiny detachment of twenty men, would likely have been swamped.

According to one chronicler of police legend, the force had been "for nearly a quarter of a century . . . been unconsciously preparing for this supreme test. . . . And—true to its long-established principles of authority, though not borrowing trouble, and providing 'protection ahead of settlement'—when the Rush developed, it was already on the ground."[3] True, the police were there at the right time largely because of fortuitous circumstance, but they were there, and that was what counted. Furthermore, they had done more than merely advertise their presence; they had established their authority by firm dealings with the miners. Constantine saw his force was not large enough and quickly appealed for an increase in strength to seventy-five.[4] He realized that this alone was not sufficient, that to meet the new challenges the police would have to become much more mobile. While the police had been at Forty Mile, it had been easy to patrol Glacier and Miller Creeks, where most of the mining was done, from one post. Now police responsibility had moved far upstream, and new methods of travel were needed. Constantine advised the purchase of a steam launch to link Forty Mile with the Klondike. This undoubtedly set the police administration back some-what, for it went far beyond their original expectations of expenditure, and they ignored Constantine's suggestion.

Constantine also urged the advisability of improving the communica-tions of the country generally—recommending that a route be opened from the south, either by way of Teslin Lake or by way of the recently blazed Dalton's Trail and, more specifically, that a trail be opened in the Klondike area connecting Dawson with the Bonanza and Hunker Creek districts. He felt that the economic potential of the country justified opening up a wagon road from the south, a suggestion which the gov-ernment eventually followed up in the Peace River-Yukon Trail expedi-tion of 1905–1906. He believed that the fact that he had collected more than $20,000 in mining fees in less than a year justified giving the miners some return on their tax money. There was considerable grumbling on this last point; many American miners resented being the milch cows of a foreign government. As Constantine put it, "the miners think that as some return for the large amount of money paid in by them increased facilities should be provided by the government."[5]

The police and the few government officials who were in the Yukon at this time had the reputation of being remarkably selfless. None of them seems to have tried to take personal advantage of the new wealth, or so says Pierre Berton, who is lavish in his praise of William Ogilvie, at that time the government land surveyor and later commissioner of the Yu-kon. Ogilvie, says Berton, was as "incorruptible as he was scrupulous" and "stubbornly refused to stake an inch of ground or to turn a single cent of profit.... Only one other man in the Yukon felt the same way, and that was Charles Constantine."[6] In this connection it is interesting to note a letter to Constantine from A. M. Burgess, on 17 April 1896:

An application has been received here signed by C. H. Hamilton, William Ogilvie and yourself to purchase 160 acres of coal lands on the south side of Coal Creek, as well as other applications for mining claims in your own name. . . . It is unlawful for an employee of the Department of the Interior to purchase Dominion Lands except under the authority of the Governor-General in council.[7]

Their incorruptibility was thus not entirely voluntary. In fact, this prohibition was a subject of bitter complaint from the police, who suggested
that their miserable salaries might be augmented by part-time prospecting, that their morale would be improved by their being given a "stake"
in the country, and that the mining claims would be better off in the
hands of loyal police than in those of Americans of dubious quality.
Moreover, evidence in the police records shows that this prohibition
against profit-making was sometimes circumvented. It was, for instance,
possible for a member of the police to stake a miner for a share of the
profits. Superintendent E. A. Snyder, who served in the Yukon during
the end of the gold rush, became rich there; when he retired in 1912, the
comptroller remarked, "he is one of the few Police Officers who have
made money in the Yukon Territory, and he is supposed to be worth
over half a million."[8] In 1897, before the practice was forbidden, Assistant Surgeon A. E. Wills staked two claims, one on Hunker Creek and
one on Bonanza, and hired two miners to work them.[9] As will be seen
later, the pay question led to serious morale problems among the police
stationed in the Yukon.

Beginning with the rush of 1897–98 the challenge faced by the police
in the Yukon became so complex that it is better examined topically.
Moreover, chronology can be confusing and deceptive. Although the
police responded quickly to any challenge, the end result—the official
reaction to the situation—was often considerably delayed. As an example: gold was discovered in 1896, the rush began in 1897, reached its
peak in 1898, and then fell off; but, for reasons to be discussed later, the
maximum number of police in the Yukon—just over three hundred—
was not reached until 1903. Similarly, some of the great expeditions to
find alternate, all-Canadian routes to the Yukon took place long after
people had stopped trying to get there. The government at times
(though not always) moved much too slowly to meet changing conditions. Moreover, if the government suffered from inertia, it also had
momentum, and once its enthusiasm was aroused, it was hard to turn it
off. Thus what went on vis-à-vis the police and the Yukon did not necessarily reflect what was going on in government circles at the time.

To deal first with the numbers of police in the Yukon—even before
the great discovery of August 1896, Constantine had requested more
men. Fortunately, this request was granted, so that by May of the next
year police strength had risen to forty. In this case the government was
not slow to react; with the news of the strike, an emergency effort was
made to get men to the Yukon as quickly as possible, to such effect that
the strength rose to ninety-five by September 1897 and to 196 by February 1898.[10] Those in charge of police policy were so keenly aware of

the new responsibilities and commitments in the north that it was planned at the time to station fully half of the entire police force in the
Yukon. This was in 1899, when enthusiasts still believed that the Yukon
had unlimited possibilities and when some senior officials of the police
believed that their days of usefulness in the Territories to the south were
clearly numbered.

This feeling is a probable reason why the police officials in the Yukon
were so reluctant to see any diminution of their force after 1900. All sorts
of reasons were given for this reluctance, such as the belief that although
criminals were reduced in number, those remaining had become craftier
and harder-working.[11] But the police, like all institutions, had a built-in
resistance to reduction of their power, and their protestations that the
Yukon still needed them reveals a desire to be needed. It may also be of
some significance that 1903, the year when the number of police in the
Yukon reached its height, was also the year of the final settlement of the
Alaska boundary dispute. President Roosevelt had sent troops to Alaska;
the increased strength of the police stationed in the Yukon may perhaps
be seen as an attempt on the part of the Canadian government to provide at least a token counterforce.

Whatever their motives, however, the police showed great flexibility in
their positioning of men and detachments during the actual rush of
1897–98. Wherever a discovery of gold was made, a community sprang
up, and the police were among its first citizens, and its first property-
owners too, for they were careful to secure a site for their post and a
timber lot in each townsite. If the community looked as though it might
be permanent, the police built cabins; if it did not, or if, as in the case of
the posts on the passes, physical conditions prevented building a permanent post, they set up their quarters in tents. By the end of November
1899, there were thirty-three posts and 254 police stationed in the Yukon
and the adjacent parts of British Columbia.

Because of the size of the force in the Yukon, it was split into two
divisions: "B" division, with headquarters at Dawson, and "H" division,
subordinate to "B". The headquarters of "H" division were originally at
Tagish, but they were moved to Whitehorse when the White Pass and
Yukon Railway was finished. Superintendent S. B. Steele was the first
commander of "B" division (and of all the police in the Yukon); he was
succeeded on 20 September 1899 by Superintendent P. C. H. Primrose,
while Superintendent A. B. Perry assumed command of the entire
Yukon on 26 September. Superintendent Z. T. Wood commanded "H"
division.

In the autumn of 1897, the rush began in earnest. After the news of
the strike became common knowledge in the south, thousands of men,

especially from the western coasts of Canada and the United States, where the news was heard first, swarmed to the north. The police were thus faced with their first new challenge in the Yukon—the sheer numbers of gold-seekers who descended upon them. It must be remembered what a furore this discovery caused in the rest of the world. "Gold" had been a political as well as an intrinsic object of worship for twenty years, especially in the United States, and the discovery of seemingly unlimited quantities, waiting in the frozen streams to be picked up by anyone who could be bothered bending over, seemed to confirm men's hopes of a new period of prosperity. Thus all sorts of unlikely people chartered all manner of unlikely craft—for passage was at a premium—and hurried north. Little was actually known of the Yukon by the general public, especially in the United States (where many thought, and some still think, that the Yukon is in Alaska), and the devices to make finding gold easier which were fobbed off on credulous greenhorns in Seattle and Vancouver would have done credit to P. T. Barnum. Of course, the flotsam of society went north as well, those whose trade it was to "mine the miners": the thieves, gamblers, murderers, and the "ladies of ultimate accessibility."[12] Some of the Klondikers got to Dawson before the freeze-up of 1897; more got as far as Skagway or Dyea, went over the passes, and waited at Lake Bennett for the spring break-up. Many, on the other hand, took one look at the passes and turned back; others never got past the flesh-pots of Skagway. But some bad characters made it; by the summer of 1897 Constantine observed that in Dawson "money, whiskey, whores are plentiful."[13]

In this transition period of 1897–98, with thousands of men poised to rush into the Yukon as soon as the weather permitted, and many more coming north by whatever means they could find, the federal government and the police braced themselves as best they could. Police reinforcements were rushed north over the Chilkoot Pass, and new posts were opened on the passes early in 1898 to control the traffic flowing into the country. This latter action, which was done on orders from Clifford Sifton, had the by no means incidental effect of drawing a *de facto* boundary across part of the disputed territory between the Alaska Panhandle and British Columbia. In Regina, Commissioner Herchmer was put to work recruiting a hundred more men for Yukon service. "The most moderate estimate of the transportation companies," wrote White, "is that there will be at least 150,000 people on route to the Yukon by the end of April [1898], and Mr. Sifton wishes to get the police on the different trails in advance of the rush."[14]

In part, the alacrity of the government's actions in the civil sphere was no doubt the result of the fact that the Yukon had become in 1896 the responsibility of the most energetic minister of the Laurier administration, Clifford Sifton. Not everything Sifton did in the Yukon has received praise from historians; although his first biographer, J. W. Dafoe, gave Sifton credit for working out a system of mining regulations,[15] a more recent study calls the regulations "controversial and ill-considered.[16] Nonetheless, he was a "doer," determined to make it clear that Canadian sovereignty extended to the Yukon and that no "American lawlessness" would be permitted there.

In August 1897 Sifton appointed a commissioner for the Yukon who was to act as governor of the Territory. The man selected, Major James M. Walsh,[17] was a crusty ex-N.W.M.P. officer, who had retired from the force under a cloud some fifteen years earlier.[18] But he was a personal friend of Sifton's, and he was still highly regarded by the public for his tactful handling of Sitting Bull and his band of Sioux when they sought sanctuary in Canada between 1877 and 1881. Walsh and a small party of officials left for the Yukon in the autumn of 1897 along with the first main body of police reinforcements. Sifton accompanied the party, partly to reconnoitre the Yukon and partly to investigate the feasibility of a pet project of his, the all-Canadian route to the goldfields. He stayed in the north only a short time, however, turning back at Tagish, and was back in Vancouver by 1 November.

J. M. Walsh was put in command, *ex officio,* of all the police in the Yukon, and Commissioner Herchmer was relieved of all responsibility for them. The police were ordered to report directly to the comptroller in Ottawa, who in turn reported to Sifton. Sifton did not wish to see the Yukon policed under a chain of command which ran from Dawson to Regina and only then to Ottawa; that was not his style. It was much simpler to cut out the middle link and to cap the whole edifice in the north with a civil administrator who was his own appointee and who would report directly to him.[19] Herchmer was not pleased to have the direction of so important a segment of the police taken abruptly out of his hands. He wrote to White expressing the hope that at least the internal business and discipline of the force would continue to be his responsibility, but even this modest request was denied by Sifton, who wrote to White, "Yes, administrator [Walsh] will be commanding officer, and all matters relating to the force must be referred to him unless he dispenses therewith."[20]

At any rate, Walsh did not last long. He was delayed at Skagway in the autumn of 1897 until the weather was too bad for travel and did not reach Dawson until the end of May 1898. By the end of July he had resigned and gone home. Although Dafoe describes him as "easy-going, well-intentioned and disinterested,"[21] he seems to have been irascible and hard to get along with. His reason for resigning was a fit of injured pride; it was

the result of Major Walsh's indignation upon learning that without consulting him a detachment of Mounted Police, under the command of Superintendent Steele, had been sent in from the outside to take possession of the summit of the passes. Mr. Sifton had to explain that this was an act of emergency to forestall the Americans. . . . Major Walsh had not been consulted because he was thought to be at the time in Dawson.[22]

Walsh was eventually replaced by William Ogilvie, the veteran of the Yukon, who handled his duties ably and got on well with the police. Walsh, in fact, seems to have held the belief, no doubt heretical in the eyes of the police, that the men of the N.W.M.P. were not suitable for service in the Yukon at all. In a report to Ottawa he recommended

that the men required for service in this country be not drawn from the North-West Mounted Police force. I find them unsuitable for the work that is to be done. They are neither boatmen, axemen, nor are they accustomed to winter bush life, three of the first qualifications for service here. . . . In their place should be called volunteers for two or three years' service in the Yukon district. They could be drawn from the districts along the Ottawa, St. Lawrence, and other rivers where men are accustomed to swift water, and to bush life. . . . In command of these should be placed one of the most competent young officers of the Mounted Police, and the remaining officers could be appointed from militia officers who have had the same experience.[23]

If echoes of Walsh's desire to set up a private force under his authority in the Yukon reached the ears of the police, it is little wonder that he was not popular or that the police chafed under his control.

With the police reinforcements was sent in a new commander,[24] Samuel Benfield (later Sir Samuel) Steele[25] the most famous Mounted Policeman of his day. Born in 1851 in Canada West,[26] son of an ex-Royal Navy officer (who was seventy years of age at his son's birth) and nephew of the assistant surgeon aboard the *Victory* at Trafalgar, he saw military service at the age of fourteen when he helped repel the Fenian raid of 1866. He served in the Red River Expedition of 1870 and joined the N.W.M.P. on its formation in 1873. By 1885 he was famous in Canada for his services in reconciling the prairie Indians to the building of the C.P.R. At the time of the gold rush he was at the height of his career with the police, yet he went on to serve in the Boer War, command the South African Constabulary, reach the rank of Major-General, and receive a knighthood before he died in 1919. His autobiography, *Forty Years in Canada,* which reflects his devotion to duty, his paternalism, his honesty, and a certain amount of pomposity is one of the best examples of the late Victorian imperial spirit at work in this country. When he came to the Yukon, he was widely regarded as the troubleshooter for the police.

At the same time, the government, realizing that the challenge which now faced the police and the general situation which threatened to develop in the Yukon amounted to an emergency, made plans to send a separate body of men, known as the Yukon Field Force, north to assist the police. It left in the summer of 1898 and established a post at Selkirk. The force comprised about two hundred all ranks, made up of men from the Canadian army. Significantly, they came not by the regular route, across Alaska, but by an all-Canadian route, north from Telegraph Creek on the Stikine River. Their job was to assist the police in some of their civil functions, especially in escorting shipments of gold out of the country. As Superintendent P. C. H. Primrose reported from Dawson, they "assisted us by furnishing sentries in the guardroom, and Bank of Commerce, head office, gold escorts, and sometimes prisoners' escorts, which duties, with the small numbers of our men in Dawson, it would have been impossible for us to perform."[27] The Yukon Field Force came under the authority of the commissioner of the Yukon, to whom the police applied when assistance was required at various posts. Fifty-three members of the force were stationed permanently at Dawson, giving the police urgently needed help. "The officers are a pleasant addition to our mess," Steele reported, "and the whole force works in harmony with us. The men are a fine athletic well trained lot, reflecting great credit on the country."[28] The entire Yukon Field Force remained in the country for a year, and half of it for two years. Its assistance to the police, by the police's own report, was essential and invaluable, especially in the performance of some of their more pedestrian duties.

Once the police arrived in the Yukon in numbers, it was not long before they were involved in all aspects of Yukon life, making their presence felt wherever activity, legal or otherwise, was taking place. Steele and his men seemed determined to avoid the example of Skagway, which was generally cited as the horrible example of what was likely to happen in an unpoliced society. In his autobiography, Steele described Skagway as a northern Sodom: "At night the crash of bands, shouts of 'murder,' cries for help mingled with the cracked voices of the singers in the variety halls; and the wily 'box-rushers' . . . cheated the tenderfeet."[29] "The town of Skagway at this time . . . was little better than a hell upon earth."[30] The motif of the evils of Skagway occurs often enough in the police correspondence and reports to indicate that the police were consciously using it as a point of contrast from which their own success in the Yukon might be measured. According to Steele, for example, the tempo of lawlessness increased as one approached the Canadian border, and then it ceased: "murder, robbery, and petty theft were of common occurrence, the 'shell game' could be seen at every turn of the trail, operations being pushed with the utmost vigour, so as not to loose[sic] the golden opportunity which they would be unable to find or take advantage of on the other side of the line in British territory."[31] This comparison reaches the height of lyricism in the work of later writers on the police, notably Harwood Steele, Sam's son, who like most chroniclers of the police of his generation, was much given to purple prose. He described the same scene thus:

straining, out of Hell, through Purgatory, the human chain kept moving —Till suddenly, a long-familiar flag blazed out, a star of Hope, in the grey skies above the summit [of the Chilkoot Pass]. And there at last were the gates of Paradise and the angels who kept it safe: The red-coats holding the passes for the North-West Mounted Police.[32]

Of course, the police were also on the passes for a much more prosaic purpose than keeping the "gates of Paradise." They were there to collect customs duties and to establish *de facto* Canadian control over the passes. The police performed the actual customs duties for only a brief period, from February 1898, when the posts were established, to 30 June of that year, when civilian officials arrived to take over the duties, though of course the police remained on the passes to enforce the various regulations.[33]

There was a bit of trouble at first with the Americans in this connection. An order had been issued by the American government requiring all goods bought in Canada to be convoyed from Skagway to the Yukon by an American official, who was to be paid eight dollars a day for his trouble. Furthermore, these convoys were to proceed as far as Lake Bennett. As soon as the police were established on the passes, they began turning back the convoys at those points. This caused some minor friction, which ceased only on 15 May 1898, when the Americans abandoned the convoy system.[34]

There was also some grumbling from the gold-seekers when the customs post was set up on the Chilkoot Pass; Inspector R. Belcher, in command, reported "great indignation among a certain class at Sheep Camp, Dyea, etc. . . . a number of meetings held . . . loud talk," but no action from the dissidents.[35] The main trouble was the weather, which was so bad that the police had great difficulty simply checking the goods passing through, collecting customs, and issuing receipts to be shown at the Tagish post. Goods were checked and receipted as they were taken off the pass. From 26 February until 30 June 1898, nearly $175,000 was collected, under very trying conditions.[36]

While providing a respite for crime-weary travellers and a source of income for the government, the police were also busy laying the physical foundations of their authority in the Yukon. Detachments were quickly set up on the various gold-bearing creeks, down the length of the Yukon River, and at all points of entry into the district. It did not take the police long to introduce a routine into their Yukon service. This was significant, for it was not only the spectacular part of police duty which consolidated their authority; a steady bureaucratic routine was also important. Thus, in cooperation with the commissioner of the Yukon, a flood of territorial orders and police general orders were promulgated and sent out with the object of imposing Ottawa's metropolitan authority over the Yukon as much as possible. All sorts of matters came under the scrutiny of the police from the reporting of deaths[37] to the problem of false weights and measures used by merchants for weighing gold.[38] The indefatigable Sam Steele settled down to a routine which would have killed a less energetic man. His description of his working day is worth quoting as an example of what was expected of an officer of the N.W.M.P. in the Yukon at that time:

my working hours were at least nineteen. I retired to rest about 2 A.M. or later, rose at six, was out of doors at seven, walked five miles up the Klondyke on the ice and back over the mountain, visited every institution under me each day sat on boards and committees until midnight, attended to the routine of the Yukon command without an adjutant, saw every prisoner daily, and was in the town station at midnight to see how things were going.[39]

The minutiae of an organization as large as the N.W.M.P. had to be attended to in the Yukon as much as in any other place. Orders were sent out, investigations made, reports submitted. Since the police were entirely without clerical assistance, the arteries of red tape frequently became clogged as a result of the inexperience or indifference of the police at the various detachments. Frequent orders were sent out from Dawson to the effect that the reports coming in were highly unsatisfactory, and numerous threats of disciplinary action were made.[40]

At the detachments, which normally comprised two to four men, the police, although expected to show initiative, were by no means left to their own devices. Each detachment had a prescribed daily routine; the one for the post at Lake Bennett in October 1898 is typical:

Reveille	6:30 A.M.
Morning Stables	7:00
Breakfast	7:30

Fatigue	8:30 or as may be required
Noon stables	11:30
Dinner	12:30 P.M.
Fatigue or exercise	2:30 or as may be necessary
Evening Stables	4:30
Supper	5:30
Last post (roll call)	10:00
Lights out	10:15

This rigorous schedule, which does not include the police duties which were part of every day, such as customs and general criminal work, was of course modified depending on circumstances and the time of year. Some of the detachments had no horses (that at Lake Bennett had only two), a fact which lightened the work considerably. Those detachments which were concerned chiefly with customs or postal duties would have followed a different routine.

In many aspects of their work the N.W.M.P. found themselves to an increasing extent involved in affairs which had little or nothing to do with keeping the peace. Sometimes they were apparently selected for tasks because they were best qualified to do them; in other cases, such as the customs service, they were likely picked merely because they could do the job with little cost to the government. An example of the police being given a job for the first reason was the matter of the trails to the Yukon, a challenge to the police which was essentially physical.

The question of developing overland routes to the Yukon involves a strange mixture of patriotism and economic self-interest, with emphasis on the latter. Almost from the moment it became apparent that there would be a rush to the Yukon, every Canadian and American community which had any pretensions of being a terminus or a way-station on a route to the goldfields began to trumpet its advantages to the world. Vancouver and Seattle, as the starting points for the water routes to the Yukon, were intense rivals, and with other Pacific towns such as San Francisco, they shared most of the traffic. But early in the rush the clamour arose for an "all-Canadian route." Why, it was asked, should Canadians have to submit to American tax-gatherers on their way to the Yukon? So asked the merchants of Edmonton, at the time an insignificant town almost literally on the edge of nowhere. The Edmonton *Bulletin* warned that the lack of an all-Canadian route was leaving the Yukon to be picked off by Americans, who thought that "if the United States does not own the earth, the United States certainly should."[41] Popular enthusiasm for the route rose to such a pitch that Clifford Sifton, who was keenly responsive to appeals from the west, ordered the police to explore a Canadian route with a view to opening it as a wagon and pack trail for the Klondikers.[42] The task was entrusted to Inspector J. D. Moodie, who left Edmonton in September 1897. His nightmare journey via the headwaters of the Pelly River lasted over fourteen months, and when he and his party finally reached Tagish in November 1898, most people concluded that the route was impractical.[43] Yet the *Bulletin,* at the end of August 1897, was congratulating itself over the number of people who had used one or other of the routes it had been touting; 102 had left since mid-June, having spent over $250 each in town outfitting themselves.[44] In a study of the Edmonton routes, J. G. MacGregor lists about sixteen hundred people who used them, about seven hundred of whom apparently reached the goldfields, though not until the rush was over.[45] Several actually died of starvation on the way. The old idea that only a handful of gold-seekers were successful in following these incredibly roundabout and impractical routes is apparently not true. The police did not seem to have given way to the rather natural tendency to think of themselves as sacrifices to Edmonton's civic greed; rather, they regarded Moodie's harrowing patrol as heroic proof of what they were capable of. As will be seen presently, it was administrative and clerical burdens which moved them to rage and resentment.

A second much-ballyhooed all-Canadian route was from the Stikine River north through central British Columbia, following the abandoned telegraph route which had been blazed thirty years before. G. M. Dawson had spoken in favour of the route, and early in 1898 the government entered into an agreement with the railroad builders Mackenzie and Mann to build a line from Telegraph Creek to Teslin Lake.[45] But nothing came of this project because it was defeated by the Conservative majority in the Senate. Sifton, who had backed it strongly, was enraged. Even Commissioner Walsh was furious; he wrote to Sifton "It is an outrage that party prejudice can be permitted to commit so villainous an act. It is treason of the blackest kind."[47] But this plan, which was not geographically practical, did not concern the police directly. Two other schemes which did affect them were the establishment of Dalton's Trail, an easier route from Haines, Alaska over the coastal mountains, and the Peace River Trail expedition, another sop to Edmonton and the "all-Canadian" enthusiasts. Although they did not open up a royal road to the Yukon, these expeditions did serve to explore a good deal of territory about which the government knew little or nothing—the Pelly River region, for instance—and, as always where the police were concerned, at little or no extra cost to the government and the taxpayer.

It was probably in 1898 that the police performed their most remarkable service in the Yukon, for that was the year of the main "rush" from the south, when most of the people who had commenced their trip in the previous year either reached their goal or gave up trying. In this year the police responded to a bewildering variety of challenges in the new Territory, many of them exceeding their original expectations, and some exceeding their authority as well. This last is easily shown by three examples.

In the spring of 1898, a motley collection of boats lay on the shores of Lakes Bennett and Lindeman waiting for the break-up of ice to permit downstream passage to Dawson. Unfortunately for the Klondikers, the narrow, turbulent Miles Canyon and the boiling Whitehorse rapids lay in their path. The inexperienced gold seekers attempted these dangerous obstacles in their crazy boats once the ice disappeared, without guides and without much common sense. Several men were drowned, whereupon Steele, who was by then in command, began a system of registration for the boats and set rules for the passage of all craft through Miles Canyon. In this latter case he acted quite arbitrarily. His much-quoted speech to the prospectors on this occasion ran, in part, as follows: "There are many of your countrymen who have said that the Mounted Police make the laws as they go along, and I am going to do so now, for your own good."[48] Here, depending on one's point of view, was an example of good British common sense or Victorian colonial paternalism at its worst.

A somewhat similar instance comes from November of the same year and had to do with the problem of destitute men in the Territory. In the winter of 1897–98 there had been a considerable danger in Dawson that food supplies would be insufficient to feed the population. Although the reality did not extend to actual starvation, there was some hardship. A repetition was feared for the following winter, especially since the population was then much greater. The police were especially apprehensive; a shortage of food inevitably meant disorder, and the destitute, for lack of anywhere to go, generally applied to the police for the aid they could not always afford to give. It was also difficult to distinguish between real and counterfeit cases of need. Hence, on 18 November 1898, Steele issued a proclamation stating that no one would be allowed to enter the Yukon without satisfying the police that he had with him two months' provisions and $500 in cash or six months' provisions and $200 in cash. Notices to this effect were posted in Skagway and the main coastal cities of Canada and the United States.[49] This ruling was quite illegal, as the Department of Justice informed Sifton the following July. Steele was told that his actions were illegal, but that this fact should not be made public.[50] By July, 1899, of course, the rush had abated, the new railway was well on its way to Whitehorse, and the ruling was no longer necessary.

An earlier instance of arbitrary action on the part of the police occurred under Constantine, when he had posted on a store in Dawson a notice which read: "This store has been appropriated by the government for the purpose of regulating the transportation of unprovided people, and is declared closed for mercantile purposes for the day."[51] This is a rather mysterious episode; no reference to it other than the piece of paper upon which the notice has been written has been found. Why Constantine picked that particular store and what was meant by "regulating the transportation" are not clear. Presumably the idea was to issue supplies to the destitute in order to get them out of the country. A store would be picked for convenience; the police would have to purchase supplies for these people (they often complained of having to do this), and the store would be the easiest place from which to issue them.

Can these actions be justified, pragmatically or in law? No one denies the police were faced with a difficult situation or that the actions they took were in the best interests of all concerned. Yet is it not a dangerous precedent to take such action, baldly admitting that the police are "making up the laws as they go along?" These were not cases of flexible interpretation of the law which is done by all police forces and was certainly to be expected in the Yukon. These were matters of actual invention of non-existent law to fit a specific situation, and apparently the police operated in such an *ultra vires* manner in the Yukon for many years after the rush; until World War II, for instance, the police enforced regulations acknowledged to be illegal, to keep Indians out of Dawson and Whitehorse.[52] The police should presumably try to be even further above suspicion than Caesar's wife, especially in this respect. On the other hand, it might be argued that extraordinary conditions require extraordinary measures; that the measures were not put into effect with the blessing of Ottawa; and that they, or at least the more flagrant examples, were officially discouraged when brought to the attention of the government. Perhaps they may be explained most easily by saying that neither the police nor any other branch of officialdom at that time was as sensitive to the many nuances of civil liberties as their counterparts are today. Canada in 1900 was more authoritarian than in our own time. It is a question of "climate of opinion." Indeed, although these are extreme examples, a great deal of the police work in the Yukon consisted of exercising a more-or-less benevolent control over the safety of others, people who were too foolish or too careless to look after themselves. From this situation a feeling of paternalism was naturally bound to develop.

The police were very directly involved in the economic conditions of the Yukon during the gold rush period. In the first place, their operations were sometimes hampered by the scarcity of material of all kinds, and they were forced to make adjustments in their methods to meet these new circumstances. Transportation, which had never been easy, became even more difficult with the onset of the rush. The price of feed for horses increased so much that many of them were killed for dog food, so that when Constantine on one occasion tried to hire a team to haul wood, he found the rate was an incredible $150 a day. The result of this inflation was that the police had to do their own hauling with dog teams. Much complaining resulted.[53]

The law of supply and demand made itself felt on the food supply of the district as well, and the police were involved in the incident in which fear of starvation had caused many people to flee Dawson in the late autumn of 1897 and led to Steele's proclamation the next year. At that time supplies of food in Dawson were so low that it was the opinion of Constantine and others that there was a strong possibility of disaster. Notices were posted in Dawson warning the miners that the only solution to the problem was

an immediate move down the river of all those who are unsupplied to Fort Yukon, where there is a large stock of provisions [this was not true]. . . . It is absolutely hazardous to build hopes upon the arrival of other boats . . . to remain here any longer is to court death from starvation or . . . a certainty of sickness from scurvy or other troubles. Starvation now stares every man in the face who is hoping and waiting for outside relief.[54]

Some men did leave, but the shortage of supplies, though real enough, did not prove as serious as had at first been feared. For a time, however, Constantine was compelled to ration his men to a diet of three-quarters of a pound of flour and four ounces of bacon a day.[55]

At one point a committee of miners and other citizens asked Constantine to take upon himself more power than he already had. On 29 October 1897, a group calling itself the "Committee of the Yukon Chamber of Mining and Commerce" presented a petition which complained that speculators were taking advantage of the scarcity of food and supplies to raise prices to an unfair level. They asked Constantine to take steps to meet "the immediate prime evil before us" and, specifically, to "establish standard selling values" for all goods in Dawson. This request for price-fixing seems a bit odd in the light of the group from which it came, some of them presumably merchants and businessmen; but it gives an insight into the reasons why there was so little complaint about the arbitrary actions taken by the police. From the beginning the Klondikers looked on the police as more than simply law-enforcement officers and public officials. They expected them to be custodians of the public will, arbiters of social justice, and solvers of problems of all sorts as well. These expectations were generally fulfilled. In this case, however, Constantine felt that matters were not grave enough to require such stringent measures. He rejected the committee's petition, remarking that "the time for this has not arrived, nor do I think it will."[56]

The general question of their own supplies vexed the police during this period of their service in the Yukon. Shipping supplies over the mountain passes was almost prohibitively expensive, and some of the cargo shipped the regular way, up the Yukon River from St. Michael's, on one occasion in the autumn of 1897 was taken off by hungry miners at Circle City. The problem of supplying the police in the Yukon was as much as anything a matter of establishing priorities with the shipping companies. It was necessary to cajole the firms which shipped goods up the Yukon River to give police goods preference over those of civilians. The police were frequently successful in doing so since the steamship companies were anxious to obtain and keep licences to import liquor and sell it to their passengers. The preferential treatment received by the police caused a good deal of grumbling, "the companies because they say they are losing money, the miners because the police seem to get so much, and the police because they do not get more [supplies]."[57] This problem tended to solve itself over the next year with the great increase of freight transported to the Yukon. Supplies never did become cheap, though they did become considerably more plentiful.

In their enforcement of the law, the officers of the police, in private correspondence and in their official reports, generally expressed a rather ambivalent attitude towards Yukon society. On the one hand, they were fond of referring to large segments of the population as the dregs of society; Constantine's celebrated phrase "the sweepings of the slums and the result of a general jail delivery,"[58] might be taken as an example. On the other hand, the same officers liked to point out how safe Dawson was for the law-abiding citizen; that a man carrying a six-shooter would look as odd in Dawson as he would in Ottawa.[59] Although the second observation was true, the first was exaggerated and reveals a certain tendency to magnify existing difficulties. The difference between the two statements, one made in 1897 and the other in 1899, also reflects to a certain extent the result of two years' hard police work. Certainly there were bad characters in the Yukon, but in his reports, Constantine seems almost to exaggerate their numbers and influence. A. N. C. Treadgold, the English mining expert who wrote a guide to the Klondike in 1898, gives a rather different picture of the type of man found in the Yukon. He divides the population into seven categories, of which the "scum of all classes and trades and nations" was by no means the largest.[60]

However, the news of the discovery of gold in 1896 did bring to the

Yukon a goodly number of criminals, and it is more than likely that the police tended to overemphasize their numbers in the community, if only because they had so much to do with them. Indeed, in the late summer of 1897, it seemed to Constantine as if the Yukon were undergoing a crime wave. The community spirit which had formerly prevailed among the miners disappeared with the influx of those, honest or dishonest, who were not accustomed to the miners' traditional code of ethics. Formerly, miners had been able to leave their supplies cached on the trails in perfect safety, but with the advent of the Klondikers, "a man has to sit on his cache with a shotgun."[61] At first Constantine simply told petty criminals to leave the country, since it was easier, though illegal, to throw them out than to feed them in jail. Many others were summarily barred from entering the country at the discretion of the police. After the quarters in Dawson were completed, the police applied corrective therapy to thieves in the form of ten hours' work a day on the enormous woodpile behind the barracks.

Although crimes were committed on the creeks and the trails, most of them, except for smuggling and bootlegging, took place in the settlements, especially around Dawson. The police tended in some respects to take a pragmatic view of this crime. Given the social conditions in Dawson, it seemed to the police that eradication of gambling and prostitution was patently impossible; indeed, perhaps it was even undesirable, despite the protestations of the local clergy to the contrary.[62] If vice was too prevalent, too popular, and perhaps too essential to suppress, then it should at least be kept under control and honest. This was the attitude adopted by the police. To this end the prostitutes were herded into their own ghetto, much to the rage of the citizens who lived there already, and they were later deported across the river to Klondike City, or "Lousetown," as it was popularly called. Women were forbidden to drink in saloons, and no liquor was served in dancehalls. All gambling was forbidden which involved the "house" getting a percentage of the stake; institutionalized gambling was thus prevented, or at least made illegal. Licenses were issued to saloons, of which there were sixteen in Dawson in 1899, at a cost of $2,500 each.[63] These measures, and the rigidly observed Sunday closing of the honkytonks, gave the police considerable control over all these operations, without making it necessary for them to be abolished altogether. Eventually gambling was forbidden, but this development, much desired by the godly, did not come until after 1901, when the issue was no longer of major importance in the Yukon. As late as 1902 gamblers were still being arrested and fined, but on a small scale,[64] and even in 1905 the officer commanding, Assistant Commissioner Z. T. Wood,[65] reported that there were several men in the Yukon who hoped that the vanished prosperity would return and the police leave, so that they could "fleece and rob the unwary to their hearts' content."[66]

The inescapable conclusion is that the police tended to regard the laws as something to be applied for the citizens' "own good." Again and again the paternalism which the police exercised may be shown by example—a paternalism strange to any American frontier settlement, but the rule in the Yukon. The police decided which laws were worthy of enforcement and which were not and to what extent. The police looked tolerantly on vice which was conducted in an orderly manner. But the toleration went further, for there is evidence that a "hands off" policy was adopted, at least for a time, by the police officials. In this respect a letter of 19 April 1901 from Wood to the officer in command at Whitehorse is significant. At Whitehorse it had been the custom to arrest and fine gamblers and prostitutes every month, but, wrote Wood, "as this practice has been the subject matter of a great many complaints . . . stating that the fining of these people . . . is a source of revenue . . . and virtually licensing them, it was stopped here some time ago, and that class of people ignored unless they openly infringed the laws. You will please act in like manner."[67] For "openly infringe the laws," we may read "make a public spectacle of themselves and openly infringe the laws which the police intend to enforce."

Orders to this effect came directly from Clifford Sifton, who had been under pressure to stamp out immorality in Dawson. Typical of the protests reaching him was a letter from Mrs. Kate Heaman, head of the Social Purity Department of the London, Ontario, W.C.T.U. She implored Sifton, "For the sake of our Motherhood, for the sake of our sisterhood, for the sake of our boyhood" to suppress the evil of prostitution in Dawson, as a "disgrace to our Christian civilization."[68] Sifton had already asked Commissioner Ogilvie if it was true that prostitutes were being issued medical certificates.[69] Ogilvie explained what had happened:

procedure adopted only after discussion in Council. . . . There was a great deal of [venereal] sickness . . . an order was made that all harlots should be examined by a physician every month and should exhibit in their rooms certificates of health. . . . it was recognized that it was illegal and was giving these characters a certain lawful standing but it was deemed in the best interests of the community to do so. . . . On the receipt of your telegram the practice was ordered discontinued; but . . . the women keep the practice up, considering it in their interest to do so.[70]

In August 1900 Sifton ordered Ogilvie to suppress gambling entirely,[71] but the Yukon Territorial Council objected that "vice would be very much worse practiced secretly"[72] and that it would be unfair to deprive the owners of gaming houses of their invested capital. Petitions from Dawson businessmen supported this position. Sifton was adamant, however, and the semi-official recognition of vice ceased in the spring of 1901, to be replaced by tacit toleration.

Of course, this distinction between crimes to be tolerated or ignored and crimes to be punished was made not only in the Yukon; the distinction is made by all law-enforcement bodies. Yet there is something almost unique in the situation in which the N.W.M.P. found themselves; they winked at the activities of the very class of people against whom the official reports thundered year after year—and moreover, without any ulterior motive of personal profit such as usually explains such behaviour. Probably the police and the Yukon government had no choice; they were not strong enough to go against the wishes of the greater part of the citizens to enjoy a more open society than existed in southern Canada. Most of the gaming houses and brothels were eventually closed down, but not until the prosperity which had supported them had largely disappeared.

In *The Developing Canadian Community*, sociologist S. D. Clark suggests that the older system of the miners' meeting was more effective in controlling these people than were the police since the "suitable sanctions" imposed by the miners had been highly effective in regulating their activities:

the activities of these parasitical groups . . . were not recognized, except within the criminal code, in the system of Canadian cultural values which had been imported [by the police] from without. The formal machinery of the state proved highly effective in dealing with the depredations of the criminal, but efforts to treat the activities of gamblers and prostitutes as crimes resulted in releasing such people from the more effective controls of the informal community.[73]

It may be true that the "informal community" was effective in controlling the criminal element before the gold rush, but the miners' meeting and the old community as a whole was not equal to the rush of 1897–98; the old system could never have controlled large numbers of unruly people and would have broken down, probably in chaos, even if the police had not superseded it. And the police did not treat gamblers and prostitutes merely as criminals; they recognized them as an inevitable part of Yukon society, at least while the rush was on, and sought chiefly to keep their activities as discreet and honest as possible. Thus the police did not release these people from effective control as Professor Clark implies; quite the reverse.

Of serious crime there was never very much in the Yukon. There were a few murders, spectacular cases which held the attention of the entire country. All were solved by the police. It was not a good country for murderers; as A. N. C. Treadgold put it, the police were "rapid, simple, severe in their methods."[74] As has been learned then and later, the north is not a good place to hide. The few exits from the Yukon were closely and constantly guarded, and it was all but impossible for white men inexperienced in survival skills to live off the land. The police kept careful track of the movements of suspicious characters and frequently advised them to leave the country even when they were innocent of any proven crime.

Thus crimes which *all* parts of Yukon society (except the criminals) felt were undesirable were either conspicuous by their absence or severely punished. Theft, for example, which was common during the gold rush, was punished by sentences which seem extremely harsh by modern standards. The records of the police jail at Dawson[75] show many men given sentences of two to seven years for theft, and they generally served every day of their sentence. Vagrancy brought from two to six months on the woodpile. Sometimes the sentences were for thefts of quite small sums; Steve B. Leslie, a British miner, got a year at hard labour for stealing ten dollars worth of gold dust and served the entire term. Also, the notes attached to the prison files show the rootless lives of many of the men attracted to the Klondike. Edward C. Mortimer, an Englishman aged 68, was given two years for stealing $1,469 worth of gold dust. He was a "Prospector, miner, and trapper. Left England when very young for New Brunswick... left in '52 for British Columbia. Followed the mining camps in Cassiar and Cariboo etc. Came to the Klondike first in '94, left for Los Angeles, Cal., in '96. Left for the Klondike in the spring of '98, arriving at Dawson in November '99. Wife died in Los Angeles 1897. Next of kin three young children in the Los Angeles Orphan Asylum." The comparison which the police liked to make between the sink of iniquity at Skagway and the model of good order at Dawson spoke volumes, they felt, for "what a motley throng can achieve under British institutions."[75] Men like Mortimer, who was early on the scene but made the mistake of leaving too soon and returning too late, thus missing his chance of fortune, made up much of this motley throng.

The actual crime statistics for the Yukon in the year ending 30 November 1899 show the kinds of offences which were the most common. The considerable variety does not, it should be noted, include any mention of gambling or prostitution.

The police were also responsible for enforcing the bylaws of Dawson and spent part of their time prosecuting the people for riding bicycles on sidewalks (for by 1901 Dawson had sidewalks) or for practising medicine

CRIME AND OFFENCE	CONVICTED	FINED	DISCHARGED	AWAITING TRAIL
Murder	5	—	—	—
Manslaughter	—	—	1	—
Attempt to rob and kill	1	—	—	—
Assault	8	13	5	2
Blackmail	—	1	—	—
Destruction of property	1	—	—	—
Intimidating a witness	—	—	1	—
Attempted suicide	1	—	—	—
Attempted escape from jail	1	—	—	—
Embezzlement	1	—	—	—
Theft and attempted escape from jail	1	—	—	—
Theft	60	2	67	5
Receiving stolen property	3	—	5	2
Perjury	—	—	11	1
Bribery	2	—	—	—
Forgery	—	—	1	—
Passing counterfeit money	—	—	—	1
Horse stealing	—	—	1	—
Smuggling	—	1	1	—
Conspiring to deprive of liberty	—	—	5	—
Fraud	5	3	16	1
False pretences	—	—	3	—
Rape	—	—	3	—
Abduction	—	—	1	—
Mutiny on a river steamer	—	—	14	—
Mischief	1	—	—	—
Attempt to shoot	—	2	—	—
Carrying concealed weapon	—	2	—	—
Obstructing peace officer	1	1	2	—
Drunk and disorderly	24	319	9	—
Fighting	—	16	—	—
Committing a nuisance	—	39	2	—
Obstruction of sidewalks	—	3	—	—
Setting bush fires	—	1	—	—
Refusing to work at fire	—	2	1	—
Cruelty to animals	—	3	—	—
Selling bad food	—	2	—	—
Selling liquor out of hours	—	1	—	—
Cutting wood without permit	—	3	3	—
Contempt of court	—	—	4	—
Capias proceedings	—	—	18	—
Refusing to pay royalty	—	—	1	—
Lunatics	19	—	—	—

without a licence.[78] Once the rush was over, they even had time to form a brass band, which was much in demand at civic functions. In the autumn of 1903 they gave an exhibit of arms at the Dawson fair and put on display some flowers from their garden. In short, as the Territory became more domesticated, the police developed all the civic virtues of the police forces to the south.

The challenges faced by the police in the gold rush period taxed their resources almost to the limit. The sheer weight of numbers of the Klondikers compelled the police to exercise their ingenuity as well as their energy. The various innovations and expedients they resorted to indicated their flexibility in response to the new problems which they encountered in the Yukon. Sometimes these solutions were extra-legal, but they were as a rule effective. They also played a critical role in shaping the development of the Territory. While these challenges were in the pattern of traditional police duty (since frontier prairie towns were similar in some ways to Dawson), along with them were arising a number of quite different ones, this time in the civil sphere, which were to give the police a taste of duties they were not much used to and to which they did not respond quite so well.

4. The Police as Civil Servants

AN IRONY of the history of the Mounted Police in the Yukon is that their most enduring contribution to the Territory lay in the duties they most heartily disliked—the performance of civil service work. Their establishment of law and order during the gold rush had caught the attention of the world and had made it clear that the Canadian government was determined to assert its sovereignty over the area. But an even more important element in the assertion of sovereignty was the more pedestrian, day-to-day civil duties which regularly made it clear that the Yukon was part of Canada.

These civil duties, as opposed to the strictly regulatory ones, were probably in the long run the most important, and thus it seems a pity that these were the duties the police liked the least. Most members of the force had come to the Yukon expecting to expend their energies catching criminals. Unfortunately, there was also a multitude of civil service tasks given to the police because they were best able to do them, because nobody else would do them at the wages offered, or because the duties were not frequent or heavy enough to necessitate the presence of regular civil servants.

At one time or another, the police performed nearly all the civil service duties in the Yukon for all three levels of government: federal, territorial, and municipal. The list is impressive: for the Department of Justice they kept the penitentiary prisoners and the lunatics and frequently acted as magistrates and justices of the peace. They looked after the welfare of the Indians and ran the Yukon postal service. They acted as land agents and mining recorders for the Department of the Interior.

They acted as coroners and as returning officers at elections. They helped the health officer of the territorial government and isolated diseases among animals for the federal Department of Agriculture. They served writs and notices for all levels of government and accompanied the tax collector on his rounds or collected taxes themselves. They acted as escorts for visiting dignitaries and provided orderlies for the courts. They assigned two men every night to guard the Dawson banks. They acted as a missing persons' bureau for the Yukon and looked after the tangled supply situation left by the Yukon Field Force when it left the country. They enforced the customs and the gold-smuggling laws.

Not all these duties were performed gladly; in fact, the complaints from the police were loud, vehement, and continuous, their main theme being that it was unfair to expect the police to prevent crime and be versatile civil servants at the same time, especially when they were as a rule not paid for these extra duties. Assistant Commissioner Z. T. Wood expressed the prevailing opinion when he wrote in 1902

It matters not whether we are shorthanded, or whether our whole available strength is required for our legitimate work . . . seemingly we are at the disposal of any department which wants to save expenses by calling upon the police to do work which properly belongs to its employees. [1]

This complaint is certainly understandable, though it may be less certainly justified. It hinges on what is considered to be the "legitimate work" of the police. They thought their proper job was to hunt down criminals and prevent the commission of crimes, but it might be argued that the Yukon was a special case and that the legitimate work of the police was to do whatever the public interest required. Since flexibility was one of the N.W.M.P.'s greatest assets and a quality in which it took great pride, it is doubtful whether the force was justified in complaining when the government sought to take advantage of it. Furthermore, some of these objectionable duties—guarding the banks, collecting gold royalties, and so forth—served to prevent crime and thus might well be considered as falling within the province of the police.

The variety of civil service duties performed by the N.W.M.P. in the Yukon is considerable but they did not devolve upon the police all at once. In some cases they became oppressive only by degrees. Nor did all the duties last for the same length of time. In general, at the very first, in 1895, the police had only the duty of establishing their authority. Then they began to act as customs agents, Indian agents, and mining recorders. Then the pressure of the gold rush increased their civil service duties tremendously in a short period of time. Finally there was a tapering-off period, in which the growth of a civil bureaucracy took much of this load away from the police, whose civil duties diminished in proportion to the growth of various government agencies in the Territory.[2] Still later, when the region declined further, the reduction in civil service personnel threw many jobs back on the police.

The history of the Yukon mail service is an example of how the police became involved in civil duties; typical, because it follows the pattern outlined above, but atypical because the police had originally volunteered for it. Mail to and from the Yukon had originally been handled by the trading companies or by willing travellers on an informal basis. It was sent out only in the summer, when the Yukon river was navigable. When the police first arrived in 1895 they took over the mail service, operating it in much the same casual way. Since no apparent urgency of communication existed, it was thought acceptable to have a situation in which no word was received in Ottawa concerning the Yukon detachment from October of one year to August of the next.[3] However, with the rush of 1897–98 unforeseen demands were put on the mail service. The matter was serious; at one point even the United States Post Office Department inquired if it could be of assistance.[4] The Canadian government hesitated to spend the enormous sums of money which would be involved in sending the mails by regular means, for Constantine had estimated the cost of a mail, employing Métis from Saskatchewan as carriers, at $1,450 each way.[5]

At this point White suggested that the police make themselves responsible for an "occasional mail" if the Post Office Department would share the expenses.[6] It was to be understood that this was only a temporary expedient and that as soon as the government developed a scheme of its own, the police would be freed of this extra responsibility. Unfortunately, the government plan, which was to let a contract for the mail to the same man who carried it for the United States government between Juneau and Circle City via the Yukon River, fell through when he defaulted on his contract.[7] The police had to shoulder the burden again. Only the winter mail was involved since the summer mail moved easily by steamer, but still the task was onerous.

Considerable resentment concerning the mail service was felt by those in command of the police on two grounds: the expense and the waste of manpower. White calculated that the mail service for the winter of 1898–99 between Bennett and Dawson alone had cost the police over $47,000.[8] This, it was felt, was money which should properly have come from the Post Office Department. And again the complaint was raised that the mail duties kept the police from their proper work. Yet in regard to the mail there were fewer complaints than in other areas.

Perhaps the element of heroism involved made this job fairly acceptable. And there is plenty of evidence in the mail service of the heroism that was building a national and international reputation for pluck and endurance in the performance of duty that was to be the force's most lasting tradition. In the report of one patrol which carried the mail from Bennett to Dawson between 27 December 1898 and 23 January 1899, for example, is found the following account, under "remarks":

delayed . . . between Bennett and Caribou owing to drifting ice and heavy wind. One dog died on route. . . . Mail delayed one day at Thirty Mile owing to horses being unable to go further. Between Five Fingers and Hootchikoo one sleigh with five bags of mail . . . went through the ice. Constable Davis and Special Constable Garson got into the river up to the waist to get the sleigh out . . . delayed one day . . . drying mail."[9]

This was the kind of service to be expected from a force which the previous year had been honoured by an invitation to the diamond jubilee of the Queen-Empress.

It would be dangerously easy to suggest that the police were keen above all to prove their derring-do in the Yukon. But it is hard to escape the conclusion that there was an element of this feeling in the attitude towards civil service duties. Those associated with the mail which did not involve a sort of outdoor adventure were far less popular with the men than those which did. It was only natural that a police constable should complain when he came north expecting to brave the terrors of the wild and found himself working instead as a mail clerk in the Dawson post office. The men at the smaller detachments complained because they had to act as the local postmasters. The extra salary for this duty at Tagish was twenty dollars a year, later a hundred; at some other posts it was three cents per day.[10] For this absurd sum the policeman, in addition to his regular duties, had to meet all the incoming steamers and mail teams and was responsible for all the mail that passed through his hands. The press of duties sometimes led to misfortunes; a staff-sergeant was compelled to make restitution of fifty dollars when a registered letter was stolen from the mail at his post of Forty Mile when he was out on patrol.[11] Such incidents were not usually the fault of the police, although there were instances of negligence on their part.[12]

Of course, there were other benefits to the police in these duties. The task of meeting steamers, though onerous, since they came at all hours of the day and night, provided a means of checking dubious characters entering or leaving the country. This was a vital weapon in crime prevention and was thus well within the province of the police. The same was true to some extent of mail delivery patrols.

These attitudes were quite marked in the case of the civil service duty the police disliked most: the customs service. The customs duties in the Yukon had been performed by the Mounted Police from their first arrival in the country. Undoubtedly, the ingenuity and stamina of the police were used to the utmost in the posts established at the White and Chilkoot passes in the winter of 1897–98.[13] But most customs work involved dull clerical routine, a task for which the police were not at all well suited and which entailed the enforcement of laws that were highly unpopular with the majority of the population. An ex-M.P. from Alberta, D. W. Davis, was appointed collector of customs for the Yukon District in the spring of 1896, but the police had to do most of the actual work. That Davis had several sub-collectors of his own at various posts only made the work more distasteful, for it galled the police to be compelled to take orders from minor civil servants.

Yet, as with the postal service, the customs work had crept upon the police by degrees, so that by the time it became onerous, it was difficult for them to escape it. In many cases, the police had pointed out to the government the need for establishing customs posts,[14] only to find themselves the prisoners of their own suggestions. Happily, their major work in this connection did not last long. The customs revenues from the Yukon were so great—in 1898–99 revenues exceeded expenditures by $450,000—that it paid the government to set up a regular collection apparatus. By the summer of 1898, civil servants had arrived to take over most of the customs operations, and the police abandoned these duties with relief, although they later had to re-assume some of them when the falling population led to retrenchment.

The chief difficulty with customs work was that it involved the police in situations for which they were not trained and for which, in many cases, they were temperamentally unsuited. Recruits seem to have been given no training in clerical duties; they found typewriters confusing and writing reports an onerous burden. In southern Canada these duties were performed by male civilian clerks, and the police recruits learned nothing of such things. The average member of the N.W.M.P. stationed in the Yukon seems to have been more than ordinarily resistant to, or inept at, office work.

The difficulties and complaints arising out of this work shed an interesting light on the self-image of the police. That officers in some cases worked twenty hours a day on the passes[15] did not bother them, but they found the friction and the petty annoyances of civil service routine exasperating. At Lake Bennett, the officer in charge complained that the two minor customs officials sent to advise the police were incompetent and spent most of their time trying to ruin the reputation of the police with "false, vile, officious" letters to their superiors.[16] Another customs officer complained when the police forgot to light his fire one morning.[17] Moreover, the customs duties caused unpleasant clashes with the public as well. There were several incidents in which the police were accused of being greedy or corrupt when they were only enforcing customs regulations. A prominent citizen, one Lieut-Col. Barwis, wrote Prime Minister Laurier, furious about police exactions at the Log Cabin post and closed by saying that the police had become a "byword for extortion" in the north. The detailed investigation which invariably followed such charges showed that the police had been exacting only the going customs rate, which was admittedly high, for the colonel's cigars (the articles in question). Wood remarked gloomily that "it is always the unfortunate policeman who, on account of his uniform and having the unpleasant duty of examining people's baggage comes in for the blame . . . these complaints . . . will continue.[18] The police were highly sensitive to attacks on their public image, and rightly so, since their authority rested to a considerable extent on their reputation. They therefore chafed at duties which cast them in the role of rapacious tax-gatherers.

The police were even more offended by civil servants who came north and expected the constables to act as their batmen. Some minor functionaries did not view the police as they saw themselves, and quarrels were frequent. In January 1899 Steele informed his men that they were "not expected to act as servants or in a menial capacity to government officials or other people travelling through the country. They are merely expected to do as much as they would for a neighbour or a friend."[19] That strikes the authentic note; the police were not unwilling to work, but their special status must be recognized—they must be accepted at least as equals. In the same spirit Superintendent Primrose declined the position of commissioner of the census in 1901 on the grounds that it would be harmful to the prestige of the police if one of their officers were to serve under a civil servant.[20]

Obviously, the N.W.M.P. had a certain image of themselves in the Yukon, and its members with enough enterprise to meet the challenges of northern service came north with a certain idea of what would be expected of them. Some had a rude awakening when they discovered that they were expected to do jobs which were so poorly paid or so unattractive that no one else could be found to do them. By such means government expenses were kept low and the Yukon was left free, for a time, of an unwieldy bureaucracy; but at the expense of police morale.

In planning for the administration of the Yukon, the government of Canada drafted its regulations with a view to making the Territory show a profit, if at all possible. Since the majority of miners were aliens and since the expenses involved in opening the Yukon and administering it were very heavy, the government wished to realize some return from the large quantities of gold being extracted. It was for this purpose that royalties on gold, and other fees, were imposed.[21] The police were the chief revenue collectors in the Yukon and were thus closely involved in the government's financial designs.

Did the police, and the Yukon as a whole, "pay their way," as far as the federal government was concerned? Certainly the Yukon showed a profit originally, but after the rush this profit turned to loss. The auditor-general's reports for the years in question show a small but significant excess of revenue over expenditure in the Yukon at first, up to and including the fiscal year 30 June 1900 to 30 June 1901, when the profit was $322,897. The big money-maker was the Department of the Interior, which collected the royalties on gold and other fees; in 1897–98 it brought in $735,485, and in the next year over $1.2 million, of which a million was "profit" for the department. After 1901, however, the Yukon ceased to show a profit. Revenues fell somewhat, but expenditures increased greatly, as the following table shows:

YEAR	REVENUES — ALL SOURCES	EXPENDITURES — ALL SOURCES	BALANCE
1898–99	1,754,974	1,682,842	72,132
1899–00	1,794,671	1,889,265	– 94,594
1900–01	1,993,982	1,671,085	322,897
1901–02	1,493,463	2,567,516	– 1,074,053
1902–03	1,339,360	2,314,433	– 975,073

The largest item of expenditure in 1901–1902 was $1,777,382 by the Department of Public Works; most of this was for capital expenditures—buildings, roads and trails, and telegraph lines.

Whether the police specifically paid their way (quite apart from the question of whether they should have) is less easy to determine. The expenditures of the N.W.M.P., including salaries, in connection with their service in the Yukon, were given as follows:[22]

YEAR	EXPENDITURES
1894–95	nil
1895–96	27,595
1896–97	22,134
1897–98	495,777
1898–99	890,018
1899–00	492,427
1900–01	498,824
1901–02	499,068
1902–03	590,702
1903–04	500,000 (est.)

Except for fines, the police generated no revenue themselves, but they did collect the greater part of the money going to the Department of the Interior and the Customs Department, especially during the rush. These sums always greatly exceeded the cost of maintaining the police, and in this rather crude sense, the police may be said to have "paid their way." Furthermore, much of the police expenditures shown in the table could properly be charged to other departments. In 1898–99, for instance, while police expenditure in the Yukon soared to $890,000, that of the Post Office Department was only $22,000. A scrutiny of the detailed statement of police expenditures in the auditor-general's report shows many items of expense incurred in carrying the mails which might well have been charged to the proper department. The question is complicated by the fact that the statistics are somewhat ambiguous.

The statistics of police expenditures which appear in the auditor-general's report are very detailed; the one for 1897–98 covers twenty-two pages of small type. In that year, just under half a million dollars was spent in connection with the Yukon service, under the following headings:[23]

Pay of force	50,673
Subsistence	66,034
Forage and dog feed	13,915
Fuel and light	2,226
Clothing	13,884
Repairs and renewals	25,361
Arms and ammunition	1,399
Horses and dogs	8,804
Hospital comforts	2,684
Books and stationery	372
Scouts and guides	54
Billeting and travelling expenses	10,159
Transport and freight charges	235,265
Contingencies	4,904
New buildings	7,017
Expenses incurred in N.W.T. chargeable to Yukon	53,020
Total	495,777

The largest expenditure was for transport, and here can be seen expenses for other departments, especially the Post Office. In the next fiscal year, 1898–99, police expenditures increased to $890,000. Unfortunately, the auditor-general's report put almost everything under "General Accounts," so it is not easy to determine exactly where the great increase occurred. The pay of the force tripled, to $150,000, which accounts for $100,000 of the increase. The largest expenditures were always for supplies and transportation, and they seem to have increased proportionately.

But the real question should be not so much whether the police "paid their way" as whether their services to the Yukon and to Canada were worth the money spent on them. Undoubtedly they were; in financial terms they were a great bargain to the federal and territorial governments.

The various challenges in the civil and criminal spheres in the Yukon gave the police an influence over the Territory which was perhaps uniquely strong for a Canadian governmental agency in peacetime. From the aspects of society over which the police exercised close surveillance or complete control during the gold rush, it would not be too much to say that the Yukon was in certain respects a rather benign police state. The police enforced the laws and sometimes made them. They kept a close watch over all the means of communication in the Territory, both in their capacity as police and as customs officers. The mails were almost entirely in their hands, for they not only carried it but also acted as local postmasters. When the telegraph line was built, the operators at the smaller posts were sometimes policemen. No one left or entered the country without passing through the police net. Everyone who left the Yukon was searched, person and baggage, for gold on which the royalty had not been paid; those coming in were searched for liquor, firearms, and gambling equipment. The police exercised considerable control over the Territory's gold industry, from staking to shipping, especially during the rush. Although they did not altogether set the standards of public morality, they rigorously enforced the compromise which had been reached between the reform element and the advocates of an open society.[24] All this power was wielded benevolently, or so the police believed, but it is rare in modern times that a police force in an Anglo-Saxon country has had such pervasive authority and even rarer in a North American setting. Whether it was wise for the government to entrust so many tasks and the concomitant power to a police force on the mere grounds of economy and efficiency is a moot point. It was a dangerous experiment, which depends largely on the quality of the men entrusted with the authority for its success; in this instance, the government was very fortunate in its choice.

By 1899, a sizeable civil bureaucracy, federal and territorial, was beginning to appear in the Yukon, and the role of the police was declining. During the crucial period of the rush, however, when the police exercising their various functions comprised most of the bureaucracy, their role was extremely important.

As agents for the Department of Indian Affairs, the police acted as intermediaries between the government and the original inhabitants of the Yukon. Not much is known of the history of the Yukon Indians prior to the gold rush since the only people who took much interest in them were transient scientists and the missionaries, in particular the redoubtable Bishop Bompas. The bishop's concern for the Indians ran deep, and he feared for the moral and physical health of his flock. Several years before the rush began, he already believed that they had been largely debauched by their contacts with whites. The police shared this view, reporting annually that the Indians were destitute. Although the police prided themselves on their reputation as the great friend of the Plains Indians, they were not sympathetic to the plight of the Yukon natives. Their behaviour towards these people was not enlightened. From their experience with the Plains Indians many seem to have derived a "noble redskin" image of the ideal Indian—that the best of them were proud, energetic people, worthy of respect. By this standard the Indians of the Yukon were judged and found wanting.

From the first the police decided that the Yukon Indians did not fit this pattern. Constantine's opinion of them, that they were "a lazy shiftless lot,"[25] was echoed and re-echoed by his colleagues and successors. Although there were not many Indians in the Yukon, perhaps two thousand in 1898, and although they were peaceful, the police found them a constant source of annoyance because of their frequent appeals for food. Perhaps they assumed that the police were in the country to be of service to them, as the missionaries were. In any case, the police tended to meet their importunities pragmatically; if the Indians were healthy, they could either work or starve, and in either case it would be simpler if they were put on a reserve, preferably far away.[25]

The Indian question also brought the police into conflict with the Territory's missionaries, especially with Bishop Bompas. Constantine had a sharp quarrel with the bishop in the winter of 1896–97 over some Indians who were squatting on land which the police had reserved for the site of a possible detachment. Constantine suspected that Bompas was encouraging them to defy the police, and wrote to Herchmer "I don't propose to be bluffed by an arrogant Bishop who thinks the only people worth considering are a few dirty Indians too lazy to work, and who prefer starvation.[27]

Here both the police and the missionaries were in error, for the Indians with whom they came in contact were not representative of the Native population. The majority of the Indians remained as nomads until the advent of the welfare state after World War II. The police dealt only with those Indians who had become ensnared by disease or urban vices, but they generalized from this sample. The police do not seem to have considered it their responsibility to help this minority cope with the onslaughts of civilization or to have regarded them as anything more than nuisances once it had become clear that they were not a threat to police authority. Even the rigorous enforcement of the prohibition of the sale of liquor to Indians was more than anything an attempt to ensure that they continued to be no threat. The police were not, and never pretended to be, humanitarians, and acting as Indian agents was only a minor part of their civil duties. They reluctantly gave food and blankets to the most miserable Indians in the settlements, but they did no more. Their handling of the Native problem is not a very glorious or enlightened side of their service in the Yukon.

5. The Police and Yukon Politics

THE YUKON was made a Territory on 13 June 1898, partly in response to local demand and partly to make it quite clear that the area was to be in no way governed from Regina.[1] The new Yukon Territory was to have a measure of local government, in the form of a council, which was appointed by the commissioner of the Yukon. As commander of the police in the Territory, Steele was a member of the first council, which was made up entirely of government administrators. The other members were the gold commissioner, the local judge, the registrar, and a legal adviser. Meetings were at first held *in camera*, but this practice proved so unpopular with the citizenry that they were declared open in August 1899.[2]

The Territorial Council concerned itself chiefly with local conditions. It passed bylaws for Dawson and regulations for the Yukon in general and in this respect worked in close cooperation with the police. When police officials discovered an abuse that was not covered by an existing law, they had no hesitation in writing to the commissioner to suggest that a suitable one be drawn up.[3] Similarly, when the commissioner received complaints from the citizens that the laws were being broken, he worked with the police to secure evidence against the offenders.[4] Many examples can be cited to show the spirit of ready cooperation which existed between the police and commissioner. Since the commissioner was *ex officio* in command of the police, his jurisdiction was clear. If a commissioner was not easy to get along with, friction would arise. Some of the incidents involving the police being forced to act in menial capacities for civil servants, for instance, seem to have originated with J. M. Walsh.[5] On the other hand, the police got along very well with both William Ogilvie (1898–1901) and J. H. Ross (1901–1905) as is reflected in the ease with which legislation was put through and the absence of complaints on both sides.

The duties of the N.W.M.P. also involved them, not for the first time in their history, in the wider sphere of Canadian-American relations. For several years the Yukon was a sensitive spot in the relations between the two countries, and events there might well serve as an example in microcosm of Canadian-American relations of this period.

Basically, the police exhibited typical late Victorian British-Canadian attitudes towards the United States. When Constantine spoke of miners as the "sweepings of the slums," he only echoed the opinions of many of his countrymen—those, at least, who did not worship the United States and its values. Just as Canadians had been apprehensive about the possiblity of Fenian raids in the 1860s and 1870s, so the authorities in the Yukon were always nervously aware of the close proximity of the "Spread-Eagleism in and about Skagway,"[6] as White put it. At the beginning of the development of the goldfields, when the activity was centered on Forty Mile, the uncertainty about where the boundary ran tended to make American sympathizers among the miners bolder than they otherwise might have been. And there was complete confusion at first as to where the boundary lay in the vicinity of the White and Chilkoot Passes. Some exponents of the extreme American point of view had it crossing Lake Bennett, and in the winter of 1897–98, with thousands of men coming over the passes, the question became much more than academic.

As in most boundary cases, both parties tried to advance their claims as much as possible. Yet the solution arrived at was typical of the new age of commonsense response. While the governments sparred, the police were faced with the problem of selecting a location for their customs post. Lake Bennett would have been unsuitable from a police point of view because of the difficulty of exercising control there. Lacking any definite instructions from the Department of the Interior, the police reached a tacit understanding with the U.S. marshall in Skagway that a temporary boundary should be established at the foot of Lake Lindeman.[7] However, in January 1898, Ottawa instructed the police to establish a post on the summit of White Pass, locating it at a spot where the water ran into the Yukon River, rather than into the Pacific.[8] These instructions made Perry apprehensive, for, as he wrote White, many Americans in Skagway and Juneau would be furious at this further advance of Canadian claims.[9] But in fact, it was a sensible compromise.[10]

Anti-Canadian feeling manifested itself again in the autumn of 1901 in an abortive plot to take over the Yukon by force.[11] But this comic-opera plot hatched by the "Order of the Midnight Sun" soon "ended in smoke."[12] Petty as the incident was, it confirmed the worst suspicions of the police. Many of the alarms and a good deal of the friction between Canadians and Americans in the Yukon were, however, on the level of common rumour. One report in the Alaska press that a crowd of excited miners had hauled down the Union Jack at the summit of the White Pass, for example, turned out on investigation to be a case of a drunken railway navvy using the flag as a blanket.[13]

The only issue which caused much reverberation on the national level was the fact that for a time the police kept a constable in uniform in Skagway as an agent to facilitate the forwarding of police supplies to the Yukon. Great objection was raised in Skagway to the presence of a uniformed official of a foreign power and to the notices giving requirements for entry to the Yukon which Steele had caused to be posted there. In answer to a note from the American secretary of state, John Hay, the Canadian government attempted to ease ruffled feelings by having the constable appear only in civilian clothes, but the Americans were not satisfied, and the representative of the police had to be withdrawn altogether, leaving police affairs in the hands of a civilian agent. The Canadian government did not feel that the convenience of a police agent was worth the dispute involved.[14]

On other levels, though, there was cooperation. In addition to the mail service, there were the efforts of the Canadian government to facilitate the progress of the Yukon Relief Expedition, an episode which resulted from highly exaggerated rumours in the American press in 1897 that United States citizens were starving in Dawson and vicinity. Pressure was put on the government in Washington, and an announcement was made in December 1897 that a large quantity of stores would be forwarded to Dawson by way of Dyea. The Canadian government was willing to do what it could to help these stores along, but the expedition was abandoned at Dyea in March 1898. An offshoot of the expedition was the sending of 550 reindeer into the interior over Dalton's Trail to be used as food for the supposedly starving miners; this also ended in failure. The Mounted Police willingly cooperated with the United States Army by making arrangments for the expedition's progress into Canada.[15]

Partly because of the presence of Americans in the Territory, the system of government introduced into the Yukon in 1898 was not democratic. The federal government did not intend it to be. Neither the authorities in Ottawa nor those in the Yukon had any intention of granting self-government to a community which was more than half American. When Steele wrote that many of Dawson's citizens "could well be spared in any community,"[16] he was expressing the official position. It was not without considerable justification that Yukon officialdom looked askance at the Americans who came to the territory after 1897. It had been easy enough to deflate the original miners' feeble attempt at assertion of their authority, but the Klondikers were a wilder breed of men, who did not "appreciate being cramped, confined, regulated, or ruled by Canadian functionaries."[17] Although there never was any serious possibility of a military takeover by the United States, the police and the government were constantly made uneasy by the American character of Dawson. The thought was never far from their minds that what "Spread-Eaglism" could not accomplish from without, a spirit of unchecked libertarianism might do from within. Although the authorities had enough sense not to interfere with harmless manifestations of republican sentiment such as the annual Fourth of July celebrations, they had no intention of letting the celebrants have a premature voice in the government.

Eventually the public pressure for a more representative form of government became insistent, and the Yukon Council was increased in size to ten members, of whom five were to be elected. This shift to a more democratic form of local government, however, took place only in 1902, after the most volatile elements of the community had disappeared in search of new goldfields or had gone home, wealthy or otherwise. The reluctance to grant wider powers to the community in the early stages of its growth was quite in line with the generally paternalistic outlook of the police and the government authorities in the Yukon.

It is not difficult to pass judgment on the efficiency of the police in the Yukon. What they set their minds to do they did extremely well, and even what they did half-heartedly was done satisfactorily. Perhaps good proof is the relative absence of public complaints, which is reflected in the Dawson newspapers and in the correspondence of the foremost political chiefs of the day, Sifton and Laurier. In 1899, three newspapers were published in Dawson: the *Yukon Midnight Sun,* which supported the government, and its two competitors, the *Klondike Nugget* and the Dawson *Daily News,* which did not—the *Midnight Sun* dubbing them the "Yellow Rag" and the "Boer Organ" respectively. The three newspapers disagreed constantly and violently, and the two opposition papers lost no opportunity to malign the administration of the Yukon in language which was strong even for the period. Yet never were the police mentioned in anything but words of great respect. The *Nugget,* the most scurrilous of the three,[18] was in fact kindest to the police; in one issue, under the editorial heading "Poor Yukoners," it stated that "the only good thing that can be said of the government of the Yukon District is that we have an excellent police and court. . . .The debit side covers several pages."[19] The same paper frequently carried a column entitled "From the Barracks," containing gossip and personal news about the local police detachment. Contemporary books on the Yukon were equally complimentary.

The police were not drawn into the so-called "Yukon Scandals," except peripherally, insofar as their absurdly low rate of pay was cited by the Dawson papers as another example of the stupidity of the government. Most of the public indignation was directed towards the unfortunate gold commissioner, Thomas Fawcett, of whom the kindest thing the *Nugget* could find to say was that he was totally incompetent.[20] The *Nugget* was instrumental in raising popular opinion against the public administration, to the end that in August 1898 a group of miners petitioned the federal government to hold an investigation into alleged irregularities in the gold commissioner's office, and other abuses. Such an inquiry was held in January 1899 under the supervision of William Ogilvie and largely exonerated the officials of any wrongdoing.

The cudgel was then taken up by Sir Charles Hibbert Tupper, who in two very long speeches to the House of Commons attacked the policy of the Liberal government in the Yukon and Ogilvie's handling of the inquiry in particular:

the uncle of the Minister of the Interior by marriage [Ogilvie] was not the proper man to inquire into charges which came so near the nephew's door. I say it was a gross scandal . . . to put a man into such a delicate position, and the fact that Mr. Ogilvie would act under the circumstances indicated his entire unfitness for that position.[21]

The odour of political partisanship hangs heavily over the whole affair, but the reputation of the police did not suffer, for they were involved only as witnesses to the supposed crimes of others. At one point in the investigation, one of the complaints which had been lodged against the police in their capacity as customs officers was brought forward as evidence of corruption, but this was old stuff and carried little weight.

In the Klondike, the Mounted Police were dealing with large numbers of white people, and thus they were subjected to a wide range of basically urban temptations. Because as individuals the police varied widely in competence, enthusiasm, and ability, it comes as no surprise that there were frequent lapses from the strict path of duty. Many traps existed to snare the susceptible police officer, but the basic problem in the Yukon was low pay, which made life difficult and strained morale. During the Klondike period the basic rate of pay for a constable was fifty cents a day, seventy-five cents after three years' service, plus fifty cents a day hard-ship allowance for those on northern service. A dollar a day plus board may have been barely adequate for the prairies, where the wage for agricultural labourers was about the same, but it was preposterously low in the Yukon, where because of the artificial economic conditions in-duced by the gold rush, a hired labourer on a claim could make between five and ten dollars a day and the cost of living was proportionately high. Of course, men did not usually join the police for profit; most of the recruits traditionally had been men out for adventure. But by the end of the nineties, the call of adventure was not enough to fill the ranks with Canadians; the force had to advertise for recruits in Britain, where young men were unaware of or oblivious to the purchasing power of a dollar in the Yukon. Of the recruits taken into the force between 1895 and 1897, 48 per cent had been born in the United Kingdom.[22]

At the same time, some men volunteered for Yukon service in order to get a free ride north in the hope of being able to get out of the force and stake a claim. It was police policy to permit men to purchase their dis-charge before completing their term of service as a good preventive against desertion, which had been a serious problem in the early years of the force—as much as 10 per cent in some years. But this policy was generally suspended during the gold rush and for several years there-afer, so that police in the Yukon wishing to buy their way out of the force were often refused permission to do so.

Thus, while there were in the force a fair number of idealists, there were also opportunists, and it was inevitable that disenchantment would set in for many. The police reports for every year noted that it was almost impossible to get men in the Yukon to re-enlist. And a few, as Hal Guest points out,[23] were simply bad or weak characters. If it had not been for the establishment of canteens at police posts where small luxuries were sold at reasonable prices,[24] the police constable in the Yukon would have found his pay able to buy him practically nothing. And as has already been noted, the police were forbidden to stake claims or to engage in any work for profit in their spare time.

With all this in mind, it may be surprising to find that examples of serious dereliction of duty among the police were rare. There were a few cases of theft; while guarding the Bank of British North America, one constable stole a small sum from the manager's desk and another stole $2,300 from the Board of Licence Commissioners.[25] A special constable embezzled $1,100 from the Dawson dog pound.[26] But there was not much of this sort of thing; most of the reductions in rank, fines, and dismissals handed out were for service offences, and there were a great many of these. The letter-books of the Dawson detachment are full of the records of police who were punished for visiting brothels, being drunk in dance-halls, and the like.

It is difficult to assess the significance of the numerous offences committed during the rush. Almost all of them were sins of the flesh—drunkenness, falling asleep on duty, "breaking barracks" (that is, staying out overnight—there were scores of these cases), and consorting with prostitutes. Certainly the police hierarchy viewed these offences seriously and they were harshly punished. The penalty for falling asleep while on guard duty in the corridor of the Dawson jail was two months' hard labour.[27] "Breaking barracks" generally bught a fine of $20, about three weeks' pay. Offences which showed the police in a bad light to members of the public brought harsher penalties. In the summer of 1901, for example, a constable was fined $15, given two months' hard labour, and dismissed for being absent from duty, drunk, and creating a disturbance in a house of ill-fame.[28] Another constable was given the same sentence for supporting a "woman of known immoral character at White Horse" and supplying her with food from the police stores.[29] Offences which might have been regarded as pranks were also punished if they embarrassed the force. One constable was given two months' hard labour and dismissed for "procuring tickets of admission to 3 prostitutes to the C.D. Docks on the arrival of his Excellency, he being on duty to receive such tickets."[30]

A few of the men put into positions of authority proved unequal to their responsibilities. The corporal in charge of the Livingstone Creek detachment in 1906 was reduced to the rank of constable, given two months' hard labour, and dismissed; he had made only three entries in the detachment diary in six weeks, "was a habitual frequenter of a house of ill-fame," did not come to the detachment when sent for by an Inspector, had to be arrested, and was drunk when arrested.[31] Anything involving theft brought severe punishment. A constable who stole $98 worth of food from police stores was given three months' hard labour and another three months of "civil imprisonment."[32] Another was given one month hard labour and dismissed for stealing a ring worth six dollars from a fellow constable.[33]

The frequency of offences involving drunkenness and "loose women" may be partly explained by the fact that during the rush the police lowered the standards for admission to the force and shortened the period of recruit training so that a number of half-trained men of unproven character went to the Yukon. Some of the recruits were barely literate and physically unprepossessing. In the Yukon they were subjected to much temptation, not the least of which was the sight of others getting rich while they worked for a dollar a day or less.

The various misdemeanors committed by the police are important not so much in themselves as in how they impaired police efficiency or affected their relationship with the community. They were certainly numerous, but it would be easy to overestimate their seriousness. As Wood admitted, "the young men must have some amusement,"[34] and there seems to have been no public outcry over any alleged police depravity. Certainly there were no complaints from the dance-hall girls, who found them good customers, as is shown by the noteworthy fact that gonorrhoea was the third most prevalent malady among the police in Whitehorse in 1901, after colds and gastric disorders.[35] The few cases of theft were reprehensible, but most of the sins of the police were ones of the flesh, and as such were perhaps more easily excused by the Yukoners than crimes of violence or dishonesty.

Despite the best efforts of the various officers commanding the police, discipline could not be kept as tight as it was to the south or as it was later to be kept farther north where temptations were fewer. Behaviour was tolerated in the Yukon which would have brought instant dismissal under other circumstances. A well-known case is that of Inspector Frank Harper, who was a veteran of nearly twenty years' service when he went to the Yukon in 1898; he promptly succumbed to its temptations. Pierre Berton quotes an old sourdough as saying, "I myself saw Captain Harper of the North West Mounted Police bet a hundred dollars that he could strip off naked, stand on his head on the stage of the Monte Carlo theatre, and eat a pound of raw beefsteak off the floor, and he won the bet."[36] This caused no official action, but eventually his public drunkenness and a liaison with a dance-hall girl (he had a wife in the south) caused him to be sent home. No punitive action was taken against him, however, for the sake of the reputation of the force and the feelings of his wife; a constable would have been quickly dismissed for similar behaviour.[37] On the other hand, Sam Steele, though a stern governor and the terror of malefactors, was popular enough in the community that the miners presented him with a poke of gold dust when he ended his service in the Yukon.[38]

Under the conditions the police had to endure, and with their miserable pay, it speaks well for the fibre of the force that derelictions of duty were so few and that the challenges of the Yukon were met as well as they were. For every record of a sergeant reduced to the ranks for drunkenness or an officer in disgrace, there are many accounts of the sort of heroism which so caught the attention of the public and the writers of popular fiction.[39]

A great deal of the foregoing examines and assesses the effect of the Mounted Police on the burgeoning frontier society of the Yukon. Others who have considered this subject have reached different conclusions.

S. D. Clark, for example, agrees that they were of "considerable importance in establishing a stable organization" of the region's social structure. But he believes that the work of the police and such other agencies
as the Salvation Army and the various churches were not the cause of
this stability, but only a manifestation of it, or at best a catalyst of it:

*Institutional controls derived from the outside, however, were effective only as a
result of the development of an underlying social consciousness favourable to the
establishment of order within the community. This was true even of the work
performed by the Mounted Police. That is to say that processes of social re-
organization were generated from within rather than from outside the society.
Lacking external aids the establishment of social order would have come about
more slowly, as the experience of mining communities amply demonstrates, but
these aids in themselves provided no solid basis upon which to erect a stable society.
Collective efforts were canalized and provided a more permanent goal of achieve-
ment; they sprang, however, from the urge of the people themselves to better their
conditions.* [40]

Certainly the Yukon possessed "an underlying social consciousness
favourable to the establishment of order"; Constantine had discovered
that as early as 1894–95 when he found that many of the miners were
"well-disposed" towards his mission. But whether this element of stability
could have prevailed over the undisciplined hordes of new arrivals for
whom, as Clark points out, "the rush to the mining frontier was something in the nature of a 'grand spree,'"[41] is questionable. Without the
police, the Yukon might have settled down eventually, as other mining
communities did, for there were other forces disposed to stability: the
merchant community, the churches, the schools, and regular family life.
But the other mining towns—in Alaska for example—did not become
stable until their days of prosperity were virtually over; speed in this
respect was essential in the Yukon for political as much as for social
reasons.

By 1899 the rush was over. Although greenhorns who kept arriving by
steamer gave the impression that Dawson was still booming, this was no
longer true. All the gold-bearing creeks had been staked, and most of
them had been worked to the point where men working by hand could
not make them pay. Dawson had ceased to provide unlimited opportunities for prospectors, so in the summer of 1899, when it was an-
nounced that gold had been discovered at Atlin and on the beaches of
Nome, Alaska, the more volatile elements of Dawson disappeared for
good, and the community started on a long slow period of shrinkage and
decline.

With the new century came new methods of mining in the Yukon.

Previously, when gold had been thick in the ground, the cost of labour meant nothing; only simple machines were needed, and a man could dig hundreds or thousands of dollars from the earth in a single day. Now what gold there still was in the ground was too scattered to make such methods profitable, and the era of the dredges began. These huge machines chewed up the old creeks and needed only a trace of gold in a cubic yard of gravel to make their operations profitable. The Yukon had changed, and the operations of the police had to change to meet new circumstances.

In the first place, the greatly reduced population of the Yukon did not need so large a police force to maintain law and order. Yet the number of police was by no means immediately reduced. There were several reasons for this anomaly. The police were performing services which had no relation to the size of the population; it made no difference to the size of the mail patrol, for example, whether it carried fifty letters or five hundred. And besides, the area over which police operations extended was actually larger in 1903 than it had been in 1898, for not all the miners left the Yukon with the decline of the Klondike area. Some went farther up the rivers and streams of the Yukon in search of new bonanzas, causing new posts to be established from time to time at places such as Duncan Creek and Gordon Landing, far from the original discoveries. As Assistant Commissioner Wood pointed out in his report for 1905, despite the fact that the population was decreasing, "each particular locality added its quota to those departing, the actual number of inhabitants at any point is not materially decreased, and therefore demands the same police protection."[42] For these reasons, as well as inertia in Ottawa, there were still three hundred police in the Territory at the beginning of 1903. But in that year it was finally decided in Ottawa that conditions no longer warranted a force of that size, and it was cut back to 228 by the end of 1905. In ensuing years further cuts were made, until by the end of the First World War, the force in the Yukon was reduced to a strength of about forty-five.

This action produced protests from two quarters. The remaining residents of the half-abandoned camps complained that the police were deserting them.[43] Wood protested that not all factors in the situation were being taken into consideration. It was true, he said, that three hundred men were not needed to keep the peace in the Yukon (thereby abandoning his argument of the previous year); a hundred men could easily police the whole Territory, "provided that they had only the legitimate work of the peace officers to perform."[44] He had a point, since other federal agencies were also withdrawing their services, throwing extra duties on the police, but this familiar refrain did not change the move towards retrenchment.

The death of the "boom" was a blessing in one way since most of the area's professional criminals left the Territory along with its prosperity, although Wood claimed that the remaining criminals filled the vacuum by spreading their operations over a wider area.[45] Also, the gold rush died more slowly than has been generally thought. Thousands left the Territory in 1899, but people still came north since there was gold to be found, if not huge fortunes to be made. The Territory's population did not bottom out until after the First World War. But by this time the duties of the police in the Yukon had become considerably less arduous than before. The centre of police pioneering in the north was moving towards the Arctic and towards Hudson Bay, and the Yukon was becoming, by degrees, once more a somnolent northern backwater.

6. North of the Arctic Circle

IN THE YUKON the police had set a precedent for further northern service by showing that they could adapt to almost any physical conditions and perform a wide variety of duties. Considering the great success with which they had handled the difficulties there, it was only natural that the police would be called upon if further northern service was required.

And soon it was, not long after the Yukon began to decline in importance, for reasons that echoed those that had brought the force into the Yukon in the first place. In 1903, the government took notice of two remote areas under its nominal sovereignty—the delta of the Mackenzie River and the west coast of Hudson Bay, and as a result police expeditions were sent to those two points.

Canada had held title to part of the Arctic islands since 1870, when it had acquired Rupert's Land, and to the remainder since 1880, when the rest of the Arctic was transferred by Britain to Canada.[1] Although the lieutenants-governor of Manitoba and the North-West Territories had a tenuous concern with these vast lands, they were in fact *terra incognita* as far as Ottawa was concerned. Diamond Jenness states the situation concisely: "Down to the very end of the nineteenth century ... Canada completely neglected her Arctic. . . . As long as no other country attempted to gain a foothold in that region they [Canadians] were content to forget it and push on with the development of the southern provinces of the Dominion."[2] The reason why the federal government displayed no interest in these lands during the first twenty years they were owned by Canada, why all the famous names in the great nineteenth-century age of Arctic exploration are British, European, or American is easy to find:

Canada had better, or at least more pressing, things to do than to worry about the north. As Jenness puts it, "The authorities . . . were carrying more important burdens than the remote and useless Arctic,"[3] a statement perhaps ironically meant, but nonetheless true.

What is of immediate concern here, however, is why the government reversed itself early in the present century and suddenly took notice of this erstwhile "remote and useless" land. Since the two areas concerned are so far apart and since the impetus leading to the establishment of government authority was somewhat different in each case, they will be treated separately in this and the next chapter.

Far to the north of any settlement, near the point where the Yukon-Alaska boundary runs into the Beaufort Sea, lies Herschel Island,[4] a barren blob about thirty-five square miles in area. Under ordinary circumstances it would probably never have attracted a moment's notice from the government, the police, or anyone else, but not long before the turn of the century, it acquired a strategic importance as a wintering place for the western Arctic whaling fleet.

Unlike the whaling ships of the eastern Arctic and Hudson Bay, which sometimes came and went each season, the ships in the west almost always came for a voyage of two summers at a time because of the short open-water seasons and the tremendous distances involved in getting home around the north of Alaska. Beginning in 1889, the captains of these ships became accustomed to wintering at Herschel Island, where they built warehouses and sometimes land dwellings for the cold season. In the winter of 1892–93 there were 160 whalers on the island. The whalers, almost all of whom were Americans, were transgressors on several counts from the Canadian point of view. They were unhampered by customs regulations and were under no restrictions in regards to liquor. The value of the whales taken was also not inconsiderable. In 1907, Inspector A. M. Jarvis, then commanding at Herschel Island, consulted four veteran whaling captains,[5] who told him that the first whale had been taken in Canadian waters in 1891, by the *Grampus*. In the same year the *Hume* returned to San Francisco after a two year voyage with a cargo worth $400,000—the most profitable voyage in American whaling history.[6] Since then 1,345 whales had been caught, valued at $13,450,000, while trading furs with the Natives had added another $1,400,000 to the revenue.[7] Although these men had no interest in making territorial claims, their very presence cast doubts on Canadian sovereignty over the island and the surrounding area; most of them doubtless neither knew nor cared that the island was ninety miles east of the international boundary. Furthermore, the whalers were suspected of corrupting the morals and, even more important, the whole social structure of the Inuit inhabitants of the area.

It was the matter of the Inuit which initially forced the reluctant federal government to pay attention to the area. Some whalers who wanted to acquire cheap servants and complaisant women had no hesitation in supplying liquor to the Inuit and teaching them to make it for themselves out of molasses or potatoes. The combined effects of liquor, disease, and general social disintegration over several generations were such that the Inuit population of the Mackenzie Delta region, which had been about 2,000 in 1830, had by 1930 declined to 200, of whom only twelve had been born in the area, the rest having migrated from Alaska.[8]

The catalytic agent in bringing this situation to the attention of the authorities was, as had largely been the case in the Yukon, the missionaries. An Anglican missionary, Rev. I. O. Stringer, reached Herschel Island in 1893, followed by Rev. C. E. Whittaker in 1895.[9] These men and their immediate superior, Bishop Bompas, forwarded complaints to the government concerning the alleged debauching of the Natives. Nor was this the government's only source of information. As early as 1895, rumours had reached Inspector Constantine in the Yukon that there were illegal and undesirable activities afoot at Herschel Island. In the fall of that year Constantine reported to Commissioner Herchmer that a man who had been an engineer on one of the whaling ships had come to him with ominous news:

The carryings-on of the officers and crews of the whalers there was such that no one would believe . . . large quantities of whiskey are taken up in the ships . . . as long as the liquor lasts, the natives neither fish nor hunt, and die of starvation in consequence. . . . The captains and mates of these vessels purchase for their own use girls from nine years and upwards.[10]

While many of the mixed-blood children who resulted from these unions were well looked after and some were taken south for education, the general effect on Inuit society concerned the authorites.

Constantine was willing to give full credence to the rumours that reached him from the coastal area. Prolonged trouble there would inevitably mean police intervention, and in 1895 the police were glad to make themselves useful wherever they could, since the future of the force was by no means secure. The Conservative administration was tottering to its fall, and the resurgent Liberals had traditionally been cool to the police.[11] It was the same situation that had taken Constantine to the Yukon in the first place.

In 1896 Constantine reported that nearly twelve hundred men were wintering at Herschel Island. Given their hard life, desertions by crew members were frequent. Because of the profit-sharing system used by the whaling companies, their pay at the end of the voyage was sometimes nothing, and they were denied the officers' privilege of living on shore during the winter with Inuit women. When the news of the discovery of gold in the Klondike reached Herschel Island, many men tried to desert and head south to the gold fields. These attempts were met by force, and sometimes led to disorder and bloodshed.[12] The sort of men who made up the whaling crews was vividly described a few years later by the officer in charge of the Herschel Island detachment. Many of the crew members, he wrote,

are not sailors at all, and have never been to sea before signing on, some are men who have come to sea to get away from the drinking habit, and a few . . . have done time for some offence in the United States. . . . Altogether they are rather a rough lot, and require to have a firm hand over them.[13]

The Canadian government looked with considerable disfavour on this situation once it had been made aware of it. It was not long since Canada had been involved with the United States in the matter of the Bering Sea seal fisheries, and she viewed the presence of American whalers in her waters with misgivings born of years of experience. It became clear to the government that in order to assert effective economic and political control over the western Arctic, some display of sovereignty would have to be made. And as an added dividend, something might be done for the Inuit, though as in the Yukon, the plight of the Natives was not uppermost in the minds of the police or the government. Comptroller White believed such conditions were natural; what was going on at Herschel Island was no more than was to be expected under the circumstances. "It is," he complained, "so difficult to convince the goody-goody people that in the development and settlement of a new country allowances must be made for the excesses of human nature."[14]

Of course, the missionaries did not agree with this "reasonable" view of the situation. Bishop Bompas, whose diocese of Selkirk included Herschel Island, did not hesitate to give the same attention to that remote spot as he had to the Yukon. In June 1896 he wrote to the minister of the interior "to call to your attention some matters which I think may probably call for the interference of your Government." These concerned the relations between the whalers and the Natives at Herschel, which were resulting in "deeds of furious violence . . . among the natives . . . to the utter ruin of those races."[15] Faced with this information, the minister asked Fred White if he thought it would be feasible for the N.W.M.P. to assume the responsibility for policing the region. White was unenthusiastic. He remarked that it might be possible to get a detachment or two into the Fort McPherson area by way of the Hudson's Bay Company supply boats, but the coastal area would best be policed from a patrol boat. However, he added, "The expense would be large, and . . . much greater than the existing state of affairs, or the results, would justify at present."[16] Meanwhile, the minister had replied to Bishop Bompas to the same effect—the project would be too expensive, and "There would be great difficulty, just at present, in getting the requisite appropriation."[17] This was an honest excuse. Sir Charles Tupper's government had fallen, and the country was just coming out of a prolonged economic depression. There was no money for Inuit welfare, which was seen as non-essential.

The late 1890s were not auspicious years for Canada to try to assert her authority in the Arctic for any reason, humanitarian or strictly political, for she already had all she could do to control the Yukon. The police were heavily committed in the Yukon from 1897 until 1903, and during part of this period they also supplied a battalion of men for service in the Boer War. Thus it was not until after 1900 that the government and the police could begin to think seriously about an extension of law and sovereignty to the north, and not until 1903 that an expedition could actually be sent out.

By 1900, Comptroller White had begun to make enquiries of his subordinates as to how the authority of the police might best be extended into the Mackenzie Delta area. "It has been urged," he wrote,

that the time has arrived when the Canadian Government should take steps to protect Canadian traders in that vicinity, and what I am most anxious to get at is (1) the facilities or means of travel between Fort Macpherson [sic] and the mouth of the Mackenzie, both summer and winter, and (2) the character and extent of the trading done by the whalers with the Natives for furs—trade which properly belongs to Canada, or upon which Canadian customs duties should be paid.[18]

White was not interested in the actual whaling operations, nearly all of which took place outside the three-mile limit, where Canada claimed no control, but coastal trading was another matter. In 1900 an exploratory patrol was sent from Dawson to Fort McPherson and back, via the Yukon and Porcupine Rivers, which route, in fact, traversed a good section of Alaska.[19] White confided to Clifford Sifton that he had "no doubt that in the early future we shall have police scattered between the Yukon and the mouth of the Mackenzie River, either directly across country, or via the Stewart and Peel Rivers." He still had qualms about the wisdom of the whole idea: "It is certainly desirable that Canada should assert her authority in the Arctic Ocean but it is questionable whether the results would justify the expenditure, at present."[20]

Possibly White was overestimating the difficulties of the proposal, for although Herschel Island was quite unknown to the Canadian government, Fort McPherson, the other suggested base of operations, should have been reasonably well known to the authorities. Having been founded by the Hudson's Bay Company in 1840,[21] the settlement was not new.

Fort McPherson is located on the Peel River, about fifteen miles south of its junction with the Mackenzie, and although it is not in the Mackenzie Delta proper, it was then the main community of the area and the only permanent one which housed white men. The post was not really inaccessible since the Hudson's Bay Company had begun running steamers down the Mackenzie in 1887, and it had been used as a jumping-off point for the Yukon by a small but significant number of miners who entered that country by the Rat-Bell-Porcupine-Yukon River route. In 1894 the Candian government had asked John Firth, the Hudson's Bay Company man at Fort McPherson, to act as an unofficial government representative; his most important duty was to keep an eye on the whalers, which he did until relieved by the police. This was not an unwelcome duty; as an employee of the company, Firth would be concerned with he activities of rival traders. He had no real authority and was probably not expected to do anything about Herschel Island, the main trouble spot. In any event, he seems to have had no ameliorating effect on the abuses that were taking place there.

Herschel Island was far more inaccessible. It could be reached easily enough in the late summer by ship from the Pacific, unless, as sometimes happened, ice conditions in the Beaufort Sea prevented ships from getting around Point Barrow. But the trip took a long time, nearly a whole season. The alternative, which was the method the police used, was to go as far as Fort McPherson by steamer and then 180 miles by small boat to Mackenzie Bay and west to Herschel Island—the last part of the trip along an inhospitable coast. This uncomfortable and sometimes hazardous voyage was to make for considerable difficulties in both manning and supplying the island post.

After 1900, planning for the new duties in the Arctic was accelerated. In this the police were aided by the efforts of those interested in the project. Frank Oliver, then the member of Parliament for Edmonton (and Clifford Sifton's successor as minister of the interior in 1905), was particularly anxious that the government assert its control over the Mackenzie Delta area, and for several years he urged action on the police and the government.[22] In 1902 Superintendent Constantine was sent to San Francisco on a confidential mission to investigate the whaling industry; a year later, Commissioner Perry went there as well to look into the possibility of obtaining a ship for police and fisheries work in the western Arctic. This came to little; Constantine reported that the whaling industry was declining, and the government refused the appropriation for a ship.[23] When in the winter of 1902–1903 the government decided to go ahead with an expedition to the western Arctic and another one to Hudson Bay, the plans were drawn up in secret by the government departments concerned, and the money was raised by passing an appropriation through Parliament to extend the fisheries protection service.[24]

The official government position is well set out in a memorandum drawn up by the Department of the Interior to justify the police expedition of 1903. It stated that there was no doubt that Canada had absolute title to the area in question, but that a show of the flag was necessary as a preventive measure:

It is feared that if American citizens are permitted to land and pursue the industries of whaling, fishing and trading with the Indians without complying with the revenue laws of Canada and without any assertion of sovereignty on the part of Canada, unfounded and troublesome claims may hereafter be set up.[25]

Probably the pleas of the missionaries carried some weight, and Ottawa's desire to collect customs duties was significant too, but the heart of the matter was the "unfounded and troublesome claims." The government desired to demonstrate its sovereignty. This was partly true of the Yukon expedition, and it was more true of the Mackenzie venture. The Mackenzie Delta, and Herschel Island in particular, were areas about which the government knew virtually nothing. Except for the Inuit and the resident missionary, there were no Canadians or British subjects living at Herschel Island and no Hudson's Bay Company post—only foreigners who were indifferent towards Canada's pretensions of sovereignty. There was little immediate danger; the whalers were not likely to proclaim a republic or to try to annex Herschel Island to Alaska. But it was damaging to Canada's concept of her own nationhood (a concept then hardly out of its infancy) to have part of her territory completely outside her control, inhabited by men who might make awkward "claims," and who certainly seemed to be up to no good.

The Mackenzie Delta expedition of 1903 was also in part a reflection of the Alaska Boundary dispute, the final settlement of which took place in the same year. "Unfounded and troublesome claims" had arisen in this affair too (though few today would deny that the Americans had the better case), and it seemed only prudent to the Canadian government that Canada's ownership of the western Arctic be made unequivocally clear. It was not that Ottawa wished to settle a question in the area; no question was to be permitted to arise.

The man selected to lead the expedition to the Mackenzie Delta was Superintendent Charles Constantine, the leader of the original Yukon expedition, who had first raised the question of policing the western Arctic. At this time, he was stationed at Fort Saskatchewan, and his orders, issued in the spring of 1903, required him to proceed to Fort McPherson via the Mackenzie River, reporting on all conditions along the route. At Fort McPherson he was to establish a detachment and then continue to Herschel Island and set up another detachment if he thought it advisable to do so. His party consisted of four constables and an N.C.O., Sergeant F. J. Fitzgerald, who was to become one of the leading figures in the subsequent history of the area.[26] The expedition left Fort Saskatchewan on 30 May 1903, travelled by rail to Athabaska Landing (now the town of Athabasca), and then by steamers, via Forts Chipewyan, Smith, Simpson, Good Hope, and Norman, to Fort McPherson.

As Constantine and his party travelled down river, he made a series of observations on the country. It was, he said, "barren and desolate, swamp, rock, and muskeg being the general character of the country. . . . I do not think that the Mackenzie district, as a whole, will ever support a purely agricultural community; the amount of arable land is very small."[27] But during the trip north, despite the rather dismal picture Constantine painted, the main idea behind the expedition—the establishment and emphasis of the Canadian presence in the area—was never far from his mind. This is clearly shown by an incident which involved an obvious symbol of sovereignty—the flag. Constantine was alarmed to see that at several Roman Catholic missions the French tricolour was being flown. This, he thought, was in very bad taste, and the sort of thing that was likely to go unchecked if the government did not assert itself. Comptroller White agreed and suggested that all police posts which might be set up in the region should be liberally supplied with Union Jacks to set an example and for distribution.[28] The issue of the flags did not end there. On a later occasion, the police actually tried to enforce the flying of the Union Jack, with marked lack of success. At Fort Simpson, there was "un incident fâcheux et bien regrettable" when a police inspector ordered the fathers to lower their flag (they were flying the Red Cross that day). Bishop Gabriel Breynat, the future "flying bishop," under whose authority the mission fell, noted the incident as showing that "même dans le Nord, nous eûmes à souffrir, quoique rarement, des activités de certains fanatiques." The fathers complied with the order under protest, but when Breynat heard of the affair he complained to friends in high places. The result was that the police had to apologize, and a constable involved was transferred to another division.[29] It is clear from the furore that there existed a certain attitude of Anglo-Protestantism among the police (though there were French-Canadians in their ranks), a feeling, common among English-Canadians of that era, which had led to the Manitoba Schools crisis and the controversy over the schools in the two provinces created in 1905.

The small expedition arrived at Fort McPherson without incident, and a detachment was established in quarters belonging to the Hudson's Bay Company—an example of the symbiotic relationship which existed between the police and the company. Here, the Hudson's Bay Company helped the police, and the police in turn provided law and order, to the Company's benefit. This happened in many places in the north, even in the Yukon, where the companies involved were American.

Constantine saw his men settled, told Sergeant Fitzgerald to try for Herschel Island that summer if he thought it feasible, and then, with what seems excessive haste, hurried back south to his wife. When White wrote Commissioner Perry the following June, he remarked that Constantine's supposedly long-term appointment to the command of the Mackenzie district had turned out "just as I thought it would." What the force badly needed, he said, was a few more unmarried officers.[30] Obtaining volunteers for the really isolated northern posts was, perhaps surprisingly in the light of legend, a serious problem in the early days of police service in the far north, and it was solved only by permitting officers and senior N.C.O.s to bring their wives with them. Once the police had been serving in the Arctic for a few years, the duties took on a glamour that ensured a more than adequate supply of volunteers. But this was, however, not the case in the beginning, as police records show. In a confidential letter to White, Perry made what must have been an embarrassing proposal for a man who had served so long in the force and who was so proud of its traditions: "In my opinion the stage has now been reached where officers must be selected for duty in the remote regions. We have failed to obtain suitable volunteers for both Mackenzie River and Hudson Bay—The public service must be carried on."[31]

Constantine's own account of his departure from Fort McPherson is considerably less prosaic; it is another of the passages of patriotic romanticism which now and again appear in the official documents relating to the police:

On July 16 [1903], at 4:10 P.M., we left Fort McPherson on the return trip. I felt for the men standing on the beach, as I well remember the feeling that came over our party in the Yukon in 1895, when the last steamer left, being cut off from the outside world, for a year at least; strangers in a strange land, but with the stout hearts and good British pluck which will pull a man through if true to himself.[32]

At first there was little for the police to do at Fort McPherson except show the flag, for Herschel Island was the main target. Officials in Ottawa believed that the difficulties of travel were so great that the island could not be reached in 1903. Writing in answer to an inquiry on the subject, White said "I do not think there is any possibility of the police reaching Herschel Island this year.... We trust that later on the government will furnish a steamer for patrolling Mackenzie Bay, and then it will be possible to reach Herschel Island."[33] White's pessimism was not shared by the man responsible for making the attempt, Sergeant Fitzgerald, whose audacity and energy were more than equal to the task. Accompanied by a constable, he made a patrol in a small boat from Fort McPherson to Herschel Island in August 1903. He decided to establish a detachment there that year and managed to persuade the resident missionary, Rev. C. E. Whittaker, to rent him the mission's steam launch to transfer supplies from Fort McPherson to the new detachment. Here his luck ran out, temporarily, when the launch was wrecked in Mackenzie Bay and part of the supplies lost. This incident later resulted in an unseemly wrangle between the police and Whittaker's bishop over the value of the wrecked steamer,[34] but the immediate effect was to leave the policemen on Herschel Island practically destitute.

Fitzgerald had been given very specific instructions by Constantine on how to manage the detachments; these give a good idea of how the police envisaged their mission. "You have been given command of this detachment," wrote Constantine, "which carries with it much responsibility; the success and the credit of the force in that part of the territories will depend upon your discretion, tact, and management." Fitzgerald was reminded of the solitary nature of his responsibilities: "There will be no one to advise and instruct you in case of difficulties; the Hudson's Bay Company officer, who ... has been many years at Fort McPherson, will be able to give you advice as to the manner of dealing with the natives, their prejudices and local customs." He was not expected to meddle with the Natives; their customs were to be respected as long as they were "consistent with the general law." Nor was Fitzgerald to be allowed to forget that he was a member of a semi-military bureaucracy; spit and polish were not to be neglected, nor was clerical routine:

Inspections of the arms are to be held WEEKLY and kits EVERY MONTH....
The men are to be PROPERLY DRESSED.... A typewriter has been
supplied ... and one of the constables or youself can easily learn how to use it ...
all your reports should be made in TRIPLICATE.[35]

Herschel Island was probably the most physically and psychologically challenging post manned by the police to that time. It was bare, desolate, and windy. There was no wood at all on the island, and coal had to be bought from the whalers. When Fitzgerald and his constable arrived, they had to find quarters. A tent, even if they had had one, was out of the question. There were only six proper buildings on the island—two owned by the Anglican mission and the other four, by the Pacific Steam Whaling Company, the chief commercial enterprise in the area.[36] As well as the frame buildings, the island boasted fifteen sod houses owned by the whaling company, various embers of the crew, and the missionary. In one of these houses, "ventilated by a hole in the roof, the same opening also serving for a window ... very damp and dark,"[37] the police spent their first winter, warmed by coal borrowed from the whaling company.

The police were in an anomalous position. They had come to Herschel Island to emphasize Canada's control over the area and to protect Canadian sovereignty from the inroads, real or imagined, being made upon it by the American whalers. Their secondary purposes were to collect customs duties from these ships and whoever else might be trading with the Natives and also to halt the flow of liquor which was so demoralizing them. It must have weakened their moral position considerably to be dependent for heat and partly for food on these same whalers and for shelter on the missionary, even though they paid for these services. In subsequent years, when for a time the police detachment was located in a frame building rented from the Pacific Steam Whaling Company, the anomaly was even more pronounced. How could the police carry out their mission, establish government authority, and enforce laws in the area when they owed their lodging to one of the "power groups" on the island and their warmth and some of their food to the another?

The answer is that the police and the whalers were not necessarily adversaries. The captains seem to have been glad to have police around who would presumably help control their notoriously unruly crews.[38] The whalers were also likely glad to have more white men to talk to. Customs duties were collected haphazardly; in 1903 no collections were made for, incredibly, no one had thought to furnish Fitzgerald with the schedule of duties.

This apparent anomaly never seems to have bothered Fitzgerald, or at least there is no reference to it in the records. He accepted without concern the premise that the success of his mission depended upon the cooperation and generosity of the people he was policing and protecting. He gave orders expecting they would be obeyed, and for the most part they were. Another reason why the whalers were cooperative was that their economic importance in the region was fast declining. Every year whales were becoming harder to find, and the market was also declining. The increasing use of petroleum products had caused a sharp drop in the price of whale-oil, and substitutes for whale-bone had been discovered. The industry would be virtually extinct by the beginning of the First World War. By 1903, most of the whalers were seeking their catch to the east of the Mackenzie Delta, and some were wintering at Baillie Island, about 250 miles to the east of Herschel. It was quite impossible for the police to get to Baillie Island, given their available means of transportation, and although they realized that they were in the wrong place to help the Inuit there, they proceeded to carry out their task by informing whatever whaling captains they could find that the laws of Canada must be obeyed. No one seems to have objected.

Thus, the police encountered little opposition because they had little real effect on the operations of the whalers. If the whaling captains wished to avoid paying customs duties or if they did not wish the police to pry into their business, it was a simple matter to bypass Herschel Island, even though it was true that little went on that the police did not eventually hear about at second or third hand. Nor did the captains object to unenforceable laws. Any successful assertion of sovereignty, insofar as it manifested itself in making the whaling captains obey the customs law, was more apparent than real. The whalers customarily employed Inuit for various jobs and paid them in trade goods, for money would have been useless to them. These goods, imported from the United States, were liable to Canadian customs duty, and getting the captains to pay it was a good way of asserting Canadian control. But two police officers could not search a dozen or so ships, especially when the police base in the area was on such uncertain foundations. Fitzgerald was therefore reduced to the expedient of asking each captain to give him a list of goods brought in for trade. The lists, honest or otherwise, were soon forthcoming, and Fitzgerald collected customs duties on that basis beginning in 1904. Ships which avoided Herschel Island could escape paying duty altogether, and on at least one occasion Fitzgerald was compelled to feign ignorance in order to conceal the weakness of his position: "I could not let the captains know that I knew that tobacco was traded, as that would show them that I could take no action at the present time."[39] Bluffing was most uncharacteristic of the way the police generally operated, and Fitzgerald's action shows how tenuous their position actually was.

Another reason the whaling captains did not object to the presence of the police arises out of the internal dynamics of the whaling industry. As Thomas Stone pointed out, the whalers' society was highly authoritarian, based on the officers' brutal control over the crews. The "system of authority... and the social stratification of the whaling community worked together to guarantee that the most significant conflicts in the community would arise where there was no genuine 'third party' mechanism to deal with them."[40] The police provided this mechanism insofar as they enforced the laws against desertion and violence. They were thus the allies rather than the adversaries of the captains.

Fitzgerald made some significant observations about the Inuit who lived at Herschel Island. His conclusion was that the stories of debauchery, in the sexual sense of the word, had been greatly exaggerated. He observed that the Inuit women did not mind being sold into temporary concubinage by their husbands—some, in fact, thought it an honour. They did not resent their inevitable abandonment by the sailors and were not thought less of by the other Inuit; if anything, they were envied. "I cannot reconcile the stories," wrote Fitzgerald, "with the eager manner with which the Esquimaux greets [sic] the arrival of the ships and go on board shaking hands with everyone they meet. If the women were ill-treated and abused as the papers say, they would surely keep away from the ships after one lesson."[41]

Fitzgerald was wrong in his assumption that all the tales of harm done to the Inuit were untrue. Diamond Jenness's research into the subject is proof enough, but there is also direct evidence from the police. Fitzgerald's cheerful denials are contradicted by a statement by the other detachment at Fort McPherson that "The numbers [of Inuit] are decreasing very fast. Last spring at McPherson out of a band of 80, whose settlement was at Herschel Island, some 70 died of measles.[42]

The discrepancy in the two accounts may be simply explained; it was the old case, as in the Yukon, of the police distinguishing between different kinds of debauchery. Because they themselves did not seem to resent it, the sexual exploitation of the Inuit was not condemned by the police, who could not understand what all the fuss in the newspapers was about. Physical deterioration, on the other hand, was obviously to the detriment of the Inuit and provoked a more direct reaction. Both problems arose from the same cause—close physical contact between Inuit and white. In the matter of liquor being sold or given to the Natives, the police took what measures they could. During his stay at Fort McPherson, Constantine tried to impress upon the Natives the fact that liquor was now forbidden. At the same time, he tried to make the new regulations as easy as possible: "one native man . . . I arrested and sentenced to two days' imprisonment, but gave him to understand that if I had not to go to Peel river he would get 30 days. I had to sentence him, if I did not it would have no effect on them."[43] It was the physical abuse of liquor—which brought disease and dissipation—rather than any moral abuse which attracted the attention of the police.

How did the Inuit respond? How did they react to this new element in their rapidly changing way of life? The police were yet another facet of the white man's society which had to be understood and reacted to. Before 1900 the Inuit of the western Arctic had encountered three classes of whites—explorers, traders, and missionaries—each of which had powerfully affected their lives. The explorers introduced the Inuit to European culture; the traders bound Inuit society to this culture; and the missionaries tried, with limited effect, to soften the effects of it. Where did the police, the fourth element, fit into the scheme of things in the Mackenzie Delta?

The police represented government and law and so introduced a new sense of order into Inuit life. No longer did the missionary have to coax the Inuit to avoid liquor; the police were now at hand to see that they were denied the opportunity to get drunk. The Inuit reaction to the new regime is difficult to assess, for few left any records. One of the Mackenzie Delta group however, a man named Nuligak, did. Nuligak was born in 1895, lived through the whaling period, and as an old man dictated his memoirs, which have been translated into English. The Inuits' initial delight in the white man's pleasures is shown clearly in Nuligak's account of his first meeting with the whalers in 1902:

When summer came Uncle Kralogark took us west to Herschel Island. . . . Crowds of Eskimos came there. That fall I saw some very large ships. The sailors we met always had something in their mouths, something they chewed. It so intrigued me that I kept staring at their jaws. One certain day that "thing" was given to me. I chewed—it was delicious. It was chewing gum. From that day I was able to recognize some of these white men's things.[44]

Herschel Island, far from being avoided, was a central spot for the Inuit because of all the delightful things that could be done there: "Finally we reached Herschel. Herschel! The great big town! I felt very happy at the sight of so many houses. . . . There were drinking bouts every day. People would drink anything; the Alaskan Inuit are renowned for that."[45] His book contains no hint of resentment towards the police for bringing all these adventures to an end; some of Nuligak's happiest memories, in fact, concern New Year's parties and games arranged for the Natives by the police and the Hudson's Bay Company at Fort McPherson.[45] It is also quite likely that the use of liquor by the Inuit continued, though perhaps on a reduced scale; the stills were easily moved to more distant locations.

The Inuit never seem to have objected to the new regulations. They were not particularly onerous, and they were not imposed all at once. The police did not expect the Inuit to obey all the laws of Canada completely and immediately. They treated the Inuit leniently and with restraint, so that later, when there were episodes of serious trouble between Inuit and whites, the police were able to take control of the situation without serious resistance. This leniency came, in part, from the fact that the legal position of the Inuit was vague; they did not fall under the Indian Act, yet they obviously had to be treated differently from whites. There was thus a large element of improvisation in police policy towards them.

In its initial stages the police expansion into the Mackenzie Delta seemed to be going well. The police at Fort McPherson had established themselves without difficulty, and those at Herschel, though partly impotent and operating under a burden of obligation to the people they had been sent to watch, had met with no serious opposition. The few laws applicable to the situation were enforced. Drunken Natives were arrested, convicted, and subjected to token imprisonment (there was no place to lock them up). Those whalers who were within reach of the police were made to obey the customs laws and to stop selling liquor to the Natives. And the government had finally put a force on the ground in that remote northwestern corner of Canada to show that Ottawa was aware of its existence and was determined to exercise control over it. Thus the initial task of the police had been successfully carried out, and the foundations were laid for a new phase of police operations in the Arctic.

7. To Hudson Bay and the Eastern Arctic

THE SECOND new area of concern for the police after 1900 was Hudson Bay. This region had had, of course, a very long history before the Canadian government bestirred itself to think about it. The bay and its coastal areas had been fairly well known since Henry Hudson explored them in the summer of 1610. Many of the names of the geographical features of the bay are now over three hundred and fifty years old; Cape Wolstenholme and Digges Island, for instance, were both named after patrons of Hudson's voyage.[1] Though the contact period in the region has been of a much longer duration than in the western Arctic, Hudson Bay presents some noteworthy parallels. Both the delta and the bay had first been developed economically by the Hudson's Bay Company. Both had a mixed population of Indians and Inuit. The two regions had both been turned over to Canada shortly after Confederation (although the Mackenzie Delta was not part of the original Rupert's Land), and there were foreign whaling operations in Hudson Bay similar to those in the Beaufort Sea. The threat to Canadian sovereignty, though less severe than in the western Arctic, was still present in Hudson Bay, there affecting territorial waters rather than land.

Two nations dominated the whaling industry of northeastern Canada. A Scottish fleet came out each summer to hunt whales in the waters of Baffin Bay; the Americans operated in Hudson Bay, on the west side, near and around Southampton Island. They had a wintering station on the coast of the bay at Cape Fullerton. The influence of these whalers on the Inuit of Hudson Bay was less deleterious than that of the Mackenzie Bay whalers on the Inuit of the western Arctic, insofar as there were fewer ships in Hudson Bay, and the whalers there did not distribute liquor quite so freely. On the other hand, the traders and whalers had been in Hudson Bay for a much longer time than their counterparts in the Mackenzie Delta, and the Inuit and Indians had had a much longer and heavier dose of cultural dislocation. Diamond Jenness describes the resulting "buckling" of native Inuit culture:

Metal pots and pans ousted the cooking-pots of stone; garments of cotton and wool overlay and underlay the native garments of fur.... The Eskimo hunters threw away their self-made bows and arrows to equip themselves with firearms, abandoned their hunting kayaks and their umiaks... and adopted the clinker-built whaleboats that the ships' captains left behind.[2]

But the issue which moved the government to take action in Hudson Bay was again not the plight of the Native people. As in the Mackenzie Delta, it was a matter of establishing effective government control. The presence of American whalers in Hudson Bay acting as if the Canadian government did not exist might be construed as casting doubts on Canada's assertion that it was a "closed" sea. And the bay was not the only area of concern; what Jenness calls the "spectre of foreign intervention"[3] had appeared farther north. Between 1898 and 1902 the Norwegian explorer Otto Sverdrup had discovered the islands which now bear his name, landed on them, and claimed them for Norway. This was an alarming development for Canada, because its claim to the Arctic archipelago rested merely on Britain's claim to all islands north of the mainland then known and any others that might later be discovered. This claim might logically be disputed by a government whose representative had been the first to set foot on hitherto unknown and completely uninhabited territory, especially as long as discovery, in the absence of further control activities in the region, was the only criterion for sovereignty. In this tricky situation, it seemed that the solution was for Canadians to go north, make demonstrations of sovereignty, and establish a presence as soon as possible.

But this expedition was not to be entirely in the hands of the police. Intended as a much grander affair than the Mackenzie Delta expedition, it was placed under the command of A. P. Low, a geologist by profession, who had done a good deal of exploring for the government in previous years. It was, in short, to be a government rather than a police expedition, showing the importance which Ottawa placed on the project.[4]

The first intimation the police had that there was something new in store for them came late in 1902, when Comptroller White was told by the deputy minister of the interior that problems of sovereignty and whalers were being considered, both in Mackenzie and Hudson Bays.[5] Far from being pleased at the opportunity to extend police control to an entirely new part of the country, White was horrified. He objected strenuously to "a plan so foreign to anything the Police have in the past been called upon to perform."[6] He held that any legal functions on the trip could adequately be carried out by a "magistrate selected from the East, with three or four of the crew sworn in as Constables."[7] White's main objections to the scheme were based on its exclusively nautical nature—that it was essentially a naval patrol and therefore foreign to police training and experience. He was also not pleased by the fact that the expedition was to be under the control of the Department of Marine and Fisheries, making the police in effect no more than passengers on the ship. This objection was an echo of the longstanding police dislike of being subordinated to other civil service agencies, which came out most strongly during their Yukon service.

White went to Clifford Sifton to plead his case, but as he reported to Commissioner Perry in August 1903, "I was bowled over in my efforts to have the Police freed from the mission to Hudson's Bay."[8] Sifton told White that in the event a landing was made somewhere in the bay, the police "would know exactly what to do in establishing a system of control—whilst anyone who might have been appointed from the East would have lacked the necessary experience."[9] Sifton's argument seems reasonable, and one wonders in retrospect what all the fuss was about. The police had performed very well in obscure corners of the Yukon and northwestern British Columbia. Why should they not do as well on the shores of Hudson Bay? Perhaps the fear in the minds of the officials was best expressed by White when he wrote, "I dreaded having any of our men landed away up in Baffin's [sic] Bay or Cumberland Sound."[10] These areas were the chief whaling grounds for the Scottish ships, and White apparently feared that police posts might be required in places where they would be completely beyond the control of police headquarters, since the N.W.M.P. did not then have a supply boat. This fear was to prove groundless, however, as the police were not assigned to that part of the Arctic for another twenty years, by which time the whalers were gone. Instead, the effort was directed at Hudson Bay, the locale of the American whalers.

White did make one sensible objection which proved to be prescient. He said, in the letter to the deputy minister quoted earlier, that the best way of policing Hudson Bay was to make the police mobile—that is, to provide them with a boat, "able to move from place to place, land where necessary, or overhaul and search a whaling schooner or trader. To make the police . . . a fixture on so long a line of coast . . .would simply be hoisting a warning signal to illicit traders to give that particular point a wide berth."[11] Although he overestimated the danger from illegal traders, White was correct when he suggested that the police would be seriously hampered in their operations by lack of mobility.

White's objections were overruled by his superiors, the deputy minister and Sifton himself, and plans for the expedition went ahead. It was made clear from the beginning that the essential purposes of the trip were scientific investigation and the establishment of sovereignty. As the deputy minister put it, the voyage was "for the purpose of patrolling and exploring and establishing the authority of the Government on the points in question."[12] But as far as the police were concerned, it was all rather vague. They were going north, but exactly where and to what no one seemed to know:

[It is] . . . proposed to send a commissioned officer . . . with four or five men who will establish the post at the place found to be most convenient. . . . The post will be provisioned for two years but it is the intention that the patrol will return and visit the post every year. . . . our knowledge of the northern portion of the territories in question being so unexact no very definite instructions can be given as to the location of the post.[13]

No wonder White had qualms.

In contrast to the Mackenzie Delta expedition, which left in the same year, the one to Hudson Bay received fairly wide publicity. In the light of the much-publicized Alaska Boundary dispute, the issue of territorial sovereignty interested the newspapers and their readers. The Toronto Globe explained the purpose of the venture neatly: "Canada claims all arctic America, but she has done little or nothing in the way of actual occupation to make good her title, so is now repairing this neglect before any diplomatic friction arises."[14] The Globe predicted, incorrectly, that a detachment would be set up that year at Chesterfield Inlet and rejoiced that "Canada's rule will be visibly demonstrated there."[15] Another newspaper said, also incorrectly, that the expedition intended to "take possession as far north as possible, raising the British flag over lands heretofore looked upon as neutral."[16] The assertion that any of the lands to be visited by the Neptune were looked upon as neutral was certainly wrong as far as the Canadian government was concerned. However, whether the reports were accurate or not, the news of the expedition met with a considerable burst of approving publicity on the part of the press, and the government was commended on its enterprise. The officer selected to lead the police contingent to Hudson Bay was Superintendent J. D.

Moodie, who had earlier proven his stamina as the leader of the party that blazed the Peace River-Yukon route in 1897–98.[17] The rest of the party was made up of a non-commissioned officer and four constables.

There is a curious discrepancy between the official purpose of this expedition and the purpose that the newspapers read into it. The press seems to have felt that the expedition was essentially punitive—that the principle of Canadian sovereignty was about to be roughly or violently asserted in the eastern Arctic. As the Ottawa *Evening Journal* put it, the *Neptune* was sailing north "with the object of expelling any American whalers found fishing in those waters."[18] But this was only wishful thinking, a popular reaction to the events of the Alaska Boundary controversy. The official attitude toward the situation was much less rigid. Moodie's instructions put the position clearly: "It is not the wish of the Government that any harsh or hurried enforcement of the laws of Canada shall be made."[19] Instead of "hurried enforcement," Moodie was instructed to "impress upon the captains of whaling and trading vessels, and the natives, the fact that after reasonable notice and warning the laws will be enforced as in other parts of Canada."[20] Evidently Ottawa did not wish to cause any incidents that might lead to a diplomatic clash with the United States, a clash which might have brought Canada's claims to sovereignty under direct and unsympathetic scrutiny.

The *Neptune* was a 465-ton Newfoundland sealing schooner, built in 1873 and strongly constructed to withstand great pressure of ice.[21] Cleaning and alterations were carried out in the spring and early summer of 1903, and on 23 August, with a complement of police, observers from the Department of Marine and Fisheries and from the Geological Survey, a photographer, and the ship's crew, the *Neptune* steamed out of Halifax harbour. The ship sailed as far north as Cumberland Sound and then back to Port Burwell (which A. P. Low thought would make a good customs station for traffic going into Hudson Bay).[22] It then sailed into Hudson Bay, stopping at Cape Wolstenholme, Cape Fullerton, and Chesterfield Inlet. Moodie decided to build his post at Fullerton Harbour, reputedly the whalers' wintering spot, and it was there the *Neptune* spent the winter of 1903–1904.

The first winter was difficult for the small detachment even though they spent much of their time living on the ship. The expedition's physician, Dr. G. B. Faribault, became violently insane shortly after the expedition set out, and he had to be given constant care and supervision until he died in April 1904. This duty must have been onerous, for Moodie requested extra pay for the men who performed it.[23] However, the only thing the police accomplished during this first winter was erecting several small buildings, scouting the immediate country, and planning for the future. No action was taken in regard to whaling activities in the bay; there was only one ship near Fullerton, and Moodie had no means of reaching any others. His instructions on this subject had been vague; he wrote to White, "I am informed that there are several American whalers in Hudson's Bay. I have no instructions as to their right to fish there, and shall do nothing in this way unless I receive definite instructions next year. I am writing to the Minister of Customs [for information]."[24]

Moodie also drew up an elaborate plan for posts in Hudson Bay and the eastern Arctic. Eight posts would be necessary, he thought—an annual visit by a government ship was not sufficient for the purposes of supervising the area and exercising effective control over it. A single visit from a ship "will give but very slight grounds on which to uphold a claim to a territory peopled by native & whitemen other than Canadians."[25] Moodie wanted the police headquarters for Hudson Bay established at Cape Wolstenholme, which he thought was the natural port of entry for the area, with detachments at Fullerton, Churchill, Port Harrison, Repulse Bay, and Chesterfield in the bay and Blacklead Island and Pond Inlet in the eastern Arctic whaling grounds."[26] Twenty-seven police would be required. He also wanted the police to acquire a steamer which could carry a hundred tons of cargo so that they would be able to supply their own detachments and not be dependent on other government agencies or private carriers."[27] Moodie's assessment of the requirements of the region proved accurate, for eventually police posts were set up at all the locations he recommended except Cape Wolstenholme and Blacklead Island. For the time being, however, these plans were too ambitious. White reported to Laurier that he was satisfied with what had been accomplished: "I gather that everything has gone on satisfactorily. They wintered at Fullerton . . . established a post there and built huts, and I feel sure that we have now made a fair start in opening up those regions."[28]

In fact the police had made only a very small start; it was not until the next year, 1904, that they began to make significant progress toward establishing themselves in the area. In July 1904, Moodie left Hudson Bay on the *Neptune,* leaving his N.C.O. and two constables behind, with instructions to make a patrol by boat north to Repulse Bay, where whaling ships were more likely to be found.[29] Moodie's task was to report to his superiors in the police and the government, and he was armed with a variety of observations, suggestions, and plans. His report was valuable to the government because it helped accomplish the goal of the police and also because it gave a good idea of some of the immediate problems involved in trying to establish effective control over the Hudson Bay region.

Moodie described the traders as a baneful influence on the Inuit, who were by nature cheerful, honest, and hard-working. "They are not beggars," he said, "but expect to pay for whatever they receive."[30] The traders took advantage of this honesty by charging high prices for their goods: a ten-dollar rifle cost the Inuit fifteen musk-ox skins worth fifty dollars each."[31] The price for a hundred primers for a Winchester rifle was one skin. The former cost ten cents in New York and the latter fifty dollars. There was an even worse result than this alleged larceny—the desire of the Inuit for trade goods was so great that they were slaughtering every musk-ox they could find, and the traders were delightedly encouraging them to do so.[32] Moodie reported that he had seriously feared that the musk-ox in the Fullerton area would be completely exterminated. He was in a quandary; there was no point in declaring a closed season on the animals since the Inuit needed them for food. So Moodie improvised and laid down his own law. Instead of enforcing a closed season on musk-ox, he told the traders that the export of musk-ox skins was now completely prohibited. This seemed to him "the only method which would be of practical use."[33] As had been the case in the Yukon, the police were "making up the laws as they go along." Under the Northwest Game Act of 1894, the animals could not be killed between 20 March and 15 October, but there was no other restriction on hunting them. They were not completely protected until 1917. Moodie justified these irregular proceedings on the grounds that haste was essential: "The *Era* was on the point of despatching a large party of natives to hunt these animals, and any action to be effective, had to be taken at once. The natives did not go."[34] Once again, boldness on the part of the police solved a dilemma where more cautious (and legal) methods—such as writing to Ottawa and waiting a year for a reply—would have failed. Of course, Moodie's writ ran only as far as he could travel; outside this area his dictates could safely be ignored.

This incident was in fact the example of a theme which ran all through the police service in Hudson Bay—the rapacity of the traders. There are many references to the traders in police letters and reports—to the Hudson's Bay Company and more especially to the independent traders—damning their greed and their tendency to cheat the Natives. In reporting on the *Era* incident, Moodie went on, "the return given the Esquimaux for valuable furs and whalebone is a mere nothing."[35] "Everything owned by the trader is valued at twenty times its price," he wrote, "and everything owned by the native is cut down in value a hundredfold."[36]

The traders would have doubtless defended themselves by saying that they had a large overhead, that the volume of trade was small, and that goods cost a great deal to bring to Fullerton from the United States. Most of the trading vessels were, however, whaling ships, and trading with the Inuit was only a sideline designed to make some extra money during the winter months; the main overhead was for the whaling operations. And even if these ships had been solely traders, as became the case later on, the margin of profit was outrageous. It might be argued, as some traders did argue, that the Inuit had all the skins they needed and that rifles and ammunition were a wonderful boon to them; if the Inuit did not feel cheated, and apparently they did not, why should anyone object to the transactions? There were two good answers. As the ethnologists had pointed out, the demand for guns and other goods had been created by the traders, who had "forced the aboriginal culture to buckle."[37] The Euro-Canadian culture, because it made life easier for the Inuit, had become as habitual to them as tobacco is to the chain-smoker, and it was the trader who was the chief purveyor of the material goods of this culture. In the second place, if the musk-oxen were seriously depleted or wiped out altogether, as seemed likely to happen, the Inuit would have lost what little independence they still retained. They would then be dependent on the traders for food as well as for everything else they needed, and the traders were likely to abandon them as soon as trading slackened. This possibility (which later became a grim reality), along with his mistrust of Americans who traded in Hudson Bay free from worries about Canadian customs regulations, moved Moodie to issue his edict.

In private conversations with police officials in Ottawa as well as in written reports and letters, Moodie emphasized the barriers which lay in the way of the police making any significant impression on the Hudson Bay area. The difficulties involved in supporting life and in travelling, he said, "are much greater even than in the Yukon."[38] The task of supplying a base from southern Canada was relatively easy in Hudson Bay, except for the storms that sometimes blew up suddenly and put supply ships in danger; the Hudson's Bay Company had supplied its posts by sea for well over two hundred years. The real difficulty lay in patrolling the coastline north of Fullerton to Repulse Bay or south toward Churchill and York Factory. In the short summer, patrols could be made by boat, but there were few places along the coast where a boat could be safe from a sudden storm, as the police were later to find out to their cost. Even in mid-winter there was often a lead of water a mile or so wide paralleling the coast of the bay; this made travel by sled difficult. Moreover, there were few trees along the coast, and for long stretches none at all; so that fuel for heating and cooking had to be carried in the form of oil or kerosene. This was in sharp contrast to the Yukon, which was thickly wooded in the valleys. Finally, the distances involved were

much greater than in the Yukon. It is more than 200 miles from Fullerton to Repulse Bay, and more than 500 from Fullerton to Churchill.
Moodie was only bing realistic when he said that "Under the existing
cirumstances and strength of the police in Hudson Bay, patrolling to any
extent is next to impossible."[39] And without patrols, any attempt on the
part of the police to demonstrate Canadian control over the area would
be unsuccessful. On the other hand, even if the police were never to
leave Fullerton, their very presence in the bay was bound to have some
value in this respect.

Moodie's solution to this dilemma—a series of posts strategically located on both sides of the bay and at the entrance to it—has already been
described. With all these posts in operation, patrols would not have to be
as long and could therefore be made more easily and more safely. The
large steamer required could supply the posts and keep an eye on the
whalers in areas where patrolling was not feasible. For liaison with the
Inuit—translating, hunting for meat, and general work—he also recommended the employment of two Natives at each post. They were to
be paid $4.50 a month and their keep, a sum which seems ungenerous,
but with which they would apparently be well pleased.[40]

Thus the first year in Hudson Bay seemed reasonably successful for
the police. They had not accomplished much, but they had done what
their resources permitted. Moodie had handled his task well; his only
false step lay in giving a newspaper reporter an interview on his return
which produced the following sensational headline: "Work Suffered
from Politics: Hudson's Bay Expedition Bungled from Start: Major
Moodie's Hands Tied: Given Incompetent Assistants, an Insufficient
Force and Absurd Instructions."[41] In response to a sharp query from
White, Moodie denied that he had said anything of the kind.[42] This
perhaps taught him not to grumble in front of reporters from Opposition newspapers.

It seemed then that the police would be required to extend their
operations in Hudson Bay. The prospect did not please Comptroller
White. Even after the first year, he was still trying to get the police
relieved from this duty. As he wrote to Perry, "I did my best to get the
Police released from this Hudson's Bay duty, but without success."[43] In
another letter he explained the reasons for his continuing objections: "I
feel sure that whilst a lot of responsibility will be thrown on the Police
Officers, we shall have very little to say about the movements of the
vessel, and general jurisdiction. However, we must bide our time and
adapt ourselves to circumstances."[44] In this fear White was only partially
correct, for the 1904–1905 voyage was entirely a police affair, rather
than being, like the first, largely scientific.

Although the friction on the first voyage to Hudson Bay was mostly a figment of journalistic imagination, on the second it was quite real. The ship chosen for the trip was the *Gauss,* re-christened the *Arctic* and commanded by Captain J. E. Bernier, a French-Canadian of great skill and experience in handling ships. Bernier, then at the height of his career, had conceived a passion for Arctic exploration, and he had raised considerable sums of public and private money to finance a "Canadian Polar Expedition" in which he and the *Arctic* would drift across the Arctic Ocean in the manner of Nansen, perhaps, he hoped, crossing the Pole. However, in the spring of 1904, Bernier was astonished to find himself "suddenly ordered to put ashore three years' supplies and proceed to Hudson Bay, practically under the orders of the Mounted Police to ascertain whether a certain . . . ship captain was engaged in selling liquor to the natives."[45] In retrospect, Bernier said "I will not dwell on the disappointment that overwhelmed me when this turn in events occurred " But in 1904 he did dwell on it, and there was much squabbling during the voyage. On his return to southern Canada in 1905, Bernier gave a newspaper interview in which he bitterly denounced Moodie, calling him "an impossible man to work with. . . . He wished to rule me and my men as he ruled his own subordinates. He even went so far as to say that he intended the boat to be run like a barracks, with himself in command."[46] The disagreement went deeper than Bernier's hurt dignity: "Just to give you one example of Major Moody's [sic] unaccommodating disposition, there were some of us wished to buy furs from the natives, not at all for trading purposes, but simply for relatives and friends. This he refused to allow us to do. . . . If they were to give me two boats like this I would never work with him again."[47]

The police themselves were guilty of the same impulses, and the matter of police trading with the Natives proved a problem in the early days of their service in Hudson Bay. There is a close parallel with the earlier situation in the Yukon. Just as the police there wished to prospect for gold and in fact did so until forbidden to, some of them in Hudson Bay saw no reason why they should not supplement their wages by a bit of fur-trading. Inspector E. A. Pelletier, who was Moodie's second-in command on the 1904– 1905 expedition, went so far as to write directly to Laurier, asking him if it were true that the officer commanding the R.N.W.M.P. in Hudson Bay had "le Monopole exclusif de la traite, ou si je puis traffiquer avec les indiens quelques articles de traite que j'ai emporté avec moi."[48] Laurier wrote to White in some annoyance, telling him that it was forbidden for the police to trade for profit.[49] Apparently it was not just a case of "quelques articles de traite," as Pelletier had suggested; Moodie reported that his subordinate had been trading for furs on a large scale until ordered to stop.[50] Eventually, the rule was relaxed to permit the police and the ship's crew to collect "souvenirs in reasonable quantities . . . for their mothers, wives, and sweethearts," but "indiscriminate trading . . . should be forbidden."[51] Since 1899 it had been illegal for a policeman to engage in trade or business, and the police had to be careful to keep their hands clean in matters of this sort for the sake of their public image and their effectiveness on the job. The memory of the "Yukon Scandals" was still fresh. Although they had not involved the police directly, neither the police nor the government wanted anything of that sort in Hudson Bay.

In the spring of 1904 the usual hurried preparations went ahead. As before, the instructions given to Superintendent Moodie were not specific. White told him that "The boarding of vessels which may be met; the establishing of police posts . . . the introduction of the system of Government control as prevails in the organized portion of Canada, will be assigned to the Mounted Police."[52]   But what did this last part mean? What exactly was the "system of Government control" which Moodie was supposed to introduce? He expended considerable effort in trying to find out, and the answers he got are worth examining for what they show of the latitude the government gave the police and of the lack of concrete purpose with which the whole project was launched.

Moodie wrote to the Department of Marine and Fisheries, asking what they wanted him to do about foreign vessels fishing in Hudson Bay. In reply, the deputy minister said that the government had not made up its mind about whether or not the provisions of the Convention of 1818 were to be applied to Hudson Bay.[53] Moodie was advised to "use your own judgement . . . it is not the wish of the Government that hurried or harsh measures with reference to the laws should be made."[54] This was not very helpful, probably deliberately so; Moodie was being told essentially to interpret laws as he saw fit. That he intended to follow this advice is clearly brought out in a letter in which he stated his intention to apply the law according to individual cases: "In the cases of offences by natives I would take chances and try them—as I have done before in the N.W.T.—but where a whiteman was concerned I would not take chances of an action for false imprisonment or whatever the penalty might be."[55]

Moodie also worried that he was on shaky ground in the matter of enforcing Canada's authority over the whaling grounds of the bay. He had been told to enforce the laws, but he had been given no assurance that he would be backed in case of dispute. Before returning south in the summer of 1904, he had issued a notice to whalers warning them that they were breaking the law and that although he was being lenient for the time being, they must be prepared to obey the laws in the next year:

My instructions are that the laws are to be strictly enforced, after due notice has been given, although it is not the wish of the Canadian Government that any harsh measures should be adopted. As I consider that in certain cases it would be such were the law put in force at once I have not done so. . . . The Government may . . . instruct that the law be enforced during 1905 and thereafter . . . you may make arrangements to meet the circumstances which may arise.[56]

Now Moodie asked the government to support him in this edict and in the one forbidding the export of musk-ox skins: "if my notice . . . is not confirmed—and it is found that it was not—law-suits may be entered to recover damages for loss of trade. Unless my action is approved and confirmed before I sail again next week—I shall on my arrival at Fullerton be compelled to withdraw the notice and allow the slaughter to continue."[57]

But no decision was immediately forthcoming, and Moodie was compelled to improvise during the next winter as well. It was not until the summer of 1906 that the government finally made up its mind on the question of asserting its sovereignty over the waters of Hudson Bay. In July 1906 Parliament passed an act to amend the Fisheries Act, which, said the deputy minister of Marine and Fisheries, "asserts that Hudson Bay is wholly territorial water of Canada, and therefore the licence fee of Fifty Dollars per annum will be chargeable on all vessels . . . British or foreign."[58] Ironically, by the time this regulation was promulgated, it no longer affected the police. In January 1905 they had reached an understanding with the Department of Marine and Fisheries by which the responsibility for Hudson Bay was divided between the two government agencies. Hampered by the lack of a patrol boat, which they could not afford to buy, the police retained control only of the western shore of the bay. The Department of Marine and Fisheries was given the responsibility of supervising the rest of the bay, including the eastern shore. This division explains why the police, during this early period, extended their operations only along the western shore and inland from this coast. The posts which are now on the eastern shore, Port Harrison and Great Whale River, are products of a later era.

One of the oddest aspects of the 1904 cruise of the *Arctic* was the way in which authority over the expedition was divided. Moodie was given wide, if unclear powers, and Captain Bernier was limited to "command and navigation of the vessel."[59] But serious decisions about the expedition's progress were to be made by, of all things, a committee:

In the event of doubt or dispute arising. . . . The senior officer of the Mounted Police, the Captain of the vessel, and a Third, to be named by the Minister of the

Interior, will constitute a board to consult and decide as to the course to be pursued: the Police officer to be President of the Board. [60]

Here was a naval operation, civil-service style; it is little wonder that disagreements and acrimony arose between Moodie and Bernier.

Lack of a ship of their own was a constant problem to the police in their operations in the Mackenzie Delta and especially in Hudson Bay. It tied them down, and when they chartered a ship, they more often than not came into conflict with its captain, as was the case with Bernier and later with the Baker Lake expedition of the First World War. It was not until 1928, with the building of the *St. Roch* and the training of a special crew, that the police finally got a satisfactory ship for Arctic work.

After hectic preparations, the second expedition to Hudson Bay left from Quebec on 17 September 1904. The police contingent consisted of Moodie, Inspector E. A. Pelletier, three N.C.O.s, and six constables. [61] The main task was to consolidate police operations in the bay, to establish new detachments, and to make patrols. Exactly where the new detachments were to be put was left entirely up to Moodie; White told him that the additional police were "to be distributed in such manner as you may deem best in the public interest." [62]

These instructions deserve comment. It is surprising to find that even after the cruise of the *Neptune*, the men in charge of the police had so little idea of the geography or the general situation in Hudson Bay that they left so important a matter as the location of police detachments to the officer in charge of the district. But it was not really a matter of ignorance or lack of concern. If the chief goal of the police in Hudson Bay was to demonstrate government sovereignty to the world, then it was not of vital importance exactly where the police put their posts; it was their "presence" that mattered. Secondly, leaving decisions of this sort to the officer on the scene was a regular part of police policy in the days before instantaneous communication. The decisions about where to locate the detachments in the Yukon had almost all been made on the scene. Not only were the headquarters in Regina and Ottawa too far away to have an intimate knowledge of the territory, they were also too far away to respond quickly to changing circumstances or emergencies. The same was even more true of Hudson Bay, though as time went on, it was true to a progressively lesser extent. As mail service and later radio service to the Hudson Bay area were introduced, and improved communications, decisions of this sort were made less often in the north.

After a stop at Port Burwell, Moodie and his party arrived at Fullerton on 16 October 1904. During his absence, a patrol had been made to Repulse Bay by boat, and as soon as he arrived, he ordered a trip made up Chesterfield Inlet to Baker Lake and back.[63] The purpose of this trip was not only to spy out the land, but also to let the Inuit who lived at Baker Lake know of the police and to try to persuade them to bring meat to Fullerton during the winter for the use of the detachment. The main activity, however, lay in the construction of proper quarters for the detachment. Assisted by a carpenter loaned by the whaling ship *Era,* the police built a barracks, fifteen by thirty feet, and a storehouse of about the same size.[64] There is a parallel here with the situation on Herschel Island. There the police had been dependent for shelter on the generosity of the missionaries and the Pacific Steam Whaling Company. In a somewhat similar way, the police at Fullerton depended on the help of the people they were supposed to be policing. The loan of the *Era*'s carpenter was of considerable help to Moodie, who noted in his report that "Capt. Comer very kindly permitted him to do his work."[65] Moreover, the detachment's storehouse was constructed from materials furnished from the *Era*'s deckhouse, which Moodie bought when it was dismantled in the spring. If Comer had chosen to be uncooperative, the police would have been placed in an awkward position.

The rather grandiose plans of the police for extending their control over a wide area of Hudson Bay were a long time maturing, and some of the details were never realized. The proposed detachments at Repulse Bay and Cape Wolstenholme were never established, and some of those which exist today were not set up until much later. Only one new detachment was founded during this early period, at Churchill, which was made the headquarters of "M" Division in 1905, and Fullerton remained for a long time the division's only other detachment. The reasons for shifting the centre of police activity to Churchill included the fact that there was a Hudson's Bay Company store there; this meant that the Inuit gravitated to Churchill, while the police found themselves virtually ignored at the more northerly post. Sometimes the police at Fullerton saw no one at all for months on end. Furthermore, it was quite possible to get to Churchill from southern Canada by land, or rather, by river. The police had already made a patrol over the old Hudson's Bay Company route from Norway House to York Factory,[66] and from York Factory to Churchill was a feasible, though not an easy trip. Churchill also had the distinction, like Fort McPherson, of being a place where the Indians and Inuit came together; the police could thus keep an eye on both races at once.

It seemed to the police and to the government that their operations in Hudson Bay between 1903 and 1905 had been an unqualified success. White wrote an inquirer in Toronto that Canada's attempt to assert her sovereignty in the eastern Arctic had succeeded even beyond the government's hopes: "We succeeded earlier and easier than we expected."[67] It seems only fair to add that the success was owing in part to the virtual lack of opposition. It remained to see how the police would consolidate this success. In the near future their ability to police this new region would be tested, and they would find that exerting real control, as opposed to token sovereignty, was not nearly so easy.

8. Expanding Activities in the Mackenzie Delta

THE HISTORY of the Mounted Police in the western Arctic and Mackenzie regions was concerned for several years chiefly with the detachments at Herschel Island and Fort McPherson. Permanent posts were opened at Fort Resolution and Fort Simpson only in 1913, and these were far enough south so that they were not really on the "northern frontier," even though all four were in the same administrative division.[1] And only in 1919 was a detachment opened at Coppermine River, marking the beginning of a new period of police expansion in the Arctic. The two small posts had no more than eight men between them between 1906 and 1915,[2] but they were important nonetheless. In the first place, McPherson and Herschel were the main settlements in the western Arctic, which meant that they were the hub of an enormous area. Secondly, the few police who manned these posts were not static. Patrols were made every year over a wide expanse of territory to the south, east, and west, all the way from Dawson to the shores of Hudson Bay. Some of these patrols were for communication, as was the case with the annual Dawson-McPherson mail patrol, which was begun in the winter of 1904–1905.[3] Some were exploratory, and some, like the two famous ones into the Barren Lands during the First World War, were made for the purpose of investigating crimes. The two posts were gathering places for the Natives, the whalers, and such occasional visitors as explorers and traders.

In 1906, the police detachment on Herschel Island finally acquired adequate quarters, not through any effort on the part of their superiors, but because one of Charles Whittaker's children had died, and the missionary had left the island. The police took over his house and his supplies.[4] As the officer in charge admitted, "This helped me greatly, as there were no quarters for us on the island, and we were unable to bring sufficient supplies to last us, on the dog sleds."[5] This was another example of how the police benefitted from fortuitous circumstance rather than careful preparation and adequate logistical support in their efforts to establish themselves in this inhospitable country.

Herschel Island was still a wintering place for whaling ships in 1906, though the industry was declining fast. In the winter of 1906–1907 only one ship stayed at Herschel,[6] but the activities of the whalers still gave the police cause for concern, as the following episode illustrates:

[Captain] McGregor complained that a nigger belonging to his crew had left the ship and was living ashore and that he had threatened to shoot him. This man had been in irons for some offence and the captain had foolishly let him go. As . . . he would be left on our hands when the ships pulled out, I had him rounded up and Sergt. Fitzgerald took him aboard and instructed the captain that he would have to look after him.[7]

Incidents such as this tended, however, to be the exception rather than the rule. There were many days when nothing happened that required the official attention of the police, and these were generally spent in performing duties which were essential if the police were to survive in such a hostile environment. All the detachments kept daily records, and some of these diaries have survived. They are far from dramatic, but they give a good idea of how the police occupied themselves. A selection from the Herschel Island diary for the autumn of 1906 shows what they are like:

Sept. 29th —Saturday. 24 [F] above, strong wind. Scrubbed out quarters.
Sept. 30th —Sunday. 24 above. Very strong gale.
Oct. 1st —Monday. 25 above, fine. Hauling wood to storehouse.
Oct. 2nd —Tuesday, 27 above, strong wind. Hauling wood to storehouse.
Oct. 3rd —Wednesday, 24 above, strong wind. Hauling wood to storehouse.
Oct. 4th —Thursday. 22 above, foggy. Cleaning up storehouse.
Oct. 5th —Friday, 25 above, fine and calm. Repairing dog harness.
Oct. 6th —Saturday. 21 above, fine and calm. Cleaning stove pipe and scrubbing out quarters.[8]

The diary is much the same throughout the year, except that the colder the weather gets, the more emphasis there is on heating. One wonders where the wood came from; very likely it was driftwood, for there were no trees on Herschel Island. The police and whalers used large amounts of coal as well for heating their quarters, coal which cost the then large sum of $32.00 a ton, $25.00 of which represented freight charges.[9]

The dependence of the police detachment and the whole community on supplies from outside is well shown by the hardships which ensued when the tender supplying the whalers was unable to get to the island in 1906 because of bad ice conditions off Point Barrow. Rather unexpectedly, perhaps, the people who seemed to suffer the most were the Inuit employed by the whalers to hunt caribou meat. When the ship failed to arrive, the Inuit could not be paid for all the work they had done in the previous twelve months. They thus had to go without the sugar, flour, and especially the tea to which by this time they were virtually addicted. The police, who also depended on the supply ship, had to buy coal and "Muck-Tuck for dog feed" from the whaling captains.[10]

Fort McPherson was a considerably more cosmopolitan centre, encompassing police, Indians, Inuit, missionaries, and the Hudson's Bay Company, but the routine of the police was much the same. Again, it was mostly a matter of repetitive duties rather than glamourous action. A brief extract from the detachment diary for late September 1906 gives the flavour of life there:

> *Sep. 26th, '06* —Const. Pritchard cooking, Corpl. and Const. Holmden sawing and cutting wood, and hauling water. . . . [Inspector Howard] went for a walk in the afternoon.
> *Sept. 27th, '06* —Const. Pritchard cooking, Corpl. and Const. Holmden sawing and splitting wood, and hauling water. Went for a walk up the river in the afternoon.
> *Sept. 28th, '06* —Const. Pritchard cooking, Corpl. and Const. Holmden sawing and splitting wood. In afternoon went for a walk up the river.[11]

It all sounds idyllic, at least for Inspector Howard. But the morale of the men was subject to fluctuations; four months later, in the middle of the winter, Howard was writing to quite a different effect: "I feel weak and run down. This country is the hardest I have yet been in during my seventeen years' service." Fort McPherson, he said, was a much more unpleasant place than any part of the Yukon, "where in nearly every place you were surrounded by the comforts of civilization to counteract the depressing effects of the climate."[12]

But little by little, events began to intrude upon the routine of the police in the Mackenzie Delta. In the summer of 1906 it was reported that a certain "A. McStephanson" had arrived at Fort McPherson on board the Hudson's Bay Company steamer *Wrigley*. This gentleman was

not Scottish; the notation referred to the explorer Vilhjalmur Stefansson, who in 1906 was paying the first of several visits to the Arctic.
During his years there he was to have frequent contacts with the police,
and they were not always amicable. From the first, the police discovered
that Stefansson was a man who had his own way of doing things and that
he was extremely stubborn and just as iron-willed as they, if not more so.
He had come to Fort McPherson intending to join the *Duchess of Bedford,*
the ship carrying the Anglo-American Arctic Expedition. The ship had
not arrived (it was eventually wrecked off Flaxman Island, aborting the
expedition), so Stefansson spent a month as a guest of the police at Fort
McPherson before setting out for Herschel Island. The police do not
seem to have welcomed their guest; supplies were not plentiful that year,
and Steffansson had, as the report put it, come "down the Mackenzie
with nothing in the way of supplies or money, and the Police have been
looking after him since last July."[13] Because the expedition had fallen
through, Stefansson was given the opportunity of living with the Inuit
during the winter of 1906–1907, an experience which enabled him to
gain an insight into their way of life surpassed by no other white man at
that time. His insights did not always agree with the opinions of others,
and Stefansson's entire career was marked by a series of quarrels with all
sorts of people, especially with civil servants.[14] On occasion he found
himself at odds with the R.N.W.M.P., and the remains of these differences may be found in his books and in the police records.

Stefansson, the great propagandist for the Canadian Arctic, believed
that it could be, according to the title of his famous book, a "friendly"
place if his rules for living there were carefully followed. His whole life
was dedicated to the proposition that, as one biographer put it, "The
Arctic Sea is not at the end of the earth, but must ... become in time a
polar Mediterranean."[15] People who did not agree with this view of the
Arctic were often dealt with scornfully. There is no doubt that although
there were members of the police who were eager for northern
service—Fitzgerald is a good example—there were others who leaned
more toward the end-of-the-earth theory. And no member of the police
in the north welcomed the possibility of an influx of amateurs wishing to
live off the land; such an event could only bring the police the task of
rescuing the unlucky and the foolish. But it seemed to Stefansson that
the southerners were always exaggerating the difficulties of life in the
north. Starvation was not always close at hand, and if it was, it was
because people insisted on eating white man's food—tea, coffee,
sugar—instead of living off the land. He bitterly resented the fact that
the Inuit had become so used to these foods that when they ran short of
them the cry of starvation was raised. In fact, he believed, the Inuit

would be perfectly all right if they continued to eat their traditional foods of fish, seal, and caribou, which never gave out, and abandoned the ways of civilization.[16] The whalers received the greatest share of Stefansson's wrath since they were the original corrupters of the Inuit, but the police also came in for a share of criticism.

A good example of Stefansson's view of the errors of the police is provided by his account of the situation at Herschel Island in the summer of 1908. The whaling industry was dying; only one ship, the *Karluk*, had wintered at the island, and supplies were running low. The Inuit began to fear starvation:

It is true, as experience has since shown, that in the absence of whalers the Eskimos of the Mackenzie River are able to live perfectly well on the game and fish of the country; but they did not think so themselves in the summer of 1908, any more than those of us used to high living think we can get along on the simple fare of the poor. The mounted police agreed with them in this, and every one therefore considered that they were facing a critical winter. . . . My opinion agreed with that of no one else with regard to the prospects for the coming winter. It seemed to me the condition was nowise serious. I had lived with the Eskimos the year before and had seen what an abundance of fish there was in the eastern channels of the Mackenzie delta, and I knew that fish and caribou were also plentiful farther east. But the whalers had never seen Eskimo living anywhere except around whaling ships and dependent on them; neither had the mounted police, and, consequently, it seemed to all of them that the district was facing a period of starvation.[17]

This was not, of course, a matter of direct conflict between Stefansson and the police. It was more a matter of a different view of the Natives and their situation and what should be done to remedy it.

Where the police did come into direct conflict with Stefansson was over the question of their responsibility for his safety. The police felt, not unreasonably, that it was part of their duty to see as far as possible that no white man starved or otherwise got into difficulties (or created difficulties) in their area. If misfortune befell an explorer, the police might be blamed for it, or at the least they would be expected to exert themselves to get him out of danger. The police had learned from their Yukon experience that the best way to avoid having to take care of indigents was not to let people into the country without ample supplies. But when they tried a similar method of prevention on Stefansson, they ran into trouble. The clash was over the matter of matches, and in this incident is clearly shown the conflict between Stefansson's view of life in the Arctic and the police, or official, view.

The quarrel, which took place during Stefansson's second trip north, may be described briefly. Stefansson and his companion, Dr. R. M. Anderson, found themselves in the summer of 1908 faced with the prospect of spending the next winter with very few supplies, since no ship had managed to get to the Beaufort Sea that season. This prospect did not worry Stefansson; in fact he welcomed it, because it gave him another opportunity to demonstrate that one could live happily in the Arctic, in close association with the Inuit and Indians, without any of the white man's goods at all. There was, however, one article of manufacture that Stefansson considered essential—matches for smoking and for lighting fires; and, unfortunately, he had run short of them. He therefore asked Fitzgerald, then commanding the R.N.W.M.P. post on Herschel Island, to give, lend, or sell him a quantity of matches. Fitzgerald refused and told him "that if I would discharge all my Eskimo . . . and if Dr. Anderson and I would live for the winter in a small house which he would assign to us near the barracks, then he would supply us with not only matches, but also everything else that we needed to eat."[18] According to Stefansson, and there is no reason to believe that he was not telling the truth, Fitzgerald admitted that his refusal was simply a way of getting Stefansson to leave. Fitzgerald thought that Stefansson's wish to live off the country in the Native manner was simple foolishness. He believed "that we were now destitute and likely to die of starvation, and it was his duty to supply us, in a way that suited him, with sufficient food to keep us from actual want."[19] Fitzgerald believed that if he gave Stefansson the matches, he would only go off on some mad venture and either kill himself or become a charge on the Natives, and Fitzgerald did not wish to become responsible for either result. "He further informed me that the laws of the Yukon gave him a right to ship Dr. Anderson and me out of the country because we had no visible means of support. But, he said, seeing he could accomplish the same result by refusing us matches, he would prefer that method, and let us go west to Point Barrow for them . . . where we should be in no danger of starving."[20] And that is what they had to do, much to Stefansson's rage.

At first glance, this episode does not seem to cast a very favourable light upon either the generosity of the police or on their intelligent appraisal of conditions of life in the Arctic. And the crowning example of the triumph of Stefansson's ideas was yet to come—the contrast between his own extremely successful journeys during the First World War and Fitzgerald's unfortunate death on patrol between Fort McPherson and Dawson in 1911, an event which confirmed Stefansson in his belief that he knew what he was doing and the police did not.

The question of the ill-fated Fitzgerald journey will be discussed later in a wider consideration of police patrols. Is Stefansson's interpretation of the events of 1908 to be accepted at face value? In the first place, it should be said in fairness to the police that over a period of years they did many favours for Stefansson. The fact that they had put him up in the summer of 1906, when he arrived without money or supplies, has already been mentioned. Stefansson did not see fit to relate this incident. Since he had at that time had no opportunity to learn the secrets of Inuit survival, he would likely have been in difficulty had the police not voluntarily assisted him.

In the next year, 1907, Stefansson had made a quick journey back to civilization—the telegraph station at Eagle, Alaska—to tell the world that despite the sinking of the *Duchess of Bedford,* he and the ship's crew were not dead. The police at Herschel Island lent him their whaleboat, in which he went first to Fort McPherson and then up the Rat River as far as the portage leading to the Bell. D. M. Le Bourdais, one of Stefansson's biographers, says, "he hired two Indians to help carry his effects across the 80-mile portage to Bell River."[21] The confidential police report on the episode, however, suggests that even here the police were of more use than Stefansson or his biographer gave them credit for being. Inspector A. M. Jarvis reported from Herschel that he had sent Stefansson "with our whale boat as far as Rat River on the Peel and got two Natives to help him track up the Rat to Rampart House."[22]

If the police were feeding Stefansson, lending him their whaleboat, and hiring Indians to carry his gear, it seems only natural, especially given the precedents of the Yukon, that they should feel it their privilege and responsibility to tell him what to do, both for his own good and because it was part of their duty to do so. It was part of the paternalistic nature of police methods in the Yukon and in the Arctic that they sought to give advice and were offended when it was rejected. This was the genesis of the quarrel over the matches. Fitzgerald's ill-tempered report of late 1908 reveals the attitude of the police and throws a light on Stefansson which did not appear in the books published about him during his lifetime:

Such men as Stefensson [sic] claim that they can live on the country, they can by someone else supplying the food. All these people are a drain on our supplies, it is impossible to refuse a white man if he is short of food. . . . [I] suggest that if there are any white men coming in the country, that they will not be allowed down the river unless they have at least one year's supply of provisions.[23]

This debate does not mean that Stefansson was wrong in his theories about Arctic survival or in his ideas on what was best for the Natives. In general, it is difficult to fault his reasoning or his commonsense ap-

1 A. Bowen Perry, Commissioner of Mounted Police, 1900-22. He ⁞mmanded the Mounted Police ⁞ring its transition from a semi-⁞itary force on the western and ⁞thern frontier to the modern ⁞ional role it plays today.

2 Sgt. Lee inspecting the guard, ⁞itehorse, c. 1900.

3 The police detachment was located in a tent at Lake Bennett, May 1898. Here the gold-seekers registered their boats before attempting the voyage down the Yukon River.

4 Sheep Camp, on the Alaska side of the Chilkoot Pass, May 1898. The police prided themselves on the contrast between the turbulence and crime of Alaska and the calm and order of the Yukon.

3

5   Frederick White, Comptroller of the Mounted Police, 1880-1913. The liaison between the Mounted Police and the government, his career in the Canadian civil service spanned forty-nine years.

6   N.W.M.P. detachment at Stewart River, Yukon Territory, c. 1900. It was from detachments such as this, manned by one or two policemen, that the government maintained law and order in the Yukon.

7 "Goddesses of Liberty Enlightening Dawson," c. 1898. The police tolerated prostitution and gambling in Dawson so long as it was orderly.

8 Members of the N.W.M.P. on duty in the Yukon, 1898. The police became part of Yukon lore, but less well known was the fact that many of them spent long hours confined to barracks for their numerous service offences.

9 Supt. Constantine's post at Forty Mile, 1901. Constantine commanded the first expedition to the Yukon in 1894.

9

7

10   Sir Samuel B. Steele, the trouble shooter of the force, the best-known policeman of his era. He typified the British paternalism in the north.

11   Members of the N.W.M.P. on duty at Chilkoot Pass, May 1898. It was the police who established the Canadian-American boundary in the region.

12   N.W.M.P. officers, Dawson, 1900. L to R: Insp. W. Scarth; Supt. Z.T. Wood; Insp. W.R. Routledge; Insp. C. Starnes; Asst. Surgeon W.E. Thompson.

13 Placer mining operations at Hunker Creek, Yukon. The police maintained detachments at all the principal mining areas.

14 Police barracks at Fort Cudahy, Yukon, under construction, 1895.

15 Police at Whitehorse with Maxim gun, c. 1900. The authorities were determined that American "spread-eagleism" would not get out of hand in the Yukon.

14

13

16 Police expedition to Fort McPherson, 1903. Supt. C. Constantine seated, Sgt. F.J. Fitzgerald standing second from left.

17 Members of the *Neptune* expedition, winter of 1903-4. By the time the government took action in the area, the whaling industry was already in decline.

16

17

19

18 N.W.M.P. barracks at Fullerton,
1904. Fullerton was the centre of whaling
operations in Hudson Bay.

19 Members of the Fullerton detachment
with Inuit employees, 1904.

20 Senior police were permitted to bring
their wives north. Mrs. S.G. Clay, wife of
the Staff-Sergeant commanding the
Chesterfield Inlet detachment, was attacked
by dogs in 1924 and died after the local
missionary amputated her leg.

21   Settlement and police detachment at Herschel Island, c. 1904. Insp. D.M. Howard said the country was "the hardest I have yet been in during my seventeen years' service."

22   Scottie, Inuit employee of the police at Fullerton, c. 1903. Supt. Moodie rejoiced that Scottie had abandoned his igloo for a "rough shack."

22

23

23 Supt. J.D. Moodie, dispenser of justice and woollen underwear to the Inuit of Hudson Bay.

24 Fullerton detachment, 1905.

25 On patrol, Dawson to Herschel Island, 1909. This annual patrol, and others like it, symbolized the role of the police to the general public.

27

26

26   Inspector F.J. Fitzgerald of the "Lost Patrol." A man with lengthy northern experience, he was killed by overconfidence and bad luck.

27   Cpl. W.J.D. Dempster preparing to search for the "Lost Patrol," 1911. Dempster held the record for fastest patrol between Dawson and Fort McPherson.

28

30

29

3

28　Burying the members of the "Lost Patrol." The Commissioner wrote that "this was the most serious catastrophe the Force has experienced in many a long day."

29　Graves of the "Lost Patrol," Ft. McPherson.

30　Last Page of Insp. Fitzgerald's Diary, found on his body.

31　Insp. Fitzgerald's will, written in charcoal shortly before his death.

33

32 Churchill detachment, 1911.

33 Hauling wood on patrol at Dease Bay, N.W.T., 1916, in connection with the Rouvière-Le Roux case. The cabin originally belonged to the priests.

35

34 Sinnisiak and Uluksuk, killers of Fathers Rouvière and Le Roux, on trial for murder in Alberta. Two trials were necessary, since it was felt in some quarters that the priests had provoked the killings.

35 Sinnisiak and Uluksuk. The case aroused intense interest, and there was considerable public sympathy for the accused. To the chagrin of the police, they were given light sentences. Sinnisiak later became arrogant and quarrelsome, and was murdered by one of his people.

36 Trial of Alikomiak and Tatamigana at Herschel Island, July 1923. The two men were the first Inuit to be executed for murder under Canadian law.

37 R.C.M.P. detachment at Craig Harbour, Ellesmere Island, N.W.T., 1925. Since there was no one except the Inuit at Etah living within hundreds of miles of the post, its function was purely symbolic.

38 Landing supplies at Craig
Harbour detachment, 1925.
The supply ship arrived once a
year, if the police were lucky.

39 R.C.M.P. detachment at
Dundas Harbour, Devon
Island, N.W.T., August 1931.

40 Inspector Alan Belcher at
Coronation Gulf, N.W.T.,
March 1931.

proach. He was right more often than wrong. But he did not give sufficient credit to those who assisted him. He depended on outside
agencies—in this case, the police—rather more than he liked to admit.

Over a period of several years, the activities of the police in the western Arctic gradually broadened. Their main duty, as set forth in the
orders issued to the men at the northern detachments, continued, however, to be of a regulatory and supervisory nature. In the summer of
1907, when Inspector A. M. Jarvis took over command of the Mackenzie
River district from Inspector D. M. Howard, the orders issued to him
show how the police assessed the situation in the area at that time. Although the whaling industry was fading rapidly into insignificance, the
police were ordered to focus their attention on it almost to the exclusion
of other duties. For this reason the headquarters of the district were to
be at Herschel Island rather than at Fort McPherson. A detailed report
was to be made of every aspect of the operations of the whaling fleet.
Above all, the Inuit were to be protected from the whalers: "Your duty is
to see that intoxicating liquors are not given to the Esquimeau. . . . [Any
ship doing so is] liable to be seized and sold. It is also your duty to protect
the natives from abuse by the whaling crews . . . forcible abduction of
native women must be rigorously dealt with."[24] Commissioner Perry was
letting his imagination run away with him to some extent; the whalers in
the western Arctic did not forcibly abduct Inuit women. It is significant
to note, though, the emphasis which was placed on the activities of the
whalers as late as 1907.

To uphold the law Jarvis was given, under the authority of the Northwest Territories Amendment Act of 1905, the power of two justices of
the peace, which empowered him to try all but the most serious crimes
which might arise in his district.[25] This seemed like a good idea, but it
had a serious drawback. When minor crimes such as selling liquor to the
Natives or trying to evade payment of customs duties were committed,
the officer in charge of the district could dispense speedy justice, which
generally proved a useful lesson to innocent and guilty alike. But with a
serious crime such as murder, the commanding officer of the district did
not have the authority to try the case. In such cases, the police had to
transport the accused and all the witnesses to Edmonton, bring the entire court north, or else ignore the case altogether.[26] An example of how
this situation tended to be detrimental to the just administration of the
law in the Arctic occurred in 1907. An Indian woman at Fort McPherson
complained to the police that she had been raped by a white man. Because the charge was beyond the legal competence of the police to try,
Howard had to forward the particulars of the case to Commissioner
Perry in Regina, asking him if he thought that the evidence was strong

enough to warrant the expense of bringing everyone concerned south for a trial. Perry conferred with Comptroller White, who asked the opinion of the Department of Justice, and after much letter-writing and delay, the decision was made that the evidence was insufficient for a trial.[27] While this decision was certainly the most practical and might even have been the best from a legal standpoint, to base it on financial considerations hardly showed justice being done to the plaintiff.

This sort of incident was not common in the Mackenzie Delta in this period, for crime there did not often rise above petty offences, especially those connected with liquor. There were, occasionally, cases which might be termed "routine"; that is, instances of crimes committed which the police investigated in much the same way as they would have anywhere else in Canada. Yet the peculiar conditions of police work in the Arctic gave even these cases a special character. A good example is the matter of Charlie Klengenberg. Klengenberg (or Klinkinberg, as his name was sometimes spelled) was a scoundrelly Dane, whom Stefansson once described as being much like the captain in Jack London's *Sea Wolf*.[28] He was captain of the *Olga,* a ship engaged in trading in the Beaufort Sea. In 1905 there was a series of incidents on board the *Olga* in which the chief engineer was shot, for mutiny according to Klengenberg, one member of the crew died, and two more drowned.[29] When the *Olga* arrived at Herschel Island in the autumn of 1905, the police ordered Klengenberg to stay on the island until a full investigation was made. He disobeyed this order and escaped in a small boat with his Inuit family, whereupon the remaining members of the *Olga*'s crew accused Klengenberg of criminal responsibility for all of the deaths.

The police had been put in exactly the awkward position that had been foreseen when the Mackenzie River posts were first established. They had clear-cut evidence of a very nasty crime, but could do little to catch the suspect for want of a ship of their own. The best they could do was to wait and beg a ride on a whaling ship going in what they hoped was the right direction. Thus, in the summer of 1907 (nearly two years later), Inspector A. M. Jarvis travelled on board the *Beluga* more than 1,500 miles to the north and east of Herschel Island in an attempt to find Klengenberg or learn of his whereabouts. In doing so, he set a "farthest north" record for a member of the R.N.W.M.P. to that time: "I have satisfied myself that Capt. Klengenberg is not in these waters.... We went as far north as Lat. 72.05 N., Long. 126.30 W., in sight of Prince Albert Land. Had Klengenberg been up there, Capt. Porter would have gone in there for me and we would have brought him out."[30] Of course, Jarvis had virtually no control over this voyage. He was on board through the courtesy of the captain and could only hope to sight his quarry wherever the captain of the *Beluga* decided to go.

Later that year, Klengenberg came to Herschel Island voluntarily. A hearing into the charges against him was held, but for lack of any convincing testimony or evidence (the witnesses had scattered), the case was dropped. The whole incident did not reflect much credit on the effectiveness of the police presence and authority in the area, and it convinced Jarvis that the police would have to expand their operations if they hoped to prevent men like Klengenberg from exploiting the Natives to the east of Herschel Island. Jarvis believed, probably correctly, that Klengenberg intended to head east with liquor to trade with the Inuit of Victoria Island, around Minto Inlet. A detachment was needed there or at Baillie Island; otherwise, police authority meant little beyond the Mackenzie Delta. His request for a new post was refused by the commissioner on the grounds that the police were not in a position to send a ship to the Arctic, and thus a post east of the Mackenzie was impossible.[31]

One requirement for a government which wishes to exercise sovereignty over a territory is that it know as much about it as possible, and the western Arctic was no exception. One of the important duties of the police was to supply information to the government on a great variety of subjects. The annual reports which the government received from the Yukon were very comprehensive, rather like the letters written by a colonial governor to his superiors, which analogy, in fact, is not too far from the truth. Reports from the Mackenzie Delta and Hudson Bay were equally comprehensive, though on a smaller scale. The activities of the whalers were carefully followed by the police for as many years as the trade continued to function. When there was a brief flurry of mining activity in the area, the police investigated and reported on it, especially when they sensed a need for government control: "There are at present three or four miners working up the Black River between Norman and Wrigley, and they are reported to have found fair pay, with what truth I do not know.... It might be well to have the officers in the district authorized to issue mining licenses."[32] Further information was provided about the activities of miners on the Black River in the annual report for 1907. Inspector Howard reported that the miners "came out on the same boat with me and I had a long talk with the leader, an American from Kansas City."[33] The miners had been trying their luck in the area between Fort Norman and Wrigley for two years, since 1905, but they had not been very successful—in fact they had found no gold at all. "The leader expressed his intention of coming back again," wrote Howard, "and I fancy he will do so, as he is a man of independent means."[34]

At the same time, some mining had begun in a small way in the extreme north of the Yukon. A "Jap named Jujiro Wada" had staked three placer mining claims "on a tributary of a river flowing into the Arctic Ocean about opposite Herschel Island."[35] Since regulations required that all mining done in the Yukon be reported to Dawson at the end of each year and since it was unfair to ask a man to travel from the vicinity of the British Mountains to Dawson just to file a report, the Department of the Interior asked the police to act as mining recorders for the northern part of the Territory. Although these attempts at mining proved to be short-lived and unsuccessful, their significance, as far as the police were concerned, was to widen their authority and sphere of activity, enabling them to send out more and more information on the district.

One of the constantly recurrent themes from this period of police activity in the western Arctic was their wish to see their authority extended over a wider geographical area. This was not just the typical "empire-building" that is so much a part of civil service activity; it was a realization on the part of the police that they could have no real influence over the population of the Arctic unless they controlled a large part of it. In his annual report for 1907, Howard noted that the authority of the police along the Arctic coast really extended only from Herschel Island to the mouth of the Mackenzie.[36] He might have added that the activities of whites had by then extended as far east as the entrance to the Dolphin and Union Straits, at the tip of Wollaston Peninsula. Thus the police were exerting effective jurisdiction over only a fraction—although the central fraction—of the whole region. Howard proposed the establishment of a detachment at Baillie Island, a location which would be perfectly suited for the exercise of police authority as far to the east and north as any white man was likely to go for some time. But in describing the requirements for such a post, Howard undermined his case. "A post at Bailey [sic] Island" he wrote, "could not be rationed from Macpherson [sic] as the distance is too great, and the coast a dangerous one, the only way would be by ship from the outside which could ration Herschel Island at the same time."[37] This was the great difficulty; the coast was so perilous that it was dangerous to supply the post by whaleboat, and the police could not afford a ship of their own. Nor were these the only problems: "Portable buildings would have to be sent in . . . as there are no trees and no buildings . . . coal would also have to be sent in for fuel as at Herschel Island."[38] In short, given the resources of material and money available to the police in 1907, it was impossible for them to establish a post at as isolated a place as Baillie Island, no matter how desirable from the police point of view such a detachment might be.

As late as 1907 the police were not even very firmly established even in their two original locations. The trouble at Fort McPherson was lack of proper accommodation. In the summer the police lived in tents, which gave some variety to their routine. But in the winter they had to fall back on a building rented from the Hudson's Bay Company, which was "in a very bad state of repair, and liable to come down at any time . . . has been up a long time, since 1872 or 1873."[39] The problem at Herschel Island was supply. Although there was no shortage at McPherson, everything for Herschel had to be carried 180 miles in an open whaleboat, subject to spoilage and loss. The Hudson's Bay Company offered to carry freight to the island, but they asked what the police considered to be excessively high rates, and they would assume no responsibility for loss or accident. Thus the police continued to supply the detachment as best they could by whaleboat from McPherson and by purchasing coal and other goods from passing whalers when the opportunity to do so presented itself. Eventually the difficulty at Fort McPherson was solved by the cooperation of the Hudson's Bay Company, which in 1909 converted a large storehouse into a barracks and guard room for the use of the police. The rent was reasonable—twenty dollars per month—and the quarters proved satisfactory for the needs of the men.[40] The problem of supplying Herschel Island was never satisfactorily solved during the years the post was in operation.

Although police work in the Mackenzie Delta in the period before the First World War did not have the extreme busyness which had been so characteristic of the Yukon period, it was not always prosaic. Extracts from the detachment diaries show the monotony of the routine, but the police were not always at the detachments. Regular patrols had to be made between the two detachments for mail and supplies, an annual patrol was made from Dawson to Fort McPherson with the winter mail, and special patrols for investigation or exploration were made as circumstances required. On patrol the police duties sometimes developed high drama of the type that helped make their reputation in the Yukon and that has been the subject of popular literature ever since. Yet police activities in the Arctic failed to achieve the same prominence. This was partly because they were on a smaller scale and partly, no doubt, because there were no journalists in the area. The police themselves felt that the hardships of northern service were not receiving sufficient publicity. In April 1908 Perry sent White an extract from Inspector Jarvis's diary for the previous winter with the suggestion that he show it to the prime minister so that some public reference might be made to the work of the police in the Arctic. The extract enclosed was for 23 November 1907, during a sledge journey between Herschel Island and Fort McPherson:

Strong S.W. wind, 15 below zero [F]. Left camp at 6 A.M., made camp for lunch and went on close to King's point [about fifty miles east of Herschel Island] where we encountered open water, and got on moving ice, and had to return about 7 miles. Found that . . . Const. Pearson F.S. had both hands and feet frozen, and had taken a bad chill. After a great deal of difficulty we got ashore after dark and had to make camp on ice. Very little wood to be found here. The stove had no legs, and we found in the morning that it had gone through the ice level with the top. A miserable camp. Const. Pearson took a second chill during the night, dosed him with brandy.[41]

The parallel with the police falling into the Yukon River while on mail patrol will be readily apparent. In each case it was the hardship involved, the atmosphere of heroism and heroics, which made the police so proud of themselves. But the student of the Stefansson method of Arctic travel may wonder what the police were doing with a stove—presumably an iron one—at all. Why not an oil lamp, which could be placed, Inuit-fashion, so that it would heat the dwelling without melting the floor? In addition, "making camp" often meant pitching a tent. Stefansson would have asked why the police did not build igloos, since they were always snug and warm. The answer is that that this stage many of the police did not know how to build igloos or were not in a place where the snow was suitable, and they were therefore compelled to suffer the discomforts of those Arctic travellers who were well supplied with courage but deficient in the special technical skills necessary for proper adaptation to the environment. Furthermore, unlike the nomadic Inuit, the police had specific goals and a set timetable and could not always afford the time necessary to build an igloo or hunt game. The Inuit, and Stefansson, could spend all the time they needed to look for food and shelter; the police could rarely afford to do so. Only later did the police become more sophisticated and more flexible in their approach to Arctic survival. Then incidents of the sort related above occurred less often, as will be seen when the great patrols of the war years are examined.

Even when they were not on patrol, the police sometimes found survival a challenge. Nearly everyone who served at Herschel Island succumbed at one time or another to what a later generation called the "blues." Howard's complaint about Fort McPherson in 1907 was quoted earlier in this chapter. S/Sgt. Fitzgerald, who was not a whiner by nature, described life on Herschel Island in equally gloomy terms two years later:

When there are no ships wintering at Herschel Island I think it is one of the most lonesome places in the north. There is no place one can go, except to visit a few hungry natives. . . . There is no white man to visit closer than 180 miles.[42]

The climate gave the men an excuse for complaint, for at times it was spectacularly unpleasant. Three days before Christmas 1908 the temperature at Herschel dropped seventy degrees Fahrenheit in five hours—from twenty-two above at 7 P.M. to fifty-two below at midnight—in a howling blizzard. Ten days later the "worst blizzard ever known in the country" blew every chimney on the island into the Beaufort Sea.[43]

All these tribulations and heroics were noted by Commissioner Perry in a rather stuffy paragraph which appeared in the annual report for 1907:

I might observe that whether bringing relief to isolated settlers in bitter cold and over the deep snow of the open plain, carrying mail to the distant Hudson's Bay posts, to the Arctic Seas, or to detachments interned in northern British Columbia, or hurrying to the relief of unfortunate persons in remote parts, our men do not fail us. They undertake the work with cheerfulness and carry it out indifferent to difficulties and hardships.[44]

The last part, about cheerfulness and indifference to hardships, seems a bit much for Perry to claim after he had read so many complaints and gloomy reports from the Arctic. But, the unwitting "interned" provides a nice touch. It is also interesting to note the difference between the realities of Arctic service and the version which was presented to the public in the published reports.

What of the primary task of the police—the assertion of Canadian sovereignty and the protection of the Natives? The duties performed by the police in 1909 were much the same as in 1903 when the two posts were established: keeping an eye on the whalers, collecting customs duties from traders, keeping liquor away from the Indians and Inuit, investigating complaints, and making patrols and reports.

The whaling industry was not quite dead; in the winter of 1908–1909 two ships hunting whales were reported to be in the western Arctic—the *Karluk*, at Herschel Island, and the *Olga*, at Prince Albert Land. The *Karluk* had taken four whales, yielding about five thousand pounds of bone, and the *Olga* had caught none.[45] The whalers gave little trouble, except for the occasional incident; in December 1909 the police tried and convicted the second officer of the *Karluk* on a charge of giving liquor to an Inuit woman and fined him a hundred dollars. "This had the desired effect," reported the officer in charge, "and a like offence has not been committed."[46] In fact, the police were grateful for the presence of the whalers for when a ship wintered at Herschel Island they had someone to talk to other than "hungry natives," as Fitzgerald put it. Inspector G. L. Jennings referred in one of his reports to the captain and crew of the *Karluk* as having made the winter of 1909–1910 pass "more pleasantly and apparently more quickly" than it otherwise would have done. He thanked them for their "strict observance of Canadian law, and ... kindness and liberality to the natives."[47] He was, however, realistic enough to admit of the whalers that "if there were no peace officers here they would quickly return to the wild times of several years ago."[48]

At this point, the federal government decided to assert its authority more strongly over whaling, using the police as agents of a policy of stricter regulation. In December 1909 the superintendent of fisheries wrote to Comptroller White saying that he understood that a good many American whalers were operating off Herschel Island and asking if the police there would help the Department of Marine and Fisheries by collecting the fifty-dollar whaling fee from the captains.[49] White replied that the police would be glad to assist, but that there were now very few vessels; furthermore, the ships did not hunt whales anywhere near Canadian territory. He asked to be informed of the extent of Canadian territorial waters so that he would know whether he had the right to require Americans to buy licences. The question of territorial waters was embarrassing to the government, for then as now there was no international consensus as to exactly how far Canada might exert her authority over the waters of the Arctic Ocean. When it was admitted that Canada had no right to ask whaling captains to buy licences unless whales were being killed within three miles of shore,[50] which was almost never done, the whole matter was quietly shelved. It was too late anyway, since the whaling industry in that part of the world was practically at an end, but the incident did not reflect well on the government's alacrity in confronting the problem, nor on its wisdom in assessing the requirements for a solution to it.[51]

The police were, of course, well aware of the sovereignty question. The reports and correspondence from the Mackenzie River posts are full of comments and suggestions on how Canada's authority might be made both more apparent and more real. Ideas put forward by the police ranged from supplying the Natives with flags to appointing judges in the area to bring Canadian law to them. One of their more perceptive suggestions concerned trade. If Canadians did not seize the opportunities, Americans would, and the trade would pass into alien hands:

With a good class of trade goods ... having no duty on these goods, selling or trading at a reasonable profit, the whole trade of our Arctic coast could easily be secured . . . but a matter of a very few years before American trading concerns open stations at Herschel Id., Kittigazuit and Baillie Id. If a Canadian firm was established first there would be no opposition.[52]

The establishment of trading posts would also help the police in two ways; it would provide an easy source of supplies for the detachments, and it would ease the problem of collecting customs.

The police were quick to assert and to extend this sovereignty—that is, their own authority, which in this period in the Arctic was virtually the same thing—as much as they could with their limited resources. This was the impetus behind a long patrol which was made in 1910 from Fort McPherson to Herschel Island by way of the Porcupine River and the extreme northern interior of the Yukon Territory. The officer commanding the district, Inspector G. L. Jennings, had heard rumours that "traders had come among the Natives bringing goods from Alaska, duty unpaid, and also intoxicants; that many individual miners were located in the district.[53] The idea for the trip was entirely that of the local officer. On his own initiative, he made a patrol of more than 400 miles through virtually unknown country in order to, as he said, "gain as accurate knowledge as possible on such a trip of the topography and general conditions of that country . . . visit as many miners and traders as could be reached."[54] This sort of initiative was one of the greatest contributions of the police to the establishment of effective Canadian control in the Arctic.

Most of the activity Jennings commented on was, in fact, transitory. The mining carried out in the country west of Fort McPherson, though it brought white men to the Bell River almost for the first time, was not lively enough to be called a "boom." "Several camps of miners" had prospected along the Bell River between 1908 and 1910, lured into the country by rumours of a big strike, but as the police reported, they found nothing and soon left.[55] In 1910, the Mackenzie Delta did not seem any more ready to be "opened up" to settlement or exploitation than it had seven years earlier; on the contrary, commercial activity in the area was declining as one by one the whaling ships left for good, to be replaced eventually by coastal traders. The police stopped asking that a new detachment be set up at Baillie Island; in 1910, Jennings admitted that there was now no need for one, "nor is it likely there will be for many years, not until more traders get into that district."[56] The police were concerned about what would happen to the Inuit. Jennings, perhaps borrowing the idea from Stefansson, suggested that a herd of reindeer be purchased for the Inuit of Mackenzie Bay.[57] Finding a replacement for the whalers in the economic life of the area had, however, to wait for a later era.

One of the aspects of police work in the Mackenzie Delta, as in the Yukon, was rendering assistance to various branches of the government. Duties associated with the post office occupied a minor but significant portion of the energy of the police. There were three mail deliveries to Fort McPherson each year; one in the summer by way of the Hudson's Bay Company steamer, one in the early winter by the police patrol from Dawson, and one in mid-winter from Edmonton via Dawson. Mail from the outside was important to the police and the whaling crews, who depended on it for news of home. Mail was also important to the Inuit, for the police, in addition to handling the "outside" mail, also carried on what they called a "rural delivery system":

Our patrol leaving Herschel Island took 184 letters, exclusive of official correspondence. 8 of them were written by Eskimo to other Eskimo along the coast, to be delivered by our rural delivery system. Some 50 letters came from the West coast as far as Flaxman's Isld., a sled having been sent to Herschel with them, as there is no winter mail in that part of Alaska. The balance is from the crew of the ship wintering at Herschel. A few letters were sent from the eastward.[58]

Carrying mail from one part of the western Arctic to another must have provided a slight but definite cohesive force in the area; in a sense, there was a community centered on the two police posts, which became clearing-houses for written news and communication. It also enabled the police to keep a close check on everything going on in their domain.

The Customs Department was also represented by the police in the Mackenzie Delta, and although there was really very little collection to be done, the duties were carried out conscientiously. It was impossible to collect customs from a trading ship which made an effort to avoid the police or argued that its supplies had been disposed of as gifts. If the police crossed the path of traders while on patrol, then duty was extracted from them, but the process was at best haphazard. Nevertheless, the principle was important, and in most years at least a token sum was collected. In 1909 just under $400 was paid to the police, in 1908 nothing, and in 1911 about $300, to give three representative examples.[59] Making ships' captains pay duty was a good practical demonstration of sovereignty—and perhaps that was all that was wanted.

The service rendered by the police to the Department of Indian Affairs was a significant part of their duties. The police reports concerning the Indians and Inuit of the western Arctic were generally complacent in tone; one from 1910 is typical: "any complaints brought to our notice have been fully investigated. The Natives have been protected on the score of morality and in regard to intoxicants."[60] This statement was true, but there was much more to the situation than that. The relations between the police and the Native people were so integral a part of their service on the northern frontier that a chapter will be devoted to it later.

Some miscellaneous aid to government agencies also took place. For example, in July 1912 two men working for the Canadian party of the International Boundary Survey, which was marking the boundary between Alaska and the Yukon, stayed for a short while with the police at Herschel Island. The purpose of the visit was to erect a signal for triangulation. However, the weather was so foul that contact with the main party on the mainland to the west could not be established. The police furnished the visitors with rations and sent a bill for them to the chief astronomer.[61] The laws regarding the conservation of game were also enforced on behalf of the department of the interior, and this occasioned the seizure of beaver pelts trapped out of season.[62]

The role of the police in establishing government control in the Mackenzie Delta region in their first ten years of service there was of great importance. But progress was slow and uncertain. The gradualness with which the police extended their control reflected the development of that part of Canada. Whereas the Yukon had sprung into sudden life not long after the police established themselves there, during the years 1903 to 1913, the Mackenzie region remained in the chrysalis stage. The police did not seem to *do* very much. In fact, the government did not want anything in particular done; the *presence* of the police was the object of the entire exercise, although the government officials of the time might not have put it that way. Had the government had any positive plans for the area, as opposed to simply laying claim to it, they presumably would have garrisoned it more strongly. However, even police work on a small scale could become complicated, and during the war the Mackenzie Delta was to become the base for a difficult expedition into territory unknown to the authorities.

$9.$ Hudson Bay

In 1906 there were only two R.N.W.M.P. detachments on the shores of Hudson Bay, at Fullerton and Churchill. This was the same number as in the Mackenzie Delta region, and it might seem that the situation in the two areas was much the same. There were, in fact, similarities, especially the difficulties of climate and transportation which plagued the police in both places. Yet there were also significant differences.

In the 1980s, with new discoveries of raw materials and plans for their exploitation, the western Arctic appears to be the new frontier of Canada. Hudson Bay, especially the Churchill region, faces a static or declining future. The reverse was true seventy-five years ago; very little thought was given to the western Arctic while Hudson Bay was in some circles a topic of constant interest as an alternate route for exporting prairie grain. The development of a port on the west coast of Hudson Bay had been a favourite project of western farmers and their representatives since the early 1880s—more than twenty years before the police set foot in the region. Their intention was to provide a shipping route to England which was shorter and therefore cheaper than the route through Montreal and to provide an alternative to the C.P.R. as an outlet from the west. By 1904 the idea of building a railroad to Hudson Bay had been endorsed by both political parties.[1] In 1907 Sir Wilfrid Laurier, speaking in the House of Commons, foresaw "towns and villages on the shores of Hudson Bay like those we see on the shores of Norway, where people will be prosperously engaged in the lumbering business, the pulp industry, the mining industry."[2] Planning and surveying the route began in 1908, and construction in 1910.

The railway was not completed until 1929, but even before that it affected all aspects of life in the Hudson Bay region, including the operations of the Mounted Police. After 1907, duties and services having to do with the new railway were a recurring features of police life in the bay area. It seems that the police established themselves at Churchill just in time since it was originally proposed as the terminus of the railway.[3] In this case the police took the initiative and offered to assist government departments concerned with surveying the route. As early as February 1907, White wrote to Frank Oliver, minister of the interior, that "As the discussion of the Hudson Bay route appears to have come to stay this time . . . we have a boat . . . which we propose to send up . . . for general patrol work. . . . If you have any surveyors you wish to get into Fort Churchill, we might manage to send them by our vessel."[4]

The boat referred to was the *Rouville*, a single screw patrol steamer, 125 feet in length, built for the police at Sorel in 1906. The police confidently expected that with a ship of their own, they would no longer be dependent on other agencies for supplies and would be able to patrol the west coast of the bay in an effective and satisfactory way for the first time. Unfortunately, the ship proved a failure. Although it was meant to carry a hundred tons of cargo, it was mistakenly built without proper cargo space. Worse still, its engines were hopelessly inefficient; during its trials on the St. Lawrence it burned nearly a ton of coal an hour.[5] The ship was not sent north. Commissioner Perry tried to put a brave face on the situation by saying that in his opinion the establishment of summer and winter patrols from Norway House to Hudson Bay would provide sufficient communication with the detachment there. The *Rouville* would be "detailed for other service."[6] But the police had suffered a definite setback to their plans for Hudson Bay.

They were not, however, cut off from communication with Regina and Ottawa. Perry was right that mail service could be maintained by patrols. Some remarkable patrols were carried out in this period between Churchill and southern Canada. One of them, in the winter of 1907–1908, involved a journey of over 1,400 miles by sled from Mafeking to Churchill and return with mail and despatches. Another patrol, made by canoe in the summer of 1908, went from Norway House to Churchill, York Factory, and return, about 1,250 miles. Both patrols were headed by Inspector E. A. Pelletier.[7]

As the Hudson Bay Railway was slowly pushed towards the bay during the second decade of the century, communications became quicker; the police on patrol made it a practice to travel by train to the end of steel and then continue by sled or canoe. But the onset of the railway complicated the work of the police in other ways at the same time.

In 1907 Superintendent Moodie, then still in command of "M" Division (the two detachments on Hudson Bay), was busy consolidating his new headquarters at Churchill. He found it more satisfactory than his previous headquarters; it was "not nearly so desolate as Fullerton."[8] But there were ways, he felt, in which the work of the police could be made more pleasant and also more effective. Although the presence of a Hudson's Bay Company store at Churchill extended the social life of the police considerably, helped solve the problem of supply, and served to draw in Inuit and Indians from a wide region, there were serious deficiencies which Moodie thought needed remedying. One was the lack of a doctor, which had adverse psychological as well as physical effects: "When anything is the matter with a man," Moodie reported, "the remainder as well as the man himself begin to look anxious and get low spirited when they realize there is no doctor within 800 miles."[9] A doctor was detailed for Churchill in 1907, but owing to the failure of the *Rouville,* he did not arrive until 1908.

One of Moodie's great concerns was the extension of police authority in his district, and in this respect, his favourite project was the establishment of a detachment at Baker Lake. Its purpose would be to establish contact with the Inuit of the "Barren Lands," some of whom had had virtually no contact with white men. But this very feature condemned the idea in the eyes of the authorities. As White wrote Moodie in turning down the proposal, "we must be careful to avoid the establishment of Police Posts as gathering places for the Natives, who would become a charge on the Government for subsistence, instead of sustaining themselves by hunting &c. as they have done in past generations."[10] Vilhjalmur Stefansson would no doubt have approved of this position, though perhaps for more unselfish reasons. Moodie persisted, however, and was told again in 1908 and 1909 that the police had no intention of becoming involved in so remote a location.[11] Several years later a detachment was opened at Baker Lake, but it was for a different and specific purpose.

Inspector Pelletier made another remarkable patrol to the Barren Lands in 1908. The proposed route was from Great Slave Lake to Churchill by way of the Thelon River and Baker Lake. The object of the patrol, as Perry described it, was fourfold: 1. To affirm Canadian jurisdiction over this area. 2. To report upon the country and the possibility of a feasible route from the Mackenzie River to the Hudson Bay. 3. To report upon the number, the location, and condition of the Natives. 4. To ascertain whether any permanent detachments of police should be established. Describing the patrol, Perry said, "Of many long and arduous patrols made by the force, this has been the most extended and difficult."[12] The party, consisting of Pelletier and three others, left Fort

Saskatchewan on 1 June 1908, and went by Fort Resolution, Pike River, Artillery Lake, Hanbury, and Thelon Rivers to Chesterfield Inlet, which they reached on 31 August. There they were met by the Hudson's Bay Company Steamer *McTavish*, chartered by Moodie to bring the party to Churchill. On the way south the *McTavish* was wrecked in a storm, and the entire party went to Fullerton to wait for freeze-up. During this part of the trip a member of the party was drowned when the small boat they were travelling in was attacked by a walrus. Leaving Fullerton on 29 November, they reached Churchill on 7 February, and then went overland to Gimli, arriving on 18 March. The time elapsed was nearly ten months, and the distance covered was 3,347 miles.[13] The information gathered was to be useful to the police when they found themselves faced with the necessity of conducting police operations over much the same area six years later. Apart from that, the patrol was an astonishing feat of endurance and survival.

As at Fort McPherson, the police at Churchill got along reasonably well with the representatives of the Hudson's Bay Company. Again, the police were grateful to have someone to talk to other than themselves, and again they found themselves dependent on the company at times for supplies and other assistance. But it worked both ways; the company men were glad to have more white men to talk to, and the police were valuable customers.

Relations between the police and the Hudson's Bay Company men were not always amicable, however. In the winter of 1907–1908 there was a sharp quarrel between the police and the clerk in charge of the company's post over the matter of several dogs belonging to the police that had been caught in traps set by company men. The tone of the incident suggests a clash between two authorities. The Hudson's Bay Company had been established at Churchill as early as 1717 and continuously since 1783.[14] Doubtless, in attempting to exercise their authority, the police encountered some resentment from those who had been accustomed to ruling the region for so many years.[15] Such is the impression given by Moodie's report of the incident:

I cautioned Mr. Alston, the clerk in charge here . . . called his attention to Section 501 of the Crim. Code. . . . His reply was a very insolent letter saying that such and such were the rules of the H.B.Co. and he would abide by them, that if Police dogs were caught it was our own fault. . . . I issued a summons and Mr. Alston then took back water . . . wrote a letter apologising . . . owning himself in the wrong and offering to replace the injured dogs . . . acknowledged that the rules of the H.B.Co. had no force in the country. On this I consented to drop the case.[16]

Moodie had won an important point in extracting from the clerk the admission that the rules of the company were subordinate to the laws enforced by the police. Nevertheless, the company had the last laugh for Commissioner Perry ruled that Moodie had erred; the traps had been set on company property, and the law forbade police dogs or any other dogs to run wild.[17] This did not alter the point that Moodie had made on the spot. While Churchill became increasingly important and increasingly civilized (Moodie's wife came to live at Churchill during the last few years of her husband's service there), the other detachment at Fullerton maintained a precarious existence. It had a very large supply of coal, which had been landed when it was still the headquarters of police operations on the bay, but it was short of almost everything else.[18] Provisioning still had to be done by whaleboat from Churchill, and by the spring of 1909 Perry reported that the stock of supplies at Fullerton was "barely sufficient to carry on the detachment."[19] He then seriously considered closing it altogether. Again the police were compelled to apply to the Hudson's Bay Company for assistance. Moodie persuaded the company to carry supplies to Term Point, halfway to Fullerton; from there they were carried north by whaleboat. Moodie strongly urged that the detachment be kept open, for, as he said, the withdrawal of the post unless it was merely moved to Baker Lake (his pet project again) would have a bad effect on the Natives: "As long as whalers and traders are north of Chesterfield Inlet, Fullerton is certainly the best place for a detachment. It is doubtful if the whalers will return to the Bay for another year . . . in which case the Natives will be entirely dependent upon the Police for obtaining ammunition &c."[20] This is exactly the situation which the government and the police wished to avoid.

The detachment at Fullerton, strangely enough, did not even have an interpreter, which made communication with the Inuit a difficult proposition. Corporal M. A. Joyce, in charge of the detachment, asked for one, remarking that "if such a man was stationed here I think it would be a very short time until the police would be looked upon as the chief authority . . . at present the Natives think the whalers can do about as they please, and that the police have very little to say about it."[21] And this was after the police had been in the region for six years. The detachment at Churchill was in a similar position. Moodie reported in 1909 that "We are still without a Chipewyan interpreter, which makes intercourse with the Indians difficult."[22] The police had to depend on English-speaking Natives and their own meagre command of Native languages, which was obviously not conducive to efficient police work. In 1910 Joyce again reported that his efforts were being seriously hampered by the lack of an interpreter. During a patrol to Wager Inlet, he had heard rumours that an Inuit man had deserted his wife in the middle of the winter. Because he could form only a sketchy idea of the situation, he was unable to pursue the matter: "had I been able to procure a competent interpreter for the trip," he wrote, "I feel confident that the patrol would have resulted in the arrest and conviction of [the man concerned]."[23]

Joyce made disparaging reference to the whalers: "The Natives appear to have a very poor idea of the reason that the police are stationed here, there is little doubt that some of the American whalers who have wintered here have done considerable to confuse the Natives in that respect."[24] Joyce singled out George Comer, then commanding the *A. T. Gifford,* the next-to-last American whaler in the bay, for particular criticism, especially in regard to the payment of customs duty:

I would judge that Capt. Comer has only paid duty on the stuff he intended trading with the Natives (exclusive of what he calls his Natives). During the month of April 1909 there was 720 lbs. of tobacco on the schooner, about 500 lbs. of this will be given to the Natives for services rendered.[25]

An amateur anthropologist who had a fine collection of Inuit artifacts, Comer was in fact on excellent terms with the police administration. A good many personal letters passed between him and White in which he expressed his friendliness to the police and his willingness to assist them where he could. In the spring of 1910, Comer was interviewed in Ottawa by a newspaper reporter, and when the interview was printed, he wrote to White, "I saw by the paper . . . that I was quoted as saying that I had by giving the Police provision [sic] kept them from starving. This you will know to be wrong and was not pleasent [sic] reading for me."[26] Later that year, White wrote Comer asking if he would do the police the favour of taking mail to Fullerton on his next voyage, and, if so, how much he could carry. Comer replied, "I can say frankly that no package will be to [sic] large for me to take. That a Mother cares to send her Son Or a wife to her Husband or a Sister to a Brother. There fore put no limit to what anyone may wish to send."[27] Here again is the anomaly of the police asking favours of the very men they were supposed to be policing.[28] On occasion, Comer even made unofficial reports on the performance of the police themselves. In the winter of 1911–1912, while he was at Fullerton, he wrote to Superintendent Starnes[29] to report on the performance on the N.C.O. in charge of that detachment: "While Sergeant Hayter was here his conduct and care of the Barracks were a credit to the Force. . . . If he had not traded for furs on the sly, I should have been able to say I would not ask for a better man for such work."[30]

Police policy on trade had not in fact been settled by Moodie's prohibi-

tion of 1903. As late as 1908, the police at Churchill were receiving
musk-ox skins from the Inuit to the dismay of the Hudson's Bay Company.[31] Moodie explained his policy:

*As Esquimaux cannot be prevented from killing for food, the Police are to pay a
small sun for any skins brought to them, merely to prevent them being left on the
ground to rot but not sufficient to induce Natives to go out and hunt them. . . . The
difference is that the Company and other traders send out Natives purposely to
hunt these animals. . . . The Police impress upon them at all times that they are
only to kill when actually in want of food.*[32]

Moodie's explanation is partially contradicted by White in a letter to a
Toronto correspondent in 1907 explaining why the police had withdrawn from trade with the Natives at Churchill:

*We shipped in a lot of material to be traded, at a little over cost price, for anything
they might have to dispose of, or in payment for labour they might furnish. The
Canadian traders then stepped in and criticized the Police for cutting the business
from them. This led us to discontinue sending in supplies, and I only protected
myself before the Public Accounts Committee by being able to show that the furs we
received from the Natives were sold in the East, by public competition, at prices
greater than the value of goods that were given in exchange.*[33]

This is a strange business. First Moodie had flatly outlawed trade in
musk-ox skins. Then he had permitted the police to receive skins of
animals killed for food so the skins would not be wasted. At the same
time, the administration of the police was sending in goods specifically
for the purpose of trade and payment for work despite the fact that such
trading had been forbidden by police regulations since the days of the
Yukon gold rush. Police policy was confusing and contradictory, and it is
little wonder that the Hudson's Bay Company was annoyed.

To give the flavour of the life of the police at the two Hudson Bay
detachments during this period, a few entries from the detachment
diaries may be quoted. First, three days from the early autumn of 1907 at
Churchill:

*28 August 1907 —Fine day. Flies very bad. Consts. Rowley, Caldwell, Verity and
Stothert working on inside of quarters being got ready for Surgeon. Corpl.
Nicholls and Const. Travers on fatigue. Const. Heaps on pass shooting with
Inspector Pelletier and party. . . . Natives banking up guardroom. . . . Indian
"David" hired to leave Barracks on 8th Janry. next to go to Split Lake with patrol
as guide. Pay 75 skins, and his wife to get rations during his absence.*

10th September 1907 —Dull day with showers. Corpl. Nicholls issuing rations &c. Consts. Rowley and Caldwell hewing logs in P.M. *In* A.M. *washing walls of barrack room. Employed Natives resacking coal on east side.*

18th September 1907 —Showery all day. Southerly winds. Corpl. Nicholls, Consts. Rowley and Caldwell on log building. Supt. Moodie performed operation on Eliza Oman taking away tumour weighing over 5 lbs. from stomach. Rev. Mr. Sevier very kindly assisted. [34]

Life at Fullerton was much less eventful:

5 January 1907 —Clear and cool, Temp. 8 A.M. *—18* [F], *at 3* A.M. *—17. N.E. wind. Arm inspection this* A.M. *Two men to their traps this* P.M., *got one fox.*

15 January 1907 —Fair and cool. Temp. —47 at 8 A.M., *at 3* P.M. *—41. No wind. Fatigue in stores, cleaning up things in general. Scottie and Pook* [employed Inuit] *to floe* [to hunt for seals]*—no luck.* [35]

Around 1910, activity in Hudson Bay began to increase. In 1909 the Hudson's Bay Company began to found new posts, starting with Erik Cove and Cape Wolstenholme in Ungava. The traders Revillon Freres founded a post at Cape Dufferin. Although these posts were not within the jurisdiction of the police, they noted their establishment with approval as tending to be of advantage to the Inuit. Moodie reported that he had been told by a representative of Revillon Freres that the Inuit at Cape Dufferin "were in a starving condition last winter, and had resorted to murder and cannibalism in consequence." [36] In 1912 the Hudson's Bay Company began to extend its operations on the west coast of the bay by opening a post at Chesterfield Inlet. Public attention was drawn to Hudson Bay in 1910 when the Governor General, Earl Grey, travelled from Norway House to York Factory, where he took ship for Labrador and southern Canada. The police were in charge of the arrangements. [37] The visit, like more recent royal tours of the north, had overtones of sovereignty. It was no coincidence that the year of Earl Grey's visit also saw the final arbitration at the Hague of the whole question of the rights of the United States to fish in Canadian waters under the Convention of 1818, an arbitration which resulted in a complete vindication of the British and Canadian position.

This new activity helped spur the police to make their own plans for expansion northward along the shore of the bay. In 1910, Fred White explained that the police had been deterred from expansion because of the cost. [38] The Hudson's Bay Company charged fifteen dollars a ton to carry supplies, and Revillon Freres charged forty-five dollars, and neither company would send its ships north of Churchill on behalf of the police. Now, however, an opportunity presented itself. Captain Sam Bartlett, a "life long Navigator" and captain of the *Neptune* expedition of 1903, had offered his schooner *Jeanie* to the police for the 1910 season at a cost of $6,000. White seized the opportunity to provision the two detachments and to send the ship north to Repulse Bay to scout the possibilities of opening a third one there.

The use of a ship for the whole season also gave the police a chance to make the route between Fullerton and Churchill more secure. Four small prefabricated shelter huts were constructed, to be placed at convenient points on the coast between the two detachments. The huts, containing a stove, lamp, bunks, and food, would make the route safer, both by sea and by land.[39] One hut was set up at Eskimo Point, and another at Rankin Inlet, but the third could not be set up at Chesterfield Inlet because of strong winds. When the ship reached Wager Inlet, the proposed location of the fourth hut, which was to serve as a way station to the new post at Repulse Bay, it was totally wrecked in a gale. The crew sailed in an open boat to Fullerton, and eventually Captain Comer took them in his ship to Churchill.[40] It was another in the long series of mishaps which plagued police shipping in Hudson Bay. These mishaps were partly the result of last-minute planning and partly of the fact that police boats in this era often had amateurs for crew. Because of the red tape involved in having plans and appropriations approved and the necessity for getting north before the end of the season, expeditions were sometimes sent off on two or three days' notice, ill-supplied and haphazardly manned. The attempt to found a new post had ended in failure, and it was not repeated for several years.

The small shelters which were successfully put up did prove to be of benefit to the police on patrol. An N.C.O. who used them called them a "great comfort," giving a patrol a "sense of security as they greatly lessen the possibility of disaster." They proved useful as well as reassuring: "They afford a great convenience for fixing your outfit and drying your skin clothing . . . this gets in bad shape camping night after night in snow houses."[41]

The attempt to extend police control north to Repulse Bay in 1910 was an almost complete failure. In 1911, however, the police did manage to expand to the south with considerably more success. The new location was at York Factory. As elsewhere, the police moved largely in response to anguished pleas from the local missionary:

Owing to the indiscriminate and unlawful use of liquor by the Officials of the Hudson's Bay Company. . . . [as] A Missionary who has the interests of the In-

*dians at heart . . . I ask the Government to station a guardian of the law here. . . .
The Hudson's Bay Company seem to be slightly wanting in their judgement when
they place reckless young men who have little idea of their responsibilities in charge
of their business at this post.* [42]

Corporal R. H. Walker, dispatched from Churchill to York Factory in
answer to this letter, reported that both the missionary and the manager
of the post had requested that a detachment be opened because of the
presence of over a hundred Indians employed each summer unloading
goods from the annual steamer. [43]

In response, a temporary detachment was opened at York Factory
(then still part of the Northwest Territories) from 11 August to 4 September 1911. The N.C.O. in charge, Sergeant C. N. C. Hayter, cancelled
all liquor permits, seized some liquor, and was able to report that "Everything has been quiet and orderly and there have been no cases of liquor
amongst Indians." [44] The company men were not pleased to see their
liquor supply dry up, and considerable correspondence ensued between
officials of the company and Ottawa. White eventually relaxed the rules
to permit them to import liquor for private consumption, but its sale was
prohibited. White wrote, "I am disposed to be generous in the issue of
permits, provided there is no abuse. . . . I am sure you will understand
what I mean." [45]

The new detachment was reopened at York Factory in the summer of
1912, but in response to the fluid conditions in the area, in the summer of
1913 it was moved around the point of land separating the Hayes and
Nelson Rivers and re-established at Port Nelson. The government had
now decided on Port Nelson as the terminus of the Hudson Bay Railway,
and already a number of workmen had arrived to begin work on the
harbour facilities. The "influx of labourers, mechanics, etc.," the police
reported, made it "extremely likely that Criminal cases will occur." [46] To
prevent the situation from getting out of hand, the complement of police
in "M" Division was doubled from ten in 1913 to twenty in 1914, of whom
eleven were stationed at Port Nelson. [47] The sergeant in charge estimated
that over seven hundred men had arrived at the railway terminus during
the summer of 1913 and reported, "we experienced great difficulty in
keeping order, especially on the ships where mutiny broke out. . . . It is
almost impossible to do police work properly." [48] It was just as well that
the police increased their strength at Port Nelson, for in the autumn of
1914 the men working on the harbour facilities went on strike when their
wages were reduced by ten cents an hour. Perhaps because of the presence of the police, no violence occurred. The police were even able to
escort one train from The Pas to the end of steel, carrying food to the

"starving foreigners." The strike ended when the company changed its mind and restored the original wage scale.[49]

A workmen's strike was an unlikely event to have occurred on the "northern frontier"; it indicated that with the influx of railwaymen, the area had reached a level of economic and technological development which put it in a class with the Yukon of 1898—geographically isolated, but otherwise quite "modern." Port Nelson was not even as isolated from the rest of Canada as it might seem. In February 1914 a wireless antenna was put up at the police detachment, and the police were thereafter able to "receive the daily news from Cape Cod, and an occasional message from Virginia. This is a great boon here, as we receive the news before it is published in the papers in civilization."[50] Sergeant R. H. Walker, who commanded the detachment, was so enthusiastic about the economic prospects of the place that he planned to take his discharge and go into business there. Apparently the railway boom had other side effects as well; for example, a number of miners had come into the country to prospect along the railway right-of-way.[51] Two new detachments were opened along the railway in 1915, one at Kettle Rapids, and the other, called "Half Way" detachment, at mile 379 from The Pas. They were closed when work on the line was abandoned. There was also a temporary detachment at Split Lake.

In 1914 Port Nelson became so important that the headquarters of "M" Division was moved there. The police bought four prefabricated structures in Ottawa and sent them north by ship, three to Port Nelson to serve as divisional headquarters and the fourth to Baker Lake.[52] But like several of the good ideas that the police tried out in the north, this one was not very successful. The buildings turned out to be "The usual sort of houses erected at summer resorts."[53] Even when insulated with beaver-board, they were cold and drafty. Whoever in Ottawa had the idea of sending summer cottages to Port Nelson caused much shivering and grumbling among the police there.

For a brief time, Port Nelson enjoyed prosperity. By the end of 1917 the entire right-of-way was finished, and a great deal of money had been spent on port facilities.[54] But then, because of the demand for steel and men in the war effort, construction was halted. The track was not finished, and some of what had already been laid was taken up during the war to be used on other lines, especially in France. In 1918 the police reduced their detachment at Port Nelson to one man, whose only duty was to guard the large amount of supplies still at the port.[55] All the labourers left. Although 322 miles of track had been built from The Pas by 1917, not a rail was laid between 1918 and 1926. By the time construction was finally renewed in 1927, the government had changed its mind and decided to put the port at Churchill. Port Nelson, which had flourished for only four years, disappeared from the map.

Twentieth-century civilization had penetrated Hudson Bay by way of Port Nelson between 1913 and 1918, but it had surprisingly little effect on the rest of the bay. Because of the continuing difficulties of transportation between points on the coast, Churchill, and especially Fullerton, remained remote from the rest of Canada. The establishment of a new Hudson's Bay Company store at Chesterfield Inlet in 1911–12 proved a great attraction to the Inuit on the northern coast, who had hitherto regarded Fullerton as the centre of their world. In the winter of 1912–13, the detachment at Fullerton was deserted by all the Inuit except the two families employed by the police.[56] In the summer of 1913 activity at Fullerton increased again when an independent trader, F. N. Monjo of New York, opened a post there, and many of the Natives returned.[57]

Although the Fullerton detachment had performed some useful services for the government—it had, for example, conducted the census in its area in 1911—[58]it really did not do enough to justify the expense and bother of maintaining it. Most of the reports from Fullerton contained passages such as "The work of the detachment has consisted of hunting for dog feed along the floe for the winter's supply. Painting the buildings and repairing the same."[59] Still, the post fulfilled the objective of demonstrating the presence of the government, which had been its primary purpose. For this reason it maintained a precarious existence, except from 1915 to 1917, when it was temporarily closed because of the extra patrol work the police had to do. It was reopened in 1918. The detachment at Churchill, on the other hand, was closed in 1915, so that by 1920 the only detachments on Hudson Bay were at Port Nelson and Fullerton.[60] Perry justified the retention of the detachment at Fullerton on the grounds that it protected the Inuit, exerted a "beneficial influence" on them by discouraging "evil customs," and was "the only point in the vast area tributary to the northern part of Hudson Bay where there is an established authority."[61] It was also a place where the police had made a large investment in buildings and supplies. But by this time the police activity in the bay was static as their attention turned to a new frontier farther to the north and east.

10. Patrols and Patrolling

PATROLLING warrants a short chapter of its own, especially because on some parts of the frontier it was not only the chief, but the sole activity of the detachments. Police patrols fell into two categories—routine and special. Routine patrols were carried out on a schedule, to deliver mail, to make a regular visit to a community, to obtain monthly or weekly supplies, to check on game,[1] or for some other usual purpose. Special patrols were sent out for particular reasons—to investigate crimes, to render aid in individual instances, to explore a certain area, sometimes with a view to the establishment of a new detachment.

"Patrol" always suggests the picture of a policeman and his dog-sled, but in police reports it describes movement on official business by any means, from foot to steamboat to aeroplane. Most of the regular patrols and the important special patrols on the northern frontier were carried out by dog team at first simply because this was the best method of travel over the greater part of the year. Later, sled patrols over the Territories were outdistanced by other kinds.[2] But this occurred only as the north ceased to be a frontier, in the nineteenth-century, non-mechanized sense of the word.

Most of the northern police detachments employed one or more Natives as dog team drivers; they were Inuit, Indian, or Métis, depending on the location of the post, and they generally lived with their families in a small building belonging to the detachment. The Natives, especially the Inuit, generally did much of the actual work of driving the sleds, which were often their own, the technique of hitching and handling the dogs being determined by the area of origin of the driver. Very often, in remote regions, their wives came along on patrol to cook and tend to the clothes. The police early adopted Inuit dress for Arctic travel, and it required nightly attention.

The police did not live off the land while on patrol unless they were forced to or unless they were going such a long distance that it was impossible to carry all the food required. In order to live off the land, one must be prepared to disregard time to a certain extent and to go where the game is; and this the police, who operated on a schedule or had a fixed objective, could not do. Whether they were chasing criminals or investigating the condition of the Inuit, they could not delay their patrols to hunt seals or search for caribou.

This being the case, the significance of the most famous of all police patrols becomes clear. The Fort McPherson-Dawson patrol of 1910–11, called the Fitzgerald or the "Lost Patrol," received more publicity than any other in the history of the police (except perhaps the one involving the "mad trapper of Rat River"), chiefly because it was the only one which ended in disaster.[3] The patrol raised issues, in the press as well as among the police, which reflected upon the method of police operations on the northern frontier, and it is thus of more than merely sensational interest.

The facts of the episode may be briefly related. Inspector F. J. Fitzgerald, two constables, and an ex-policeman acting as guide left Fort McPherson for Dawson in December 1910, carrying mail.[4] It was unusual for a patrol to follow this route; the regular mail patrol went in the opposite direction. The men became lost in the Richardson mountains because the guide had never travelled the route in that direction, and they spent a dangerous amount of time looking for the right way to Dawson. Fitzgerald decided to retrace his steps to Fort McPherson, but too late, and all four men died, three of starvation and one by suicide, only a good day's journey from that post.[5]

What had happened? This question was asked not only by the police, who hastened to make an investigation into the disaster, but also by the public and the press, which criticized police methods as being wasteful of lives. When Commissioner Perry wrote to White, "this is the most serious catastrophe that the Force has experienced in many a long day,"[6] he referred not only to the loss of men, but also to the damage done the reputation of the police. It was difficult to understand what had gone wrong. Fitzgerald was an experienced and resourceful man who had first come to the Mackenzie Delta in 1903. It was not a case of an amateur making mistakes which led to the tragedy; rather, it was a case of over-confidence, summed up concisely by the Anglican missionary at Fort McPherson:

They went off short provisioned, for the sake of travelling light, but their dogs were not of the best, and they had no Indian for guide. Carter had been over the trail [in the other direction], four years ago, but was not sure of the crossings. [7]

Although the records do not say so directly, the impression is strong that Fitzgerald was trying to set a speed record and therefore did not take enough provisions to guard against disaster.

The police hierarchy now found itself in the unpleasant position of having to defend itself against newspaper criticism of their established methods. Superintendent A. E. R. Cuthbert, an officer of the force stationed at Edmonton, unwisely gave an interview to a reporter from the *Bulletin* in which he was quoted as saying that Arctic patrols were useless. [8] A sharp query from Regina brought anguished denials, including the logically dubious assertion, in regard to such patrols, that "the fact of their being carried out showed they were necessary." [9] More to the point, Cuthbert explained that he had told the reporter that "The question was a much wider one than appeared to the casual observer, owing to the desireability of Canada asserting sovereignty over every foot of the far north." He continued, "I was aware that considerable criticism was being made of the Northern patrols, among friends of the deceased especially." [10] The tone of his apology shows that the reprimand, which has not survived, was a sharp one; the police felt more irritation from the bad publicity they received over this incident than from anything which had appeared in the newspapers for many years.

Perry replied to his critics in his next annual report. The gist of his argument was that dangerous patrols were going on all the time, but that the police did not object to them, so why should anyone else? "In spite of every precaution," he wrote, "a tragedy may occur at any time. It does not deter our men from seeking service there, and it is to the north that many would like to go." [11] He also quoted from a letter written by the Hon. G. W. Brown, lieutenant-governor of Saskatchewan: "While the event brings deepest sadness to all, we feel that it is only an event such as this which can give greatest lustre and enduring remembrance to the splendid Force." [12] This seems rather insensitive, but perhaps it was of comfort to the relatives of the deceased; it apparently comforted Commissioner Perry. Nevertheless, to disarm his detractors and to prevent a repetition of the tragedy, Perry ordered a number of shelter cabins built on the route between Fort McPherson and Dawson and also between Fort McPherson and Herschel Island. [13]

The most interesting criticism of the episode came from Vilhjalmur Stefansson, who heard of it while he was still in the north. For Stefansson, the fate of the Fitzgerald patrol was proof that the police method of Arctic travel was inferior to his own. The irony of his earlier quarrel with Fitzgerald was not lost on him.[14] When he commented on Fitzgerald's death in 1913, his tone was self-satisfied:

the last conversation I had had with Fitzgerald was one in which he told me his thorough disapprobation of my methods of travel, and that if I tried to follow them I should surely come to grief. And here we were in comfort and plenty listening to the story of his tragic death.[15]

Stefansson's general criticism of the police method of patrolling is worth quoting in this context:

They had failed through the essential weakness of their system of travel, which was to take with them all the food they thought they could possibly need on the journey, without making any preparations for gathering more from the country when their stores should become exhausted. The result was in that case, as it has been in so many others, that when unlooked-for circumstances stretched the time of the journey beyond the limit reckoned on at first, supplies ran out . . . then came death through cold and starvation . . . it had always seemed to me that so long as you are travelling in a country supplied with game, you are safer to start with a rifle and with the resolution to find food (but without a pound of food on your sled), than you would be in starting with a sled heavily loaded with food and with no provision for getting more when the sled load has been eaten up.[16]

Stefansson's method of Arctic travel certainly worked well for him, keeping him alive under all sorts of conditions, thus proving its worth pragmatically. What should be questioned is whether his comments on the Fitzgerald patrol really fitted the facts of the case and whether they can be applied to police patrols in general.

Stefansson says that Fitzgerald's main mistake was taking his food with him instead of living off the land, that "in a country supplied with game" there was no reason why anyone should starve. But much of the region through which the police had to pass does not teem with game. There were few caribou and, of course, no seals, which were the staple in Stefansson's diet. There were a good number of rabbits, but they hardly repay the energy required to catch them, and as Stefansson knew, a man living on rabbit meat will starve for want of fat. Secondly, and this is the important point, Fitzgerald died not because he failed to follow Stefansson's formula for success, but because he deviated from the regular police method of patrolling. His party did not take with them "all the food which they thought they could possibly need." On the contrary, they travelled as light as possible.[17] The Fitzgerald patrol was an incident outside the ordinary pattern of police operations and reflects not on police methods but on the bad luck and poor judgment of Fitzgerald himself. The fact that the incident was unique among the hundreds of similar patrols carried out by the police—a fact well emphasized by Perry—is further proof of this assertion.

Of the many special patrols carried out by the police, two are representative; both were made during the First World War to investigate bizarre murders. They were of special importance for several reasons. They were journeys of discovery for the police; few white men and no member of the Mounted Police had seen the territory which was to be covered. They were significant from the point of view of police-Inuit relations, for the police on these patrols met men who had never before seen a white man, let alone a representative of the government. The patrols were important in emphasizing Canadian control over the central Arctic coast. Nothing establishes sovereignty over an area more clearly than effective policing of it. If murderers could be successfully tracked down and arrested near Coronation Gulf, then Canada's right to the area would seem clear and certain.[18]

The first case was that of H. V. Radford and George Street. Radford was an American explorer of considerable experience who had been active in the north at least as early as 1909.[19] His companion Street was a young and inexperienced man from Ottawa. In June 1912, they were murdered by Inuit at the southern end of Bathurst Inlet, apparently because Radford had threatened and struck an Inuit who was acting as a guide and servant to the expedition. As anyone who knew anything about the Inuit was aware, threatening an Inuit was never safe. Many Inuit believed that a man who spoke harshly had it in his mind to commit murder, and that it was thus reasonable and proper to kill him first. This is what happened to Radford, and Street was the victim of his stupidity. Radford had a reputation in the north for being bad-tempered; at one point he had threatened the police with a lawsuit because they would not let him shoot a wood-buffalo.[20]

News of the murders reached the police and the public about a year after they occurred when an Inuit who had been with the party told H. H. Hall, the Hudson's Bay Company officer at Chesterfield Inlet, what had happened. Hall passed the news on to the police at Churchill.[21] There was considerable public interest in the crime partly because of its bizarre details and partly because it had taken place in such a remote spot. Press reaction was mixed. One school of thought held that the whole incident should be ignored, that the murdered men had brought their fate on themselves: "Men who go into a country like that must take chances of such a fate, and can hardly look for governmental protection ... [if they are tactful] they are not likely to be exposed to any serious danger."[22] The other point of view was just the opposite: "Justice in Canada is supposed to be administered without regard to cost.... If the slayers of these men go unpunished, no man's life will be save [sic] hereafter in the far northern Frontier.... They should be brought to trial if it costs a million."[23]

Fairly quickly a decision was taken by the police, in consultation with Prime Minister Borden, to carry out a patrol. It was not to be a punitive expedition, but one to "establish friendly relations with the tribe, secure their confidence, and carefully inquire into all the circumstances."[24] This policy would be most beneficial to the Inuit and would probably be the most popular with the Canadian public, whose view of this particular racial minority was sentimental and generally approving.

The long, complicated story of the expedition to investigate the murders is fascinating even in a brief account.[25] When they learned of the event in June 1913, the police decided that the best way to investigate was to establish a base at Baker Lake and send a patrol from there overland to Bathurst Inlet, the scene of the crime. At the end of July 1914, a schooner, the *Village Belle*, purchased by the police for the work, set out from Halifax. It arrived in Hudson Bay too late to reach Baker Lake that season, so the expedition, under the command of Inspector W. J. Beyts, wintered at Port Nelson.

The season of 1915 was spent in getting to Baker Lake, and in the winter of 1915–16 an advance camp was set up on the Thelon River. In 1916, nothing much was done, since Beyts allowed himself to be overwhelmed by the tremendous difficulties of moving a ponderous lot of equipment and men through such difficult country. Dissatisfied with the pace, the police replaced Beyts with Inspector F. H. French. Finally, in the winter of 1917–1918 a successful patrol was carried out; and the murderers were found when the crime was nearly six years old.

The police did more than simply solve the crime; they accomplished a good deal in the way of exploration and surveying. One member of the party, Constable A. B. Kennedy, an ex-Royal Navy man with a good knowledge of map-making, made an extensive survey of the Baker Lake-Chesterfield Inlet area between 1915 and 1916, covering 1,154 square miles:

Upwards of thirty islands have been located and charted for the first time; these vary in size from ... 100 sq. miles in area to mere islets. ... Native names have been obtained wherever possible.[26]

A new chart was made of Baker Lake itself. Kennedy wrote, "If this sheet be compared with the previous existing survey, that of Tyrell [sic], 1900, it will be seen that there are very great alterations, more especially in regard to distances.[27] This work was in connection with the police base at Baker Lake, but it also had a wider usefulness in increasing the government's knowledge of that part of the Northwest Territories.

The police also came into contact with Inuit who had previously had no dealings with whites. As Inspector French reported, "I came upon large bands . . . on Kent Peninsula and around Bathurst Inlet who had never seen white men before."[28] It should be re-emphasized that the government and the police intended the patrol mostly as an investigation of the case. They realized that the murderer or murderers had probably acted in what the Inuit would consider self-defence. Before it set out, Borden conferred with Laurier, seeking the benefit of his experience and asking his advice as to what the attitude of the police should be towards the guilty parties. Borden passed on Laurier's advice to the police:

He considers the Eskimos a very peaceable race and thinks that . . . no Jury would convict them. He thinks the way you suggest —to quietly bring these people under the influence of the law —is the only course to be followed.[29]

This was the principle on which the entire expedition was carried out. The police met with no opposition from the Inuit, therefore, beyond a certain natural suspicion which they bore towards strangers.

The upshot of the affair was that after an extensive investigation, including interviews with the Inuit who had witnessed the murders, the police came to the conclusion that the original explanation was correct. Radford had precipitated the murders by his foolishly harsh treatment of his Inuit companions. As one police officer put it, Radford's action was "not a safe way to deal with Esquimaux."[30] The band of Inuit among whom the murders had occurred (the Killinimuits) were finally found, and the culprits confessed willingly, but in accord with the government's policy, the matter was not pressed further.

The other murder case was remarkably similar, and it is also worth commenting upon for what it shows of police operations in the Arctic. The chief difference was that the second case was not so drawn out, and the eventual treatment of the Inuit involved was also different, partly because the victims were priests and partly because the authorities were not prepared to be as lenient a second time.

The case concerned the murder of Fathers Rouvière (sometimes spelled without the last "e") and Le Roux, two Oblate missionaries who had been working among the Inuit of the Coppermine River region.

They had a small cabin at the northeast end of Great Bear Lake, which they used as a base camp for expeditions to these relatively unknown people.[31] They were last heard of in 1913, and the first intimation of their fate was in the summer of 1914, when a man named D'Arcy Arden, who was exploring the Dease River near Great Bear Lake, met an Inuit who was wearing a cassock.[32] The priests, it was eventually learned, had been killed late in 1913 near Bloody Falls on the Coppermine River. The cause of the murders was very similar to the Radford and Street case. One of the priests, Father Le Roux, had become impatient with the Inuit who were acting as their guides and servants and had threatened one of them. The confession of Sinnisiak, one of the killers, shows clearly what happened:

Ilogoak [Le Roux] was carrying a rifle. He was mad with us when we started back from their camp and I could not understand his talk. I asked Ilogoak if he was going to kill me and he nodded his head. . . . he pushed me again and wanted me to put on the harness and then he took his rifle out on top of the sled. I was very scared and started to pull. We went a little way and Uluksak and I started to talk and Ilogoak put his hand over my mouth. Ilogoak was very mad and was pushing me. I was thinking hard and crying and very scared and the frost was in my boots and I was cold. I wanted to go back. I was afraid. Ilogoak would not let us. Every time the sled stuck Ilogoak would pull out the rifle. I got hot inside my body. . . . I was very much afraid. . . . he looked away from me and I stabbed him in the back with a knife.[33]

At the first news of their disappearance, it had been thought that the priests might turn up alive and well, but that they might have been robbed, since their small cabin had been ransacked. In this case, the officer in charge of the investigation, Inspector C. D. La Nauze, was ordered to catch the thieves and impose a small fine. Harsher treatment would not be necessary since "this is the first occasion enforcement of the law has taken place in this remote district."[34]

The truth became generally known in the spring of 1915, and the police prepared to send out a patrol in the next year. In the summer of 1915 a patrol from Fort Norman established a depot at Dease Bay on Great Bear Lake. Between the end of March and the end of May 1916, a patrol was made from this depot to the Coppermine River and beyond. All circumstances were investigated, and the culprits were arrested. By the end of June 1916 the party had arrived at Herschel Island with the prisoners. This case was solved more quickly because the distances involved were much shorter, the police had a ready-made base camp at Dease Bay (the priests' cabin), and the patrol was fortunate enough to fall in with the Canadian Arctic expedition, who helped them with fall in with the Canadian Arctic expedition, who helped them with supplies and information and lent the police their ship for the journey to Herschel Island. The two Inuit prisoners were taken south and charged with murder. The eventual disposition of this case is significant from the point of view of police-Inuit relations and will be discussed in the next chapter.

The actual patrolling "technique" bears some examination for it shows the way the police adapted themselves to Arctic conditions, borrowing ideas and methods from the Natives which seemed suitable for their purposes. Details vary from one patrol to another, depending mostly on its purpose and where it was going, but a good example is the patrol made in the spring of 1917 from Baker Lake to the Arctic coast in connection with the Radford and Street affair. It shows all the features which appear in reports of police patrols—the daily record of events and comments on the Natives, game, and geography. The main report is accompanied by shorter crime reports, giving the statements of several witnesses in the case.

The patrol was made up of two members of the R.N.W.M.P., Inspector F. H. French and Sergeant-Major T. B. Caulkin, two "police Natives" (that is, regular Inuit employees), one "hired Native," and an Inuit woman. The patrol also took two canoes and twenty-five dogs, enough for three sleds. The party left Baker Lake on 21 March 1917 and reached Bernard Harbour on 13 June. There they spent the summer, returning to Baker Lake in the following autumn and winter. The distance covered by foot and sled was 2,483 miles; 1,835 "over routes" in direct pursuit of their objective, 284 miles hunting for caribou, 114 miles hunting seal, and 250 miles in various directions searching for Inuit camps.[35]

The chief difficulties facing this patrol, as with other similar patrols in the Arctic, were not the Inuit, who were almost uniformly cooperative, but supplies, terrain, and climate. The men could take only a month's rations with them, and after the end of April, they were compelled to live off the land. In this they were quite successful as far as procuring game was concerned; French reported no shortage of caribou until they reached the coast, and then they were able to kill seals and trade for meat (and fish for the dogs) when they encountered bands of Inuit. It can be seen from the report, however, that it was not easy for the police to acclimatize themselves to an Arctic diet; one made up entirely of meat disagreed with them, and "going on two meals of half-raw deermeat during the day . . . 14 or 16 hours between meals" told on their health. Nor did they have much luck with cooking over a stone blubber lamp when they ran out of coal-oil. In general, though, partly because of the assistance rendered by their Inuit companions, they were reasonably well supplied with food; no worse, at least, than the indigenous population.

The climate and terrain proved difficult chiefly because of the season in which they travelled. By the end of May the weather was warm enough to melt much of the snow, and the patrol was inconvenienced by having to travel along the sides of the creek beds, where the snow was deeper. The sun made the sea-ice treacherous, and the last part of the outward journey, along the coast from Bathurst Inlet to Bernard Harbour, was the most uncomfortable, because the men were continually wet. The patrol lived in igloos until the heat brought down the roof and forced them into their tent.[36] But these misadventures happened regularly to everyone in that country, white and Inuit alike. In general, the report shows that the members of this patrol (and this is true of most other police patrols in the Arctic) coped with the difficulties of supply and geography as well as, or better than, any other white man, and perhaps nearly as well as the Natives themselves. This was largely because they relied on Inuit technology and experience wherever circumstances permitted. If the police were going rapidly from one specific point to another, as was the case with the Fitzgerald patrol, they might run into trouble. But wherever they could adopt the customs and procedures of the country through which they were travelling, they were remarkably successful.[37]

11. The Police and the Native Peoples of the Northern Frontier

"CANADA ... was integrating that region [the Arctic] with the rest of the country, and would enforce there her laws. But what plans she entertained, if any, for the welfare of its Eskimos she wrapped in silence."[1] Diamond Jenness's trenchant comment on Canadian government policy in the Arctic is a good place to begin an examination of the relationship between the instruments of that policy—the police—and the Native peoples.[2]

Jenness says that the basic premise of government policy was erroneous because it accepted the responsibility for maintaining law and order in the Arctic while refusing to accept any of the responsibilities which go with sovereignty: "The administration of the Arctic, handled in the end entirely by the police, was as static and unprogressive as police-run states generally are."[3] The fact that the comptroller of the R.N.W.M.P. was also for a time the commissioner of the Northwest Territories did not mean that the police had any great influence of government policy towards the Arctic. The government had so little positive interest in the north before 1920, apart from its rather static conception of sovereignty, that it found it convenient to have the police and the token government administration handled by the same man. Frederick White, the comptroller, was commissioner of the Northwest Territories from 1905 until his death in 1918, but the position was a sinecure; his main duty was to distribute small sums to various church mission schools. The astonishing fact is that government expenditure on the entire Northwest Territories in this era, exclusive of the cost of the police, was only about $5,000 a year. Though they administered the Territories, the police did not set policy for them;

they "were only the instruments of a policy (or lack of policy) which they neither planned nor formulated. . . . They merely carried out the broad functions assigned to them by the Minister of the Interior, the Prime Minister, and ultimately Parliament."[4]

The fate of these people was left entirely in the hands of the traders, the missionaries, and the police. And it was not the fault of the police, either by wish or by deed, that there were no government schools, hospitals, or any other services for the Native peoples of the north during this period. Constant and repeated appeals for doctors, health services, schools, and financial assistance for the Natives came from police detachments in the north. The usual reply from Ottawa was either silence or instructions for the police to do the best they could with their own resources to ameliorate the suffering they saw among the Indians and Inuit with whom they came in contact. Diamond Jenness realized this fact. Even Farley Mowat, no friend of government agencies, dealt fairly gently with the police when he condemned the government for its neglect of the Inuit.[5] In *Canada North,* he even speaks warmly of them.[6] Not every writer has held the police in high esteem; R. A. Davies, in *The Great Mackenzie,* wrote that the police were "great white fathers" instead of "counsellors and aides" and claimed that they "held back the stimuli of self-development."[7]

The police detachments quickly became centres for some Natives (though many avoided all settlements and continued to pursue a successful nomadic way of life). Here they found casual employment, trade (if there were traders present), and, in hard times, places to go for assistance. The detachments at Herschel Island and Fullerton attracted Inuit only, those at Fort McPherson and Churchill attracted Indians and Inuit, and those in the Yukon and at Port Nelson and York Factory only Indians.[8] As a general rule, the police behaved in quite a different way towards the Indians than towards the Inuit. Because they made a conscious distinction between the two races, the relations between the police and the two Native races will be treated separately, the Indians first.

The Mounted Police were no strangers to Indians. Since the founding of the N.W.M.P. in 1873, one of its primary tasks had been to interpret Canadian laws for, and enforce them on, the Indians of the plains. The approach taken to the Indians of the far north was much the same. By 1900 these Indians were generally quite accustomed to white men. On the shores of Hudson Bay for two hundred years, and in the Mackenzie Delta for sixty, they had become increasingly involved with traders and missionaries. Since the police were accustomed to dealing with Indians and the Indians were used to the ways of whites, there was virtually no conflict between the police and the Indians in the new areas where the police began to establish their power after 1903. The chief effect of the advent of the police on the Indians way of life was that one more set of rules was added to it. Laws which the Hudson's Bay Company factor had not bothered with were now to be enforced. If the Indian obeyed them, he was left alone by the police, for better or worse.

How did the police view the Indians of the north? The evidence in the police records shows that they looked upon them with a mixture of paternalism and contempt. The evidence of contempt is massive. As one example, a report from Fort McPherson on the conditions of the Indians there at the end of 1906: "There are about thirty . . . around the post this winter. . . . They all complain of game being scarce, but the most of them are too lazy to hunt."[9] There may have been any number of reasons why these Indians did not hunt: perhaps they were sick or did not think it worthwhile; perhaps they were what sociologists call "alienated" by the white man's culture. In any case, these Indians were not representative of the general Native population. But for the police they were always "lazy"; the word reappears like a Calvinist refrain through their reports.

There is also ample evidence of the paternalism. A good example, which incidentally shows how the police explained their mission to the Indians they were meeting for the first time, is an account of two speeches made by Inspector E. A. Pelletier, while on a patrol from Norway House to Churchill in 1907. The first was made at Cross Lake to a band of what Pelletier called "good Indians" and reveals the patronizing tone the police adopted when speaking to them:

I want to tell you something about us. We, the Police, have just come into this territory. We have not come here to trade, we are wealthy; we have come here to look after everything to see that everybody behaves well. We have always been the great friend of the good Indians. We are just the same to white men; we punish bad Indians and bad white men just the same. . . . Whenever you and your councillors have trouble with your people, come to us and explain matters; have confidence in us for we are here for your good. Whenever white traders ill use you or steal from you come to us without fear and tell us. We are not properly settled here and have no suitable buildings as yet, but perhaps next year we will build proper buildings for ourselves.[10]

There was another band in the same area which was not so well-behaved. Pelletier said that they were beginning to discover that the local Indian agent had no real power over them and, in consequence, were increasingly becoming "immoral, lying, unscrupulous, and thieving." To this group, he made a sterner speech:

I am very sad to hear these reports. We were under the impression that the Indians in this country were good Indians, obedient to their Chief and councillors, but I see now that this is not so. If this keeps going on amongst your tribe we will be compelled to build a jail at Norway House and will get after the bad Indians. I want you to go round your people and tell them that we have had nearly enough of their bad behaviour, that we are keeping track of all those that do wrong. . . . It is for them to behave themselves well so that we may be inclined to forget and forgive them their bad conduct up to the present. [11]

Nowadays such speeches would be considered ludicrous, not least by the Indians themselves, who are far too sophisticated for the "great white father" approach. But in 1907 this was the accepted way of talking to Indians, especially ones who had had little contact with the police or other government officials.

The attitude of the police towards the Indians they encountered in the Yukon was generally that they were a lazy, dirty nuisance, to be given meagre aid if they were actually starving, but to be ignored as much as possible. Relations with the Indians occupied only a small part of the attention of the police in the Yukon. They were, however, a much more important part of their service in the Mackenzie Delta and in Hudson Bay; but the attitude of the police there was much the same. As an example, here are Inspector D. M. Howard's comments on the hardships of the Mackenzie Delta Indians in 1907:

These Indians are to blame themselves for a good deal of the shortness now prevailing, as they can easily put up enough fish to last them over the winter, but they are too lazy to do it, and the more you do for them, the more you may. [12]

Still, Howard did issue enough supplies to keep the Indians alive.

Police comments on the Indians were not entirely negative; they did have a vague but positive idea of what the Indians ought to be doing. Most members of the force in the north seem to have felt that the Indians would be best off giving up the white man's vices and concentrating on hunting, fishing, and trapping and that the virtues of hard work would be the best preparation for coping with the rest of the world. How the Indians were supposed to rise above the subsistence level (and what they were supposed to do if they did) was never made clear: the police fixed their attention on the first stage of the process as they saw it—self-discipline—believing that if the Indians would only buckle down to honest work, the rest would come naturally. The Indians did not think this way at all, which perhaps explains some of the lack of understanding between the two groups.

Were the police satisfied that the Indians' "laziness" was the sole cause of their misfortune, or did they look beneath the surface to determine why they were in such a miserable condition? Certainly the Indians' own supposed failings were judged to be a major cause of their distress. But the police were not as superficial in their assessment of the problem as might be supposed at first. Many realized that the Indians were victims of circumstances over which they had no control. In this respect, the activities of the Hudson's Bay Company came in for a good deal of criticism. Superintendent Moodie, for example, speaking of the Indians at Churchill, reported that "The H.B. Co. has the Indians so completely in its power that they are afraid to work for others and every effort is used to prevent them from meeting the police." He went on to describe how he had defeated the company's attempt at Churchill to increase its profits by one-third at the expense of the Indians; he had threatened to trade with the Indians himself until the company capitulated and agreed to take the usual profit.[13] Over the course of many years, the company had established a relationship with the Indians which reduced them in some instances almost to the level of serfs. The manner in which the company advanced credit to the Indians against the next year's catch often bound them to the company by a continuous debt. But the company's practice in this respect was dictated both by economic necessity and long experience; to regularize the trade, it was found necessary to keep the Indians in the company's debt. Some of the police also realized that there were two sides to the question. Giving credit to the Indians always involved a certain amount of risk, for sometimes they would "procure goods for their season's hunt and forget to return with fur in the spring," and when there was more than one trading concern in the area, the Indians would not hesitate to play them off against each other.[14]

What happened to some northern Indians during the First World War is a very good example of how they were victimized by circumstances. When war broke out, the price of furs fell dramatically, and the Hudson's Bay Company stopped giving the Indians credit, or "debt" as it was called. At York Factory the company, as an economy measure, ceased its usual practice of giving supplies to destitute Indians and informed the local missionary that it would not be "responsible for any cases of want amongst the Indians in the future."[15] The result of this new policy was severe privation for some Indians; as the police at Athabaska Landing reported, they had been caught "absolutely unprepared, and consequently many of them had a somewhat hand-to-mouth existence."[16] It is dangerous, perhaps, to generalize on a few examples, but the observations made by this officer are not untypical. He found a ray of hope in the economic problems faced by the Indians; from present adversity they might learn the virtue of self-reliance: "The Indians are not a provident race and possibly the inexorable terms under which they are obliged to trade now, 'nothing for nothing,' may teach them the value of laying by for a rainy day."[17]

Another example of such thinking on the part of the police comes from the Mackenzie Delta. In 1909, there was talk of making a treaty with the Indians of the region. The police officer in charge advised against a treaty on the grounds that the annual payment of money would only harm the Indians: "They would spend the cash in a day, eat all the provisions in a week, and then be worse off than ever." Here is a typical attitude of the police at the time. How would the Indians have been worse off? They would have paid off some debts, bought some supplies, had a good meal or two, and probably a celebration. What they would not have done is put something aside for a rainy day as the police were always urging them to do—a course of action that the Victorian middle class was always urging on the working class. The admonitions of the police sound like the dictates of nineteenth-century self-help manuals. The officer went on to say that what the Indians really needed was a good spell of adversity, which would strengthen their character: "The traders . . . all informed me that during the past two years when the traders were compelled to curtail the large advances usually given against fur, that the Indians had never worked so hard and so well."[18]

What was the Department of Indian Affairs doing for the Indians of the Northern frontier? The answer, in the Northwest Territories as earlier in the Yukon, was—very little. The Indians of the northern Mackenzie, not being under treaty, were left to the care of the missionaries, traders, and police until an agency was opened at Fort Simpson in 1913. Those at Churchill, York Factory, and Port Nelson were covered by Treaty No. 5, which was extended to them in 1909. Under it the Indians received the usual payments and nothing else. What few administrative duties were required—payment of treaty, taking the census, distribution of land scrip to the Métis—were carried out by the police. For all the good that these services did the Indians, the police might as well not have bothered; Superintendent C. Starnes's account of the distribution of scrip at Churchill in 1911 shows clearly that the aid provided by the government was of no lasting use to the Natives:

I also received a parcel containing scrip to be issued to half-breeds here and at York. . . . Two buyers arrived here from York . . . for the purpose of securing these scrip. . . . They were rather annoying to me and commenced to worry me even before I had received the scrip. . . . I am informed . . . that most of the scrip was secured by the men for $450 each.[19]

Nor did it seem to the police that the money distributed as annuities was of much use. In 1915, for instance, $3,300 was distributed to the Indians at York and Churchill, but almost every penny of it immediately went to the Hudson's Bay Company for payment of debt, and because the police disapproved of debt, they reported that the Indians were no better off than before.[20]

In the public and private reports of the police concerning the Indians of the northern frontier during this period, the impression is one of squalor, disease, and neglect. The police did what little they could— distributed supplies, sparingly, and sent their doctor to look after the sick—but they always seem to have become quickly annoyed by the Indians' stolid refusal to follow their well-meaning advice or to show appreciation for their help. In 1915 the police doctor at Churchill reported that the Indians there were suffering badly from tuberculosis. "I have repeatedly explained to them," he wrote, "the infectious nature of the disease, how it spreads, and how it could be lessened. My advices seem to have been of very little use, and results have been very discouraging."[21] It does not take much imagination to picture the scene—the police doctor talking earnestly about germs and sanitation and the Indians staring at him, indifferent and probably uncomprehending. The story was the same in every place where the Indians lived near police detachments or trading posts. At Port Nelson, Howard reported that the Indians were "full of consumption" and that it was "impossible to get them to take the most ordinary precautions to guard against it."[22]

Such exasperation often quickly changed to contempt. The police were not sociologists or anthropologists and none of their formal training equipped them to deal sensitively with the northern Indians; this was decades before "Native awareness seminars" became part of the education of police recruits. In any case, no means of assistance was made available by the government. The pattern repeated itself again and again. A young policeman came to the north, saw the squalor of the Indians who clustered around the posts, was horrified, and gave the Indians what assistance he could and much advice. The Indians seemed to squander the aid and ignore the advice. Very soon the policeman decided the Indians were not worth bothering with. Copious evidence of all these stages exists in the police records.

The result was often, though not always, a callous attitude towards the problems of the Indians. The sentiment expressed in the observation, "I do not think it the right thing at any time to issue rations to Indians, it encourages them to be lazy," was widely shared. Sometimes this attitude hardened into startling insensitivity. In an incident at York Factory in which an Indian baby was eaten by dogs that had been allowed to run loose, the police officer reported "The accident has had a salutary effect upon these easy-going Indians" because "it had taught them to keep their dogs tied up."[23] This attitude was in striking contrast to that displayed when the victim was white. In September 1924 the wife of the N.C.O. in charge of the Chesterfield Inlet detachment died after a dog attack. No silver linings were discovered in this tragedy.

The police were generally not popular with the northern Indians. As the only government agents in many areas, they had to bear the brunt of the Indians' dissatisfaction with government policy. Thus, at York Factory in 1915, for example, the Indians were angry because the treaty promised them an annual visit by a doctor, and they had not seen one for two years. They were also dissatisfied because of what they considered neglect on the part of the police. The local chief petitioned the Department of Indian Affairs for an investigation: "I and my councillors . . . would like to have a visit of an Inspector of Indian Affairs . . . the present Indian agent, the commanding officer of the R.N.W.M. Police, takes no interest in us, and we feel very much as if we were not wanted."[24] The chief had probably sensed the situation correctly; nevertheless, as with all complaints about the police, an investigation was made, and a doctor eventually visited the band.

Another glimpse, perhaps more revealing, comes from Churchill. In 1911, Superintendent Starnes reported that the Indians of that region had their own name for the police; they called them "the imprisoners."[25] This translation is expressive of one facet of police work, but it is more significant insofar as it shows how the Indians of one locality viewed the police—not as lawgivers or protectors.[26] Starnes believed that the Indians had been deliberately encouraged to look on the police as unfriendly, presumably by the traders. He thought that the police had made progress in overcoming the reluctance of the Indians to deal with them: "They are beginning to understand a little better what the aims of the Government, and the duties of the Police are towards them, and are less backward in approaching us."[27]

These northern Indians had less experience with Euro-Canadians and their laws than those living in the more southerly parts of Canada. Those around Hudson Bay had dealt with white men for generations, of course, but their lifestyle had not been nearly as altered by Christianization, education, and "civilization" in general as that of the Indians in, say, Ontario or Quebec. The Cree of Hudson Bay knew all about traders and what to expect from them, but the police were a new phenomenon. The northern Indians could probably not perceive any sensible reason for the police being in their country. Unlike the missionaries, they were not there specifically for what they perceived as the Indians' good; unlike the traders, they were not there for their own. It should thus not be surprising if the police were to come under suspicion and hostility, even if they had had nothing but kind feelings towards the Indians.

This hostility did not provoke any open assaults by Indians on members of the R.N.W.M.P.; it was sullen rather than active. But it did produce a lingering suspicion of the police and all their works. A good example comes from Churchill in the winter of 1917–18. The police had gone there to give the Indians their annual treaty payments, an event which was generally well attended. On this occasion, however, on arriving at Churchill the police found that many Indians had not waited for them, but had gone inland to their hunting grounds. On investigation, it was found that the Indians had in fact fled. A rumour had been started, possibly by the Métis, that the police were going to conscript all the Indians they could catch into the army and send them overseas to fight.[28] That the Indians would believe such a story shows what they thought of the government and its agents.

There were few criminal cases involving Indians in this period; the Indians of the northern frontier were generally "quiet and well behaved."[29] Serious crimes among them were infrequent enough to deserve individual mention in the annual reports, or, perhaps, serious crimes which came to the attention of the police—for no doubt many things went on in the bush that the police had no inkling of. In handling criminal cases involving Indians, the police tried to make public examples of the culprits in order to discourage similar crimes. For instance, in 1913 "Crazy Thomas," a councillor of the Churchill band of Chipewyans, who had been debauching young girls and widows, was charged with common assault. He was held in jail for two days and then discharged on payment of a fine and costs.[30] The comment of the police was that "this case will have a very salutary effect on all natives in this locality, as they were not quite aware of the powers of the police. The two days that 'Crazy Thomas' spent in custody have had a very marked effect on him." It was the example set rather than the actual punishment that the police believed to be important.

It is clear that police officers and Native women at these northern posts were involved in what a more genteel generation called "liaisons," but documentary evidence is not plentiful, for unless a formal complaint was made, nothing was put on paper. And the attitude of the police hierarchy was liberal in matters of this sort. Examples do exist, however. In 1912 the Methodist missionary at Norway House complained that a police constable there was improperly involved with an Indian girl. An investigation was carried out, and it was found that the girl was quite satisfied with the relationship. However, to placate the missionary, who was the only complainant, the constable was transferred to Regina, but he was not otherwise punished.[31] Another incident, involving the cruise of the *Arctic,* is more revealing. Apparently complaints had been made to Prime Minister Laurier that there had been incidents of immorality between the police on the *Arctic* expedition and the Natives. Comptroller White was asked to investigate and reported that Moodie had informed him that "there was no conspicuous immorality—nothing more than what always occurs between white men and native women in spite of all possible precautions."[32] What these reports were based on is made clear by some unpublished documents. In his private papers, Captain Comer later alleged that the men of the police detachment at Fullerton had fathered six children between 1903 and 1910. In January 1904 Moodie charged Constable Jarvis with taking a Native girl into the barracks room "for the purpose of prostituting her, she being of the age of 14 years or under." Jarvis was given six months' imprisonment with hard labour, but had half his sentence remitted since the girl, according to Moodie, "altho' young, was by no means innocent. She and virtue had been separated for many a day."[33]

Another example concerns Inspector Fitzgerald, the leader of the "Lost Patrol," who in 1907, as sergeant in charge of the detachment at Herschel Island, requested permission to marry an Inuit woman. The sad denouement of the episode was recorded by the local Anglican missionary:

The members of the NWMP Force, now resident at Herschel, had followed the practice of the American whalemen, in that several of them supported Eskimo mistresses. Sergeant Fitzgerald had fallen hier [sic] to one named Unalina. During my visit in August, he had requested me to marry them, and arrangements were made to do so. But he must obtain the consent of his Officer Commanding before he could marry, and this Inspector Jarvis declined to give, saying he would prefer reporting to Ottawa that Fitzgerald had blown his brains out, rather than that he had married a native woman, though he did not at all protest the current relationship. From the Eskimos' point of view, to be taken into residence by a man and treated as a wife, constituted real marriage and when later Unalina gave birth to a daughter, the real bar to her legitimacy was the Inspector's refusal to allow the marriage. The child, Annie, later was injured in play, and became deformed, and was the subject of an application to the Police Department for compassionate consideration which was declined on the ground that there was no marriage certificate, though the facts are plain enough."[34]

Rev. Whittaker suggested that the police hierarchy had no objection to a liaison but that formal marriage was unthinkable, as indeed it was to remain for many years after 1907. Members of the police were expected to adhere to the strict code of Victorian morality; on more than one occasion, married officers were "allowed to resign" because of their association with other women, and divorce generally cast a cloud over an officer's career. Yet it is evident from White's comment that the hierarchy was much more tolerant of the sexual conduct of unmarried policemen who were stationed in the north, often for years at a time.

In summary, then, it can be said that relations between the police and the Indians of the northern frontier were peaceful but not cordial. The police took an unsentimental view of the Indian; they assumed that all northern Indians were like the ones who clustered around the white posts, and they judged them inferior. They sometimes ascribed other causes to the misery they saw, such as the bad influence of the traders, but they never tried to do much for the Indians except to give them periodic handouts. And, after all, why should they have? They were not the Department of Indian Affairs. Although they did the work of that department in the Hudson Bay and Mackenzie Delta areas, they did it not by choice or because they were trained to do so, but for the usual reason—because they were on the scene and would do the work for nothing. They were not social workers and never pretended to be humanitarians; they reacted to the Indians as might have been expected. The sins of commission and omission in regard to the Indians were, as Jenness and others have recognized, not the fault of the police, but of the government.

The case of the Inuit is remarkably different. One might reasonably suppose that the police would lump the Indians and Inuit together since they were all "Natives." Nothing could be further from the truth. To the surprise and evident delight of the police, wherever they came into contact with them—at Churchill, Fullerton, Herschel Island, Fort McPherson, and on patrol—the police found in the Inuit cheerful friends rather than sullen adversaries. As one policeman put it, "The more you get acquainted with them, the better you like them."[35]

The reason the police gave for this admiration, which was universal among members of the force, was that the Inuit had all the qualities which the Indians lacked. They were "quickly learning the lessons of thriftiness, cleanliness, and morality" from the missionaries.[36] It was the marked contrast between the Indians and the Inuit which so surprised the police and which they remarked upon so frequently. Commenting on his trip down the Mackenzie to Fort McPherson in 1910 Fitzgerald said of the Inuit: "it was a pleasure to see their pleasant faces, after the sulky looks of the Indians. All the Eskimo had good clean clothes and looked far superior to the Indians in their dirty rags."[37] Inspector

G. L. Jennings commented earlier in the same year that "The Eskimos as a race are the most interesting of any I have seen. They are quick to learn, good manual workers, hospitable in the extreme, and are in almost every way the direct opposite of an Indian."[38] Superintendent Moodie, speaking of the Inuit at Fullerton in 1903, reported that "In intellect and quickness in picking up ideas the Esquimaux are in advance of the ordinary Indians."[29] Inspector A. M. Jarvis, writing in 1908, compared the Indians and Inuit of the Mackenzie Delta:

The Indians here, they are too lazy to hunt or trap and live all the year on fish . . . any money or debt they can procure goes on their backs, and then their stomach is thought of. Different with the Esquimaux; one need only go 100 miles down the Mackenzie River, and he will find the men either out trapping, or fishing through the ice. The women are either making skin boots or clothing, or smoking cigaretts [sic] and laughing. . . . They are not improvident like the Indians. They very seldom take debt, [but if they do] . . . the first thing they do is to come in with the furs to pay what they owe.[40]

Why this remarkable difference in attitude? The Inuit of the Arctic coast had been in contact with Europeans for a far shorter time than the Indians farther south, and their culture had taken much less buffeting; they were therefore more secure in their ways. Some of the things the police liked—the Inuit hospitality to strangers, for instance—were integral parts of their culture. The survival of the Inuit race required that its members be generous and hospitable; this was not true to the same extent of Indians. The police were also pleased to find that Inuit commercial and acquisitive values coincided more or less with theirs. They could not be fobbed off with shoddy goods, and they were generally conscientious about settling their debts.[41]

Because they liked the Inuit and because they realized how little contact they had had with European culture, the police adopted liberal views about how to deal with them. From the first the police maintained an open mind on how to approach this new-found race. Moodie, the first officer of the police to establish contact with the Hudson Bay Inuit, had very enlightened opinions as to how they should be introduced to Canadian laws. Referring to a murder which had taken place among the Inuit at Fullerton a few years before the arrival of the police, Moodie said that he did not want to punish any Inuit who acted in ignorance of the law. "All superstitions have to be handled gently," he wrote, "and it is worse than useless to attempt to upset old customs in a day. It is a matter of time to change these, and it can only be done by first obtaining the goodwill and confidence of the natives."[42] This may be taken as a concise statement of the police attitude towards the Inuit for it was the policy they followed consistently throughout the first twenty years of this century.

Yet with a change of perspective a different view of police-Inuit relations in Hudson Bay emerges. Dr. L. E. Borden, the surgeon and botanist on the *Neptune,* wrote in his memoirs a description of a speech made by Moodie to a group of Inuit in November 1903 in which Moodie told him about Edward VII, the big chief, who wanted them to do right and good, questioned them about infanticide, parricide, and cannibalism (the answers were evasive), and presented each adult with a suit of woolen underwear. W. G. Ross's comment on this episode is worth quoting:

The irony of this situation, although not apparent to Moodie, was abundantly clear to Borden, Comer, and most certainly to the Eskimos. Here were a people who had maintained intimate ties with foreign whalers for more than forty years being treated as simple, helpless, credulous savages. Here were men who possessed whaleboats, darting guns, shoulder guns... who hunted with telescopes and powerful repeating rifles, and who normally wore American trousers, shirts, jackets, hats and sunglasses. Here were women... who made up clothes on sewing machines, who attended shipboard dances in imported dresses.... To these people an officious, uniformed stranger was distributing underwear as if it were a priceless treasure and lecturing them on morals and allegiance to a big white chief. When Moodie suggested that the Eskimos might wish to travel 500 miles to Churchill to send joyful messages to the king, no one responded.[43]

This text refers to a select group of Inuit regularly employed by the whalers, but the cultural misunderstanding displayed by this episode is indeed startling.

Moodie's comments on the unfair prices given the Inuit for their furs and whalebone have already been mentioned. He did not content himself by condemning the traders, however, for he had a positive system in mind to replace the existing one. He thought that the regime that prevailed among the Inuit of Greenland, in which all trading was conducted by the government for the benefit of the Inuit and freebooters were excluded, would do very well in Canada.[44] Moodie's opinion was shared by Diamond Jenness, who came to much the same conclusion.[45]

As far as "civilizing" the Inuit was concerned, members of the police often expressed the opinion that they were better left uneducated and un-Christianized. Some of them were, as W. G. Ross points out, more civilized than the police knew or would admit. As one officer put it, the Inuit "do not require to be educated, and will be far better left alone to their aboriginal life"; education would only train the girls for domestic service and boys for manual labour, which was no progress at all.[46] There were two schools of thought on the question of whether the Inuit should be educated or left alone; the latter course seemed feasible because it was assumed in 1910 that the Arctic would never attract large numbers of white men. Vilhjalmur Stefansson would have liked to have seen the Inuit left undisturbed. As he said, "I am so great an admirer of the Eskimo before civilization changed them that it is not easy to get me to say that civilization has improved them in any material way."[47]

However, this was probably a minority view, owing to the obvious fact that the Inuit had been changed by civilization and still were being changed. The Inuit would need to be educated, if only in self-defence. This was the point made by Diamond Jenness when he compared the Canadian and American approach to the Inuit. The Americans, he said,

had dotted the coast [of Alaska] not with needless police posts, but with government schools, believing that the only policy consonant with the dignity of the United States was to educate and train her Eskimo wards until they could be wholly absorbed into the social and economic life of the nation. [48]

The police were aware of this aspect of the problem. Even Jennings, who was opposed to education of any kind for the Inuit, is also on record as considering "a government school similar to those in Alaska an urgent necessity."[49] He believed that it was essential that the Inuit "should learn English, and the values of trade, if only for their own protection. They themselves are most anxious for this."[50] This contradiction illustrates all the more the strong concern of the police for the welfare of the Inuit. They had a genuine desire to see the government and others do what was best for them. They did not look upon the Inuit as nuisances or as failures, but as wards, to be protected and encouraged as much as possible. There was much confusion about what was best for the Inuit, but the police wished them well, in marked contrast to their attitude towards the Indians.

Sometimes, police enthusiasm for the Inuit had unfortunate results; the assistance given to them was not always in their best interests. An example can be found at Fullerton in 1905. Superintendent Moodie belonged to the school of thought which believed the igloo a cold and drafty place and pitied the Inuit who had to live in one. Moodie reported with pride that one of the Inuit employed by the police at Fullerton had begun to live in a house:

Scottie . . . has a small shack made of rough boards and tarpaper, and with a stove in it. I can assure you he appreciates thoroughly the warmth and comfort of such a place, humble as it is. It is my intention to erect similar shacks at each post for all employed natives. Realizing the comfort of such will do more to civilize these people than all the preaching in the world unaccompanied by care of the body also. [51]

Although well-meaning, this is just the sort of action which bound the Inuit to the white man's culture. The Inuit became disdainful of his old ways. But the shack was hard to heat, unsanitary (because unlike an igloo it was permanent), and bred disease, particularly tuberculosis. Moodie also suggested that a small building be put up to serve as a hospital for the Inuit, to be staffed by Inuit women in lieu of nurses; this, of course, was never done. The policeman believed that he was doing the Inuit a great favour when he gave him enough discarded materials to build a small shack. It was the first step in his "civilization." The wisdom of this step has been hotly debated by many "experts" on the Inuit; there have been as many shades of opinion about the question as there have been writers, though in the past twenty years the Inuit have settled the question themselves by moving off the land and into government-built settlements. Stefansson abhorred the practice of abandoning the igloo, seeing it as a step in the dissolution of Inuit culture. Farley Mowat believes that there is no other choice for Inuit survival. [52] The topic, now only of historical interest, is open to endless debate, but the police did not operate on a philosophical level. They thought in 1905 that they were improving Inuit life by putting them in shacks and did not see the implications of such action.

In the years before 1920, the police rarely had to fulfil their primary function of enforcers of the law when dealing with Inuit. When they did act in a police capacity, it was likely to involve not the investigation of a crime, but the settlement of purely Inuit disputes. A typical example comes from Herschel Island in 1909. An Inuit and his wife had died from eating bad whale meat, and the family boat, as was apparently the custom, was claimed by the wife's father. A quarrel arose over the boat, and Inspector Jennings was asked to adjudicate:

I explained the law to them and gave the whaleboat to Varwuk [the man's father]; Ilyaki [the woman's father], though not liking to give up the boat in the presence of his people, did so at once, and the Esquimaux were all pleased at the outcome. These people have implicit faith in the Mounted Police, and it is a pleasure to deal with them. I find that they are very anxious to live according to the law of the white man. [53]

The Inuit generally accepted the white man's customs, however odd, without question, and his laws, as interpreted by the police, were no exception. The Inuit were genuinely friendly and anxious to please, and they may well have felt that the decrees of the police, like those of the missionaries, were powerful magic that should be followed to the letter.

As a rule the police tried to deal with the Inuit in terms that they could understand; that is, they tried to make justice a concrete rather than an abstract idea. Because the idea of confinement was foreign to the Inuit mind, they were rarely put in jail during this period. Instead, on occasion, the police followed their old habit of "making up the laws." A good example is one of the infrequent instances in which Inuit stole from whites. In the summer of 1916, a family of Inuit stole a case of pemmican from the Canadian Arctic Expedition at Bernard Harbour and headed east. A police corporal, who was staying with the expedition at the time, set out in pursuit and soon caught up with the thieves. Rather than make an arrest, which would have involved endless bother, the corporal invoked the *lex talionis* and demanded that the head of the family make restitution. The man offered a seal pup in payment, but the corporal refused it and took instead two boxes of cartridges. These were the culprit's most valuable possessions, and he protested, but to no avail. As the policeman later reported, "Something had to be done, however, to show these people that they could not steal with impunity."[54] This irregular method of enforcing the law was justice that the Inuit could readily understand once they had accepted the white man's concept of private property.

By this time some had been more influenced by whites than others. In 1910, there were Inuit at Herschel Island who had been in constant contact with white civilization for more than twenty years. At the same time, there were others, notably in the area south of Coronation Gulf, who had never seen a white man. Some therefore remained strong in their traditional ways, while others were well on the way to forgetting them.

By 1910 the situation which had been predicted for several years had come to pass in the western Arctic. The whaling ships no longer came north, and the Inuit who relied on them for employment now found themselves without flour, tea, and sugar. Their situation, while not as bad as that of the Indians, was beginning to sound ominously familiar:

I visited all the natives on the island . . . issued some of them flour and bacon, and then tried to give them a square meal about once a week. There was [sic] 47 natives on the island and it was impossible to try and feed them from our supplies . . . but we filled their stomachs now and then . . . they had to eat a number of their seal skins. . . . One family had to eat their dogs. . . . It was very hard on the children, they could not go the seal skin and the seal oil. From now on they will pull through alright and there was no deaths from starvation.[55]

What happened to the Inuit at Herschel Island in 1909 was a foretaste of the fate that befell most of the others in the Canadian Arctic in the ensuing forty years. The police were to find themselves more and more in the same relationship to the Inuit as they were to the Indians — dispensers of relief to starving, demoralized Natives.

Although this trend was apparent by 1910, it did not become really serious until after 1920. Before then, throughout most of the Arctic, the Inuit remained self-reliant, which was an important reason why the police thought so much more of them than of the Indians. Almost everywhere the police met the Indians, it was on the white man's terms. On the prairies their civilization had been defeated by the farmer, and in the north the white trapper was beginning to encroach on their territory; in many places they had been reduced to dependence and beggary. But when the police met the Inuit it was on the Inuit's home ground and, at least in the beginning, on the Inuit's terms. The policeman who could cross the prairie by train or automobile, or go down the Mackenzie on a steamer, could feel superior to the Indian on foot or in a canoe. But it was difficult for the police, faced with conditions in the Arctic, to feel superior to the Inuit. The Inuit were perfectly adapted to their environment. They had invented the igloo and the sled, the two essentials of Arctic life. If the police wanted to venture away from their detachments and live to return, they had to adopt the Inuit method of travel. Not until well after 1920, when the aeroplane was introduced to the Arctic, did the police have anything better.

Realizing their debts created in the police an attitude of admiration and respect. Even if they considered the Inuit to be children intellectually, the police were forced to respect their skills and to admire their code of behaviour.

This attitude of the police towards the Inuit underwent a perceptible change during and after the First World War, particularly as a result of a number of murders, two of which have already been mentioned. Everyone seemed to agree that the Inuit who murdered Radford and Street could not be held accountable for their actions, but in the Rouvière-Le Roux case opinion was divided. Sinnisiak and Uluksuk were brought to Edmonton in the summer of 1917, and Sinnisiak was tried for the murder of Father Rouvière. To the amazement and chagrin of the police, he was acquitted. Inspector C. D. La Nauze, who had arrested the two, wrote indignantly to the commissioner:

There seems to have been a campaign of public sympathy for the "poor Eskimos"
and the public seem to be on the side of the defence. . . . we are hoping for a
conviction of the two murderers on the second charge. . . . If both murderers are
found "not guilty" we have nothing to do but send them back FREE MEN to their
own land to let their tribe know that NO PUNISHMENT will be meted out to
those who murder white men. [56]

La Nauze was not alone in his indignation; Bishop Breynat, who did not
believe that his priests had given offence to the Inuit, quoted in his
memoirs a letter which attributed the acquittal to anti-Catholic prejudice:

Pour eux [the public], les Esquimaux étaient des braves gens, les meurtriers,
presque des héros; la responsabilité du crime pesait presque sur ces "papistes" qui
étaient venus les troubler dans leur primitive innocence! Je ne puis chasser de mon
esprit la répugnante image d'un individu que je vis, au milieu de beaucoup
d'autres: il fouillait ses poches, en tirait des cigarettes et, les offrant aux meur-
triers, disait "Jump in again." [57]

They need not have worried. The Inuit were taken to Calgary, tried
together, and found guilty of murdering Father Le Roux. The judge
told the bored and uncomprehending accused, dozing in the August
heat, that the "great White chief" had decided to be kind to them: "Because they did not know our ways . . . he will not have them put to
death . . . for the future they now know what the law is . . . they must let
their people know."[58]
    The sentence of death was commuted to life imprisonment at the
police detachment at Fort Resolution, but after two years the men were
freed and taken back to their people. Commissioner Perry hoped that
they would "no doubt have a salutary influence on their tribe as they will
be able to inform them of the power and justice of the government."[59] In
fact the lesson learned was that crime paid, for the two Inuit became
favourites of the police at Fort Resolution. They made themselves useful
around the detachment, and they were employed as drivers when the
Tree River detachment was set up in 1919. By the time they returned
home they had acquired enough "style," money, and cast-off goods to
make them the richest men among their people. Later, one was killed by
his band, apparently because of his arrogance. The Rouvière-Le Roux
case marks the end of the initial phase in the police attitude towards the
Inuit—an age of innocence in which the Inuit were objects of wonder.
After this time, there are occasional derogatory references; Inuit were
"born thieves and liars . . . any one of them would sell his soul to possess a
rifle."[60] The incident that really aroused the police, however, was the

murder of one of their own men, Corporal W. A. Doak, who was shot by an Inuit prisoner at the Tree River detachment in April 1922. This was a very different matter from the earlier cases. First, the murder was totally unprovoked and could not be excused as a matter of cultural misunderstanding. Second, the victim was an official representative of the government; his murder therefore could be viewed as a challenge to Canadian sovereignty on the Arctic coast. Thus, no proposals were forthcoming from the force to handle the killer gently or to respect his superstitions.

The case of Alikomiak and Tatamigana, the two men who eventually received the death sentence,[61] illustrates the debate between those who still considered the Inuit to be primitive innocents who had to be tutored as children and those who saw them as dangerous savages who had to be inspired with the fear of the white man's justice. In this case the trial was held in the north; a judicial party went to Herschel Island in the summer of 1923, but the government was set on punishment before the trial began. Before the trial, the lawyer appointed for the defence, T. L. Cory,[62] suggested that mercy was wasted on the Inuit: "as kindness has failed in the past I strongly recommend that the law should take its course and those Eskimos found guilty of murder should be hanged in a place where the natives will see and recognize the outcome of taking another's life."[63] Commissioner Cortlandt Starnes of the R.C.M.P. had similar opinions. He observed in a letter to the Department of the Interior that "Kind and generous treatment of the Natives who have committed murders in the past has apparently had the opposite effect to that intended, and I am afraid there is a danger of the Natives concluding that crime is a thing to be rewarded by the White man."[64] This situation was partly the fault of the police. In the infrequent cases when Inuit were imprisoned, they were sent to northern detachments where they were treated more like mascots than criminals. Alikomiak, the man who shot Cpl. Doak, was already under arrest for the murder of a trader. He had been given the run of the detachment and had shot the corporal while he was sleeping. Now the policy of the police and the government turned from kindness to sternness, though the attitude towards the individual Inuit continued to be friendly.

The two Inuit were convicted, and they were hanged at Herschel Island on 1 February 1924, after a protracted debate in the press as to whether or not clemency should be shown to them. Some newspapers asked the government to show mercy, on the grounds that the Inuit had not been properly educated in Canadian law and should not be punished for their ignorance.[65] Others believed that any trial held at Herschel Island could not be fair[66] and that the peculiar circumstances of the case warranted mercy.[67] On the other hand, it was felt in some quarters that "Human life is precious—even the lives of these two Eskimo savages; but the public welfare is of more importance."[68] Other newspaper comment ranged from the melodramatic ("the gallows yawns on the already ice-locked shores of the Arctic, and in many an igloo this winter will be discussed the white man's law"),[69] to a sensible suggestion from the Toronto *Star:*

It is up to the parliament of Canada to see whether the "foreign" policy of the government in regard to these people is coherent and reasonable, whether there is any thought-out policy, or merely a "mandate" to the police to run things the best they know how.[70]

The *Star* had put its finger on the great fault in government Inuit policy—that there was no policy and the police had *carte blanche* to do whatever they thought best. The press reported that before the two men were hanged, they had said that "the police had long been enemies of their people."[71] This was not true, but by 1924 relations between the police and the Inuit had substantially altered. In particular, the police no longer thought of the Inuit primarily as lovable children, but now also took into account, realistically, the darker side of their character.

12. Ultima Thule

THE YEAR 1919 was in several ways a turning point in the history of the Mounted Police. It was the year in which Parliament by statute changed the name of the force to the Royal Canadian Mounted Police.[1] In February of the next year their headquarters moved from Regina to Ottawa. In general, the role of the police was changing, as the new R.C.M.P. became less a force of the prairie and the frontier and more concerned with the sophisticated problems of an increasingly urbanized nation.[2] The Winnipeg General Strike of 1919, in which the police were pitted not against outlaws or Indians but against putative Bolsheviks indicates this change.

There was, however, one new frontier left to challenge the police in the period following the end of the First World War—the far north, the most remote parts of the Canadian mainland and the Arctic archipelago. During the 1920s the R.C.M.P. extended its operations over the last remaining areas of the inhabited Canadian north and over some of the areas too far north to support even an Inuit population. In these regions the political aspect of the police was paramount, for their main task was to establish a "presence" in the interests of Canadian sovereignty rather than to carry out regular police duties. This period of the history of the police and northern frontier illustrates the final stage in their pioneering work there; it also provides an excellent example of the way in which the Canadian government determined its northern policy and put it into practice.

In 1895, by order-in-council, Canada had claimed the Arctic archipelago as far north as 83¼ degrees north latitude,[3] but before 1920 she had been far from energetic in prosecuting her claims. A. P. Low had reached Ellesmere Island in 1904, and in 1909 Captain J. E. Bernier had landed on Melville Island and claimed the entire archipelago for Canada, extending her claims to the Pole in the wedge-shaped sector which appears on some maps today.[4] But as one student of the period has put it:

Canada was content to permit the residual Northwest Territories to remain a deserted and forgotten national attic. The Government might be striving to extend that attic to the North Pole, but it had no intention of furnishing it with meaningful government if the expense could be avoided.[5]

The trouble was not only the government's "unfortunate parsimony,"[6] but also that it had more pressing matters to attend to. As a result, nothing more than gestures of sovereignty, and fleeting ones at that, were made until a foreign country showed an interest in the Arctic. Then, as Stefansson remarked, Ottawa came alive, "for it is human nature to want whatever someone else wants. The Government actually began to spend money."[7] The "someone else" in this case was Denmark, and the catalyst was *ovibos moschatus,* the musk-ox.

Concern had been expressed in Canada as early as the turn of the century that the musk-ox was in danger of extinction. Inspector J. D. Moodie had warned in 1904 that the traders in Hudson Bay were encouraging the Inuit to slaughter the animals and had prohibited the practice in his immediate area. Yet although all members of the police had in 1903 been given the power to try game offences summarily,[8] it was not until the new Northwest Game Act of 1917 that musk-oxen were protected completely by law; after that year they could be shot only for scientific purposes, by special licence. Further government interest in these animals was shown in 1919 by the establishment of the Reindeer and Musk-ox Commission, which investigated their economic as well as their biological potential.[9]

There was one group of hunters who did not, however, come under Canadian control. These were Inuit from the northwest coast of Greenland, around Thule, who regularly crossed Smith Sound to hunt musk-ox on central Ellesmere Island, which was in 1920 quite outside the sphere of effective Canadian control. In 1910 a trading post had been established at Thule[10] by Knud Rasmussen, a Dane who combined the energy of a Stefansson with the insight into Inuit affairs of a Diamond Jenness. Rasmussen was a sort of father-figure to the Inuit of Thule,

and he was also the semi-official representative of the Danish government, which did not proclaim its sovereignty over North Greenland until
1921.[11]

On 31 July 1919,[12] while the Reindeer and Musk-ox Commission was
beginning its work, the Canadian government sent a request to Denmark
(through the British government) asking the Danes to restrain the Inuit
of Thule from killing musk-oxen on Ellesmere Island. The Danish government put the matter to Rasmussen, who was neither a lawyer nor a
diplomat; his reply contained this ominous sentence:

*As everyone knows, the land of the Polar Eskimos falls under what is called "No
Man's Land" and there is, therefore, no authority in this country except that which
I myself am able to exert through the Trading Station.*[13]

In its reply to the Canadian government of 20 April 1920, the Danish
government said that it could "subscribe to what Mr. Rasmussen says."[14]
In fact, it was questionable whether the Inuits' aboriginal hunting rights
were affected by Canada's sovereignty claims, especially since there was
no governmental authority of any kind in the area.

While the government hastened to protest to the Danes that Ellesmere
Island was not a "no man's land,"[15] the civil servants concerned with the
matter were privately worried. A confidential memorandum prepared
for the Department of the Interior suggested that Canada's title to Ellesmere Island was by no means certain since much of the island had
been neither discovered nor occupied by British subjects—only claimed,
from a distance, for the British Crown:

*The situation as to sovereignty in the northern islands, therefore, appears to be
that Britain has had an inchoate title which now probably through the lapse of
time may be considered to have terminated; that the Low and Bernier expeditions
may have established a "fictitious" title which also has probably lapsed; and
therefore, that apparently Denmark or any other country is in a position to acquire
sovereignty by establishing effective occupation and administration.*[16]

The next question was, as J. B. Harkin put it, whether Ellesmere and the
other islands were worth bothering about. "Do we want them, or do we
not?" he asked. "Apparently if we want them we have to do something to
establish our title."[17] At a meeting of experts on the north, including
Stefansson, it was decided that Canada ought to assert its authority over
Ellesmere Island for two reasons. First, the island might be worth something; the analogy of Alaska was suggested. But the most important
consideration was a "sentimental" one: "Ellesmere and the other north-

ern islands have always been regarded in Canada as Canadian, and there doubtless would be a strong sentiment against their being taken possession of by any other flag."[18] The government did not want to leave itself open to accusations of letting the Arctic go by default.

How was sovereignty to be established? Harkin had suggested that a number of Inuit could be moved from Fullerton, where food supplies were failing, to Ellesmere, where a couple of police constables could protect them and the musk-ox as well.[19] Stefansson enthusiastically supported the idea of sending the Mounted Police to Ellesmere Island and said that at least two detachments should be established there because if the police were to stay at the south end of the island, the Danes might well claim the north end anyway.[20] After some discussion, both ideas were adopted, and on 27 October 1920, the advisory board recommended to W. W. Cory, deputy minister of the interior,[21] that three permanent posts be set up by the police on Ellesmere Island, that some Inuit be transferred to the island, and that the Hudson's Bay Company or some other trader be encouraged to extend operations to the area.[22] At the same time, the suggestion made by A. P. Low in 1903 was adopted; in the summer of 1920 an R.C.M.P. detachment was set up at Port Burwell, the gateway to Hudson Strait and Bay. The two policemen involved lived with the Moravian missionaries the first year, patrolled to the Inuit camps, and checked the navigation markers at Button Island and Cape Chidley.[23]

The next step was to include the police in planning the Ellesmere Island expedition. Assistant Commissioner Cortlandt Starnes was asked to estimate the cost of establishing these three detachments, plus two more on Devon and Bylot Islands. He suggested a cost of $45,000 for two years, not including the expense of transportation.[24] The decision was then made to go ahead with the expedition in the summer of 1921.

In fact, no police posts were set up until the summer of 1922; the reason for this delay, although it had nothing to do with the police, is an interesting example of the government's hesitant, rather devious approach to the actual implementation of its policy. There were a few bold spirits in the government; Loring Christie of external affairs advised Prime Minister Meighen that Denmark would give no trouble if Canada acted firmly since it would be expensive and troublesome for her to dispute Canada's claims once the Mounted Police were on the ground.[25] One enthusiast suggested that the police could travel to Ellesmere Island by dirigible from the Imperial Air Station in Scotland in the middle of the winter of 1920–21 in case of a sudden move by the Danes.[26] In general, however, the official attitude was cautious. J. B. Harkin, who co-ordinated the planning for the expedition, wanted its purpose to be secret from the outset, chiefly to forestall possible rival expeditions from Denmark or the United States, which latter country, by virtue of the work of Greely and Peary, might also feel it should assert some claim to Ellesmere Island. Harkin suggested to the deputy minister of the interior that the public be told the expedition had to do with reindeer; this would be "good camouflage" as far as the Americans were concerned because Stefansson had paved the way for such an idea with his "propaganda" about the animals.[27] Stefansson, who had at times manipulated others for his own ends, now became a stalking-horse for the Canadian government. With the approval of his minister, Harkin told Stefansson that the Canadian government was considering another scientific expedition to the Beaufort Sea and suggested he might like to command it. Stefansson jumped at the chance and began to make preparations.

The true purpose of the Beaufort Sea expedition, however, was not exploration, but to prevent Stefansson, who had been a member of the committee planning the Ellesmere Island project, from revealing the government's intentions to the Danes or the Americans. Harkin warned Cory, "I feel quite sure that entirely apart from the Denmark danger Stefansson could very readily convince the United States to send an expedition to Ellesmere Land. That country has probably a better title at present . . . than Canada has."[28] Harkin felt that this expedition should actually go ahead, although it would cost $100,000; the "sop to Stefansson's pride and selfishness" was not "too high for the assurance it gives us."[29] It would be "unwise to bank on his loyalty too much," but he could be kept in line through self-interest.[30] To complicate the matter, some members of the government were suggesting that Sir Ernest Shackleton rather than Stefansson should command the expedition.[31] The immediate result of all this chicanery was that both plans fell through, and no expedition was sent north in 1921. Stefansson was understandably angry, and it was reported to Harkin that in the summer of 1921 he had given interviews to American newspapers about a proposed expedition to "islands and country lying north of Canada"[32]—just the result those who felt there was nothing "north of Canada" had feared. Harkin trembled to think of the public reaction if the worst should come to pass:

One has but to recall the outburst of public indignation and protest in Canada at the decision of the Alaskan arbitration to realize what public opinion would be if any neglect on the Government's part resulted in the loss of an area thousands of times larger and more important than was involved in the Alaskan case.[33]

Harkin was apparently motivated in part by fear of becoming a latter-day Lord Alverstone. Having abandoned duplicity, he quickly made preparations to send a real expedition north in the summer of 1922.

The 1922 expedition, which took the police farther north than ever before, was under the command of J. D. Craig, the advisory engineer for the Northwest Territories Branch of the Department of the Interior.[34] As far as the R.C.M.P. was concerned, the scope of the expedition had diminished, for only two detachments were to be established, one at Pond Inlet,[35] and one somewhere on the east coast of Ellesmere Island, the actual site to be determined by Craig himself.[36] The government refurbished the old *Arctic* for the voyage and to command the ship called on the imperishable veteran, Captain J. E. Bernier. The voyage was without serious incident. A detachment was set up at Craig Harbour, at the extreme southeast corner of Ellesmere Island, on 28 August 1922, and on the return to the south, a second post was established at Pond Inlet. Craig Harbour was commanded by Inspector C. E. Wilcox, and Pond Inlet by S/Sgt. A. H. Joy; each detachment had two constables and one or two Inuit families, hired at Etah, Greenland—Peary's former base. In contrast with the Hudson Bay expedition of 1903, in which there was some squabbling between the police and the other members of the crew, the 1922 voyage was totally harmonious, possibly because it was chiefly a police venture, whereas the earlier one had had an important scientific purpose, and interests and personalities had clashed over the division of authority. At Craig Harbour, Wilcox and Craig exchanged warm personal letters,[37] and Captain Bernier gave a speech to the police advising them on how to survive the physical and psychological challenges of the winter—be sure to pack snow around the buildings in November, he said, and "do not make a hill out of a mountain" in personal relations.[38] When the *Arctic* returned south at the end of the summer, the Canadian press welcomed the expedition as a demonstration of Canada's rights: "Canada's Northern Empire Within 850 Miles of North Pole, Making our Sovereignty Certain," reported the Ottawa *Journal* of 17 October 1922. In fact, the Canadian government did not feel entirely certain until it settled Otto Sverdrup's claims eight years later,[39] but the expedition was a large step in the right direction.

Pond Inlet, the other detachment set up in the summer of 1922, was to serve a somewhat different purpose since Canada's claim to Baffin Island had never been questioned. Pond Inlet was established simply to provide police supervision over an area which seemed to be in need of it. As with the Coppermine region, it was murder which brought the police to Baffin Island. The victim, a trader from Newfoundland named Robert Janes, had set up a post in 1916 on Eclipse Sound, not far from Pond Inlet.[40] He had had little success and had grown morose. In the spring of 1920 he attempted to return to civilization at Chesterfield Inlet, and while he was at Cape Crawford, he was shot by the local Inuit, apparently because he had frightened them by his attitude. In contrast to the earlier Rouvière-Le Roux case, this affair was fairly easy for the police, for transportation was available. The Hudson's Bay Company planned to open a post at Pond Inlet in the summer of 1921 and readily agreed to take Joy on the S.S. *Baychimo* to investigate Janes's death. Joy experienced little difficulty in finding the murderers and bringing them to Pond Inlet; he was thus already on the scene when the police post was set up in 1922. The result of the affair was that on her next trip north, in 1923, the *Arctic* brought a judicial party to Pond Inlet; one Inuit was sentenced to ten years in Stony Mountain penitentiary, another was acquitted, and a third was sent for two years to the Pond Inlet post.[41]

Following the establishment of Craig Harbour and Pond Inlet in 1922, the police extended their operations over new parts of the eastern Arctic. The C.G.S. *Arctic,* refitted at a cost of $105,000,[42] landed a detachment at Pangnirtung, Cumberland Gulf, in 1923, and in 1924 another was set up at Dundas Harbour on the southeast coast of Devon Island. In the next few years detachments were set up in the eastern Arctic as follows:

1920—Port Burwell
1922—Craig Harbour (closed 1926, reopened 1933)
1922—Pond Inlet
1923—Pangnirtung
1924—Dundas Harbour
1926—Bache Peninsula (closed 1933)
1927—Lake Harbour

In 1924 the *Arctic* managed to land supplies at Cape Sabine at the southern end of Kane Basin, so that the members of the Craig Harbour detachment could patrol north to where the Thule Inuit were actually hunting the musk-oxen.

The government thus showed it had not forgotten Stefansson's warning that a police post at the extreme southern end of Ellesmere Island could not exercise sovereignty over the whole island, especially because the alleged encroachments were taking place some two hundred miles to the north. Ottawa's concern with sovereignty had not ceased with the establishment of the Craig Harbour post. On 24 April 1925, the first meeting of the "Northern Advisory Board" was held.[43] The board comprised representatives of most government departments which had interests in the Arctic; members included W. W. Cory (chairman) and J. D. Craig from the Department of the Interior, Charles Camsell from the

Department of Mines, O. D. Skelton from External Affairs, R. M. Anderson, a naturalist from the Victoria Memorial Museum, Duncan Campbell Scott of Indian Affairs, G. J. Desbarats of the Fisheries Department, and Cortlandt Starnes of the R.C.M.P..[44]

The immediate impetus for the formation of the Northern Advisory Board was the proposed Arctic expedition of the American explorer Donald B. MacMillan.[45] MacMillan, who had discovered much of Greely Fiord and had proven that "Crocker Land" was a chimera between 1914 and 1917,[46] was preparing an expedition for 1925 which would be based at Etah, with stations on Ellesmere and Axel Heiberg Islands. Its chief purpose was to carry out aerial exploration of the Polar region under the leadership of Commander Richard Byrd. When the Canadian government heard of this expedition, it informed MacMillan through the British ambassador in Washington that Canadian licences were required if he wished to secure specimens of Arctic fauna, but letters to that effect had been ignored.[47] The Northern Advisory Board met this situation by adopting a triple course of action: gentle suggestions to the Americans, surveillance of MacMillan and Byrd's activities in the Arctic, and a widening of police activities to forestall any possible difficulties. In May 1925, W. W. Cory went to Washington to tell the secretary of the navy, Curtis Wilbur, and the Naval Bureau of Aeronautics that Canada's permission should be obtained before MacMillan landed on Canadian soil.[48] In the same month the Americans were told that the R.C.M.P. and the Hudson's Bay Company were more than willing to assist MacMillan's expedition and would be happy to "furnish the necessary permits" for exploration in Canadian territory.[49] An officer of the R.C.M.P. was sent with the Arctic in 1925 to call on MacMillan and see what he was up to. Finally, it was decided to try and establish a permanent detachment at Bache Peninsula, near Cape Sabine, to emphasize Canada's ownership of that sensitive area.[50]

The government's awareness of every nuance of the sovereignty issue is shown by a minor incident involving the MacMillan expedition. In August 1925, following the recommendations mentioned above, the Arctic, with Inspector Wilcox on board, visited Macmillan at Etah, on the northwest coast of Greenland. G. P. Mackenzie, in command of the Canadian party, had a conversation with Commander Byrd, in which Byrd asked whether any Canadian had ever been to Axel Heiberg Island. Mackenzie replied in the negative, but the implications of the question worried him. In consultation with Inspector Wilcox and Staff-Sergeant Joy, who was then in charge of the Craig Harbour detachment, it was decided to send a patrol from that post to Axel Heiberg Island the next winter to rectify the omission.[51] The question of the new detachment was resolved in 1926 when the Craig Harbour detachment was closed, its buildings abandoned, and a new one opened at Bache Peninsula.[52] Its latitude, just over 79 degrees north, made it the most northerly detachment in the history of the force,[53] and probably the most northerly post office in the world at that time.

The MacMillan-Byrd expedition was only partly successful. The base at Etah was established, but Byrd was not able to set up camps on Ellesmere or Axel Heiberg Island owing to difficulties with his aircraft and bad flying conditions. The expedition remained at Etah for only three weeks and then returned to the United States.[54] In retrospect the attitude of the Canadian government representatives may seem extreme; the United States government had never moved to consolidate any claims it might have had to Canadian territory by virtue of the explorations of its nationals. Canadian nervousness may best be seen as an overreaction after several decades of inaction.

This official apprehensiveness, however, led to a series of remarkable police patrols in the mid and late 1920s; they covered most of the remaining parts of the Arctic archipelago which had not previously been visited by a Canadian. Two of these patrols deserve mention in this context for they were entirely for the purpose of sovereignty and exploration, going through territory which was completely uninhabited. The first was the result of Commander Byrd's question. On 26 March 1927, S/Sgt. Joy, with one constable, three Inuit, and four dog teams left Bache Peninsula, crossed Ellesmere Island, and visited Axel Heiberg, Amund Ringnes, King Christian, Cornwall, and Graham Islands, returning to the post on 18 May; the distance covered was 1,300 miles.[55] Two years later, Joy, now an inspector, made an even longer patrol from Dundas Harbour to Bache Peninsula via Melville Island (Winter Harbour), Hecla and Griper Bay, and Lougheed, Ellef Ringnes, Cornwall, Axel Heiberg, and Ellesmere Islands. The patrol lasted from 12 March to 31 May 1929, covered 1,700 miles, and was rightly hailed by Commissioner Starnes as "the most noteworthy event of the year in the north."[56] Although none of the land traversed by Joy could be classed as *terra incognita,* since it all had been discovered by others, the patrols were remarkable for their length and their speed; even Stefansson, it is fair to say, could not have done better.

These were the two longest patrols, but there were several others which were scarcely less important. The police at the Bache Peninsula[57] and Dundas Harbour detachments, since there were no indigenous inhabitants near except for the Inuit families from Etah hired to work for them, spent most of their time on patrol and covered a great deal of territory. In one instance new land was discovered; in 1928 Constable

T. C. Makinson of the Bache Peninsula detachment discovered the large inlet off Smith Sound which now bears his name.[58] In 1929 Corporal E. Anstead of the same detachment patrolled nearly 1,100 miles along the west coast of Ellesmere Island as far north as the Bjorne Peninsula. In 1932 Corporal H. W. Stallworthy, with Joy the most successful of the police in carrying out these long patrols, made a journey completely around Axel Heiberg Island in search of Dr. H. E. K. Krueger, the German explorer; the distance covered was 1,400 miles.[59] In 1934 and 1935, Stallworthy, on loan to the Oxford University Ellesmere Island Expedition, reached the site of Fort Conger and Hazen Lake. He got as far as 82 deg. 25' N., a record for the police at that time. In October 1935 he was made a fellow of the Royal Geographical Society.

These splendid patrols, which took the police to almost all the islands of the Arctic archipelago, fulfilled one of the main requirements of sovereignty—that of exercising control, insofar as control could be exercised over uninhabited territory. Between 1922 and 1932, therefore, Canada had

exercised jurisdiction in and over the Arctic islands by establishing police, customs, and post offices at strategic and necessary points and by conducting patrols over the surrounding territory.... The title of Canada to the Arctic islands was recognized by Norway in 1930; and the claims of Denmark and the United States have been nullified by Canadian occupation of the territory.[60]

The customs and post offices referred to were of course police operations since the police were the sole government presence in the area.

In the more southerly parts of the eastern Arctic, where there were trading posts and Inuit, the police had more functions to perform than their fellows in the far north. Patrols were regularly sent out from Port Burwell, Pangnirtung, Pond Inlet, and Lake Harbour to take the census, report on the health of the Natives, advertise the presence of the police, and do a little exploring. In 1924 the patrols to the Inuit camps took on a greater importance when the government at Ottawa at last decided to assume a formal responsibility for the Natives of the Arctic. By a revision of the Indian Act which came into effect on 19 July 1924, the superintendent of Indian Affairs took charge of Inuit affairs as well.[61] While this change was of no immediate benefit to the Inuit, it did mean that the government had taken official notice of them and would perhaps eventually do something for them. In the meantime, they were visited by the police and ministered to in a rough and ready fashion. The R.C.M.P. patrols, along with the reports of explorers, were cited by the Department of Indian Affairs as the chief sources of information on the Inuit.[62]

Reading the reports of the R.C.M.P. from the eastern Arctic in conjunction with the government's reports on Inuit welfare makes it evident that police comments were ignored. Hardly a report from Baffin Island in the 1920s was without reference to "lung trouble," "tuberculosis," and "pneumonia" among the Inuit. In 1925 the Department of Indians Affairs reported that it had "not undertaken any large outlay in regard to medical attention, as we are informed there is surprisingly little sickness throughout the north."[63] In the R.C.M.P. report for 1926 Inspector Wilcox at Pond Inlet warned that "unless medical assistance is given these people at once, inside ten years the native population of North Baffin Island will be wiped out."[64] While the government spoke glowingly of the services performed by the doctor on the yearly visit of the *Arctic*, the actual care provided (by the police) was more rudimentary:

a young married woman . . . temperature was around 106, and the natives all told me it was no use doing anything for her . . . I treated her as I did the others [several were ill] . . . hot tea . . . a ration of tea and biscuit . . . Dover powders, poulticed their chests and gave them a laxative . . . in a few days she was well and around again . . . illuminating what effect a cup of tea, a little laxative, coupled with a lot of faith, would have on the natives.[65]

Faith or not, it was a fact that in 1925–26, among the three hundred Inuit around Pond Inlet, there were twelve deaths, eight owing to an "unidentified disease," while only three children were born, all of whom also died.[66] At Wakeham Bay in 1927–28 there were eight births and thirty-two deaths in a population of two hundred and eight.[67] The contrast between the plight of the Inuit of the eastern Arctic as reported by the police and traders and the "cloak of deceptive or pious phrases"[68] which the government published annually is striking. It shows that the government's only concern with the region was the establishment of sovereignty. Once this had been done, its only remaining interest was in rigid economies of expenditure, especially during the great depression of the 1930s.

The role played by the police in the eastern Arctic did not change in essentials between 1922 and 1940. Beyond a certain reshuffling of detachments, the routine of the police did not vary much; survival occupied much of their time, and patrolling took up most of the rest. These patrols eventually became "routine"—that is, regularly scheduled; by 1928 the patrol from Pangnirtung to Home Bay and return, a distance of 537 miles, was so commonplace that details of it were no longer considered of interest to the public.[69] Besides the medical benefits the Inuit derived from these visits, the police believed that they prevented outbreaks of violence, such as the Home Bay murders of 1923, which were caused by a form of Christian religious mania. Missionaries had visited the settlement at Kivitoo, Home Bay, and had left behind an enthusiasm for, but an imperfect understanding of, Christian principles. A self-styled messiah caused the death of two men and was himself murdered. The police patrolled from Pangnirtung in 1924 but took no action other than to explain the Inuits' error to them.[70] The yearly patrol, it was believed, "breaks the current of these unhealthy thoughts" by giving the Inuit something new to occupy their minds; it also instilled "some real respect for the big white man outside whose servants the police are."[71] But given the policy of the government—to spend only what the bare essentials of sovereignty demanded—the police could do no more than dispense a few relief supplies, try a little amateur medical treatment, and preach the secular gospel of "a wise, unselfish, but very powerful directing authority outside."[72] This was the pattern of the 1920s and the 1930s in the eastern Arctic.

13. The End of the Frontier

AFTER THE MID 1920s the Canadian Arctic underwent rapid change, both social and technological. Technological change manifested itself in the arrival in the north of the aeroplane and the radio, two innovations which did much to alter the pattern of police response to the challenges of the frontier. In 1921 Commissioner Perry, in his last report before retirement, noted the first aeroplane journey by a member of the R.C.M.P. on duty. Surprisingly, perhaps, this did not occur in southern Canada but between Fort Simpson and Edmonton, when a police sergeant investigating a murder case travelled in a plane belonging to the Imperial Oil Company.[1] In July 1929 Aklavik saw its first plane, flown by "Punch" Dickens, who took the Inuit for rides at ten dollars a head, and by the end of that year plans were made to carry mail by plane from Fort Resolution to Aklavik.[2] On Dominion Day 1930 the first commercial plane landed at Herschel Island with a load of sightseers. Technology had given the western Arctic a new link with the rest of Canada.

Another link was provided by radio, which spread all over the Arctic in the 1920s. Wireless stations were built at Aklavik (1924), at Port Burwell, and at more southerly places, manned by the Canadian Corps of Signals.[3] By 1928 every police detachment in the north had a receiving set (though not a transmitter; these were too expensive), so that messages could be sent over the ordinary broadcast band as far north as Bache Peninsula. The R.C.M.P. had an arrangement with station KDKA in Pittsburgh to send messages to the Arctic detachments on a regular schedule.[4] The radios must have been a godsend to the men at the isolated posts; for several years in the late 1920s most reports from the

Arctic dwell at length on the domestic and foreign stations received, with comments on the quality of the music and the humour.

A good example of the way in which technology affected the operations of the police on the frontier is the case of the notorious Albert Johnson, the so-called "mad trapper of Rat River," which took place during the winter of 1931–32.[5] Radio was extensively used in the case; when it was thought that Johnson might try to flee from the Fort McPherson area to northern Yukon, radio messages were relayed through Dawson, Anchorage, and Fort Yukon to the R.C.M.P. detachment at Old Crow, ordering the police there to block his route. Significantly, it was found that the old method of sending out a patrol by dog-team did not work well. The contrast with the Bathurst Inlet patrol of the First World War is striking. In the earlier instance, the police had set out into the virtual unknown, had met a reasonably friendly reception, and had eventually accomplished their mission. This had always been the pattern; Inuit and whites on the northern frontier had never offered the police serious resistance.[6] When in the Johnson case the police encountered a man who fired at them without warning, and accurately too, they found that the old methods had to be supplemented by modern ones. Four major patrols were sent out; one policeman was killed, another policeman and a member of the Signal Corps were badly wounded, but the episode ended only when a plane, piloted by the experienced bush pilot "Wop" May, was chartered for search and supply purposes, and the final patrol was provided with a low-powered radio transmitter-receiver. Without these expedients, the affair might have been indefinitely protracted, for Johnson was as resourceful as the police, and far more ruthless.

Another application of new methods began in 1928 when the police finally acquired a ship capable of navigating the waters of the Arctic archipelago and wintering in the north. This was the motor schooner *St. Roch*, built in Vancouver and sent north in the summer of 1928.[7] The *St. Roch*, which patrolled the northern coast of Canada from 1928 to 1948, performed several useful functions for the police. It freed them from their old dependence on others for supplying posts such as Herschel Island, Coppermine, Tree River, and Cambridge Bay. It also removed them from the anomalous position of having to depend on traders for transportation to check on their activities at remote spots. It permitted the police to bring accused criminals from remote areas in the western Arctic to trial at Herschel Island or Aklavik and the sick to hospital. It was a demonstration of sovereignty; fixed during the winter and mobile during the short navigation season, it was the answer to the problem posed as early as 1900 by Comptroller Frederick White—how to make the police on the Arctic coast more mobile and thus more effective. Fitzgerald had recognized the problem at Herschel Island in 1903 when he was compelled to ask traders to give him a list of their goods and to ignore those who bypassed him altogether. Now, after twenty-five years, the R.C.M.P. could make effective summer patrols in the western and central Arctic without the assistance of anyone.

By 1928 the pre-war pattern of Canada's northern frontier was set. Despite the new technology, it was in some ways similar to the old one. The government still did as little as possible, leaving, as before, the souls of the Natives to the missionaries, their trade to the Hudson's Bay Company, and their welfare to the police. As in previous decades, the R.C.M.P. performed a variety of services for the government, not the least of which was to enable Ottawa to tell itself that everything necessary was being done for the Inuit. The exterior forces at work on the far north did not change in essentials between 1910 and 1940; it was not until the Second World War and especially the ensuing Cold War that the Arctic frontier began to take on the importance to Canada that it now holds.

An essential fact about the northern frontier between 1894 and 1925 was that it was always moving. If the frontier is thought of as the limit of penetration of government control, it lay in 1885 at the level of the Saskatchewan River, and in 1900, at Herschel Island and Churchill. By 1920 it was at Coronation Gulf, north Baffin Island, and Ellesmere Island. By 1925 there was no longer a northern frontier in the sense that the government, through the police, had spread its influence over the whole of the inhabited Arctic and some of the uninhabited parts as well. Thus, in any given year there was a wide variation in the level of "civilization" in the Northwest Territories, generally depending on the length of time the white man had been at a particular locality. In 1925, for instance, the Mackenzie Delta had grown considerably, with two missions, two hospitals under construction, the police, the Hudson's Bay Company, and several private traders in the area. Some of the Natives were even becoming wealthy, for the 1920s marked the high point of the white fox trade, and by 1929 a good skin brought fifty dollars at Fort McPherson. A few Indians and Inuit made enough money to be called "plutocrats";[8] they owned their own schooners, and in some cases were rumoured to have earned $10,000 in a year from trapping. At the same time, the police were encountering Inuit around King William Island who had hardly seen a white man and were still virtually in the stone age.

Because of the diversity of conditions in the north and the changing nature of the frontier in the 1920s, the challenges facing the police varied widely according to their location. There were posts in the inhabited Arctic where these challenges were of the traditional kind. At the

Tree River detachment in 1925, for example, the main work carried out by the police was to make two long patrols by dog sled—one east to investigate a murder at Perry River, and one even farther east to investigate another murder on Adelaide Peninsula.[9] The four detachments which made up the "Arctic Sub-district"—[10] Aklavik (headquarters), Herschel Island, Baillie Island (moved to Cambridge Bay in 1926), and Tree River—were responsible for a stretch of Arctic Coast which lay between the 95th and 141st degrees of west longitude, about 1,200 miles in a straight line. In it the police were involved with Inuit who had been heavily influenced by white culture at one end of the line and with those who were almost completely uninfluenced at the other.

In the parts of the Yukon and Northwest Territories where the police and whites had been established longer, administrative duties loomed larger. As had been the case during the Yukon gold rush, the police filled a large number of civil posts, and these duties sometimes took up much of their time and energy. At Herschel Island, the police collected $14,588 in income tax during July and August 1925; Superintendent G. Ritchie, commanding "G" Division, commented, "Our men had to prepare the intricate forms, the persons concerned not having the faintest idea thereof. This in itself takes up time, valuable at that particular season."[11]

In the early days of police service in the Northwest Territories civil cases greatly outnumbered criminal ones. Offences against the Criminal Code were few in the 1920s—only twenty-nine in 1925—and increased only when the white population of the Territories began to grow. By 1947 the number of criminal charges had increased nearly seventeen times, to 489; the commissioner attributed this rise mostly to the increase in the population of the town of Yellowknife.[12] Although crimes were few in this period, they continued to receive most of the public attention directed toward the police on the northern frontier; the case of the "mad trapper" got all the sensational publicity at which the newspapers of the 1920s were so skilled. But it was also the solid acts of administration which established the police on the frontier—the settling of the estates of deceased persons (which required a good deal of work), the numerous services performed for the Department of the Interior (for which specifics are unfortunately not given in the records), and the rest of the investigations carried out.

In 1949, Commissioner S. T. Wood[13] commented on the passing of the northern frontier:

[T]he time has now passed (in fact it passed several years ago) when a large part of the Territories can no longer be looked upon as really isolated, and in that part of the Territories some of the detachments situated therein are just as busy and have *as much real police work to do as the average detachment in the provinces and in addition have the Government Administrative work to do.*[14]

It is striking how the distinction between civil duties and "real" police work persisted in the R.C.M.P.; Wood's words are almost an exact echo of those used by his father in the Yukon fifty years earlier.[15] He was probably thinking of the old age pension and the new family allowance, which the police began to distribute in remote areas at the end of the war, involving them in much extra paperwork. The old police prejudice against this sort of work survived the passing of the old frontier. The fact that the Territories were no longer isolated by the 1940s did not mean that the old techniques of policing had disappeared altogether, but the new ones which had been introduced in the 1920s were becoming increasingly more important. The report for 1950 included a table of patrols carried out by "G" Division[16] which shows the old and the new way of doing things:

PATROLS	N.W.T.	YUKON	QUEBEC	HUDSON BAY	TOTAL
Dogs	34,507	3,333	1,330	7,690	46,860
Boats	29,390	12,008	1,291	8,211	50,900
Plane					
(public)	92,085	42,771	10,375	3,096	148,327
(police)	31,256	—	—	—	31,256
Auto	60,170	173,796	—	252	234,218
Rail	7,504	7,500	750	2,842	18,596
Foot	2,088	6,351	364	371	9,174
Totals	257,000	245,749	14,110	22,462	539,331[17]

By the mid 1920s, as the frontier period of Canada's north drew to a close, the role of the Mounted Police also changed as its focus shifted southward. Popular literature about the force concentrated for many years, as it still does, on tales of brave deeds in the frozen waste. Indeed, in 1920, Hollywood was about to make the archetypal Sergeant Preston a household word.[18] The reality of the force, on the other hand, was that although its northern service continued and even expanded, it was in the south that the major part of its future growth evidently lay. After the First World War, the R.C.M.P. absorbed the Dominion Police, became responsible for national security, and eventually became the provincial police force in eight of the ten provinces. Much of this new work had a distinctly urban flavour, such as activities in the Winnipeg general strike in 1919 or wartime investigations of enemy aliens on the prairies.[19] Yet it was their northern service that remained central to the public image of the police. As the R.C.M.P. spread throughout Canada, it was not strikebreakers the public envisioned when they thought of the police, but the crew of the *St. Roch,* the pursuers of the "mad trapper," or Inspector Joy's remarkable patrols of the later 1920s.[20] Until the Canadian north fell under the iron grip of the civil service after 1945, there was no lack of melodrama from the boreal regions.

And the Mounted Police have, of course, been perfect subjects for Canadian mythologizing, particularly in respect to their northern service. All the elements necessary to create heroes were present: climate, difficult terrain, exotic Natives, unruly foreigners. Although there were individual heroic figures—Sam Steele is the best known—the police were essentially group heroes, a team in the Canadian tradition of collective heroism.[21] The police were well aware of their image and took pains to cultivate it. Though they writhed at the absurdities and inaccuracies of the popular media—they could never convince the Americans that their motto was not "we always get our man"—they were at the same time always ready to lend technical advice to screenwriters and film producers, realizing that the heroic image which came out of Hollywood and elsewhere was one of their greatest assets. The image of the police that began on the prairies in the 1870s and was reinforced a generation later in the Yukon and Northwest Territories has proved impervious, as far as Canadian public opinion is concerned, to all assaults by latter-day debunkers and muckrakers.

It was suggested at the beginning of this book that the Mounted Police served as agents of metropolitanism in the Canadian north, imposing on the hinterland the policies and controls devised in the far-off metropolitan centre. This statement is qualified by the fact that the forces of metropolitanism in the north were not as urgent as on the southern prairies, where the police first acted in this role and where, as David Breen has pointed out, they were "pervasive and unrelenting."[22] The reason for this gentler or at least more gradual imposition of metropolitan control is that the government had no long-range plan for the north; there was no northern equivalent of John A. Macdonald's "National Policy." What the government wanted the Mounted Police to do in northern Canada was to demonstrate sovereignty and make a gradual start at enforcing Canadian law there. There were to be no "hurried measures."[23] R. C. Macleod has shown the careful nature of this process as it was applied to the southern prairies.[24] In the north, at least outside the Yukon, it was even slower—the policy there was one of symbolic gestures such as the pursuit of the Inuit who killed explorers, priests, and government officials—but otherwise, it was largely a policy of benign (or indifferent) neglect. Using the police as its main instrument, the federal government slowly spread its metropolitan web of laws, regulations, economic and cultural policies, and finally a well-intentioned but arguably suffocating welfare system over much of northern Canada.

Appendix

THE BATHURST INLET PATROL

"M" Division, R.N.W.M.Police,
Bernard Harbour, N.W.T.,
Dolphin and Union Straits,
June 16, 1917.

The Officer Commanding,
R.N.W.M.Police,
Port Nelson,

Sir,—I have the honour to forward to you a general report of a patrol made from Baker Lake Lake, N.W.T., to Bernard Harbour on the Arctic Coast.

On March 21, 1917, I left Baker Lake Detachment with Reg. No. 4557 Sergt.-Major Caulkin, T.B., Police Natives "Joe" and "By and By," and hired native "Quash-ak" and native woman Solomon, taking three teams of police dogs (25), sleds, and two canoes.... We proceeded west across Baker Lake, calling at our first cache, where we took up most of our supplies, and coal oil for the patrol. One month's rations for six were all we were able to leave with, as with all our camp equipment and coal oil we were heavily loaded. After the month's rations were finished we were to subsist as best we could...

On the morning of March 23 I sent Sergt.-Major Caulkin to a Kinipitoo encampment on the northwest end of the lake, and here he was able to purchase 10 large deer, and also to procure the services of a native with a dog-team to accompany us as far as Schultz lake and to assist in carrying our dog-feed and coal oil....

The weather from March 21 to March 26 had been clear and cold, but on this latter date it commenced to storm and continued to do so till April 2, when we were able to break camp, proceeding to Aberdeen Lake.... there found an encampment of the Shan-ing-i-ong-muits and one Pad-i-muit family. We built our igloo alongside and camped with them....

On April 10 our native guide and his son returned to their camp, and we were now alone in a strange country, with which none of my natives were acquainted, so we had to travel by compass and endeavour to pick our way as near as possible by this means. . . .

We finally came out on the Arctic coast on the night of May 7, and as far as I am able to judge from the map we hit the coast about 15 miles west of the mouth of the Ellis river. The river . . . is known to the natives as Coog-nay-ok, but this I did not find out until I got a copy of Hanbury's map at Bernard Harbour. . . .

On May 14 we saw several sled tracks going in a south-westerly direction toward Bathurst Inlet; these we followed and eventually came upon a large Eskimo encampment situated on an island in the mouth of Bathurst Inlet.

These natives were Killin-o-muits, and we were received in a very friendly manner, although we had to go through the formula of showing friendly intentions by extending the arms above the head upon approaching the camp, and our natives were soon engaged in conversation with them.

May 15 was spent in investigating the Radford and Street case, and we traded with these natives for footwear and seal-line, etc., our own being pretty well played out. We also traded and procured a native stone lamp and some blubber, but this method of cooking was so slow that after several attempts to boil a kettle, consisting of an all-night vigil, we eventually abandoned the lamp and found small twigs growing on the islands in the inlet, sufficient to make a small fire. . . .

From May 18 the travelling got very bad; the sea-ice became bare and jagged and cut the dogs' feet, so that the majority were lame. I had an outfit of sealskin boots made and put on all the dogs, but the ice was so sharp that they would wear out a pair in one night, as was also the case with our own footwear, and it was fortunate that we were constantly coming in contact with natives and able to trade for footgear and to get repairs made. . . .

At all these encampments I stayed and gave them a lecture on the murdering of the white men, and regarding pilfering from them and also dwelling on the laws of civilization generally. They appeared to be greatly impressed. They had heard of Inspector LaNauze's patrol in there and the taking out of the murderers of the Roman Catholic missionaries, and this seems to have created a great impression amongst them, the extent of which remains to be seen in the future. . . .

We reached Tree river on the night of June 4 . . . At this point we traded for some barren ground grizzly bear meat from the natives and were made very sick from eating it; although the meat tasted pretty good there was something about it that was not good for the stomach. . . .

We reached Bernard harbour on June 13 and were met by Mr. Phillips, post manager of the Hudson's Bay Company, who showed us every kindness and assisted us in every way possible.

Mr. Phillips informed me that it would be impossible to proceed farther west by sled as the breakup was liable to occur any time now, and that if I attempted it I would get stranded somewhere along the coast. He further informed me that the Hudson's Bay Company boat would arrive as soon as the ice cleared and that our best way out was to go out on her to Herschel island. This I decided to do . . .

It is needless to say that this was a hard trip, for I must say that it has been the hardest trip I have ever made, and we suffered much from cold and exposure. These we felt all the more when our supplies ran out and when towards the end of our journey our deerskin clothing got the worse for wear and the hair started falling out and the winds pierced through the seams and holes.

Most of us were continually frozen about the face and hands, and with regard to snow blindness we were suffering from this more or less during the whole journey, the natives particularly showing a weakness in this direction even when wearing snow glasses, which I must say was due to the inferior quality of our glasses, but which were the best I could procure before we started.

Both myself and Sergt.-Major Caulkin were in very poor shape as regards health; this was undoubtedly due to the straight meat diet which we had been on for the past month or six weeks, eating only quantities of deer, seal and bearmeat, to which we were unused, and even this eaten mostly half raw ever since the time of our being out of coal oil for our lamps. . . .

Dogs: . . . our dogs kept in good travelling shape and at no time did they show signs of becoming leg weary until the last stages of our journey. This was unavoidable when taking the heat of the sun, long hours of travelling and the sharp ice passed over into consideration, although even with these to our disadvantage our dogs all stayed in harness to the finish, and we did not have one casualty. This I think is remarkable when one considers the length and conditions of the patrol generally. . . .

Game: . . . Our total kill of deer during the journey from Schultz lake, where we first came into contact with them, was 168, and these were used for dog-feed and our own consumption.

Also in the vicinity of Bathurst inlet and along the Arctic coast to Bernard harbour we had shot nineteen seals up to the time of our arrival here.

Natives: . . . Some of the Killin-e-muits had not seen a white man before, and had very few white men's goods in their possession . . . Most of their arrow heads were made of bone or native copper which they obtain in Bathurst inlet. Those natives appeared very clean, seemed industrious, and well clothed, and the men were tall and of fine physique....

Some natives I met I did not like the looks of, and these were the Wad-le-ar-ing-muits of the Coppermine river; they were altogether too familiar, and I do not think they would hesitate to try to take advantage of a lone white man travelling amongst them. It was from this particular tribe that the murderers of the two Roman Catholic missionaries hail. I gave them a long lecture respecting our laws.... from different sources I found out that it is correct that they do away with the majority of female born babies. I lectured them severely on this matter... steps should be taken to stop this practice as the result is that polyandry is now resorted to among them, and I noticed a huge number of marriageable huskies who were without wives....

White settlers: We met no white settlers during our journey until reaching Tree river on the Arctic Coast on June 4, when we met one, Albin Kihlman, a Norwegian engaged in fishing and trapping....

The next white persons we met were Capt. Bernard and one of his crew on the schooner *Teddy Bear,* frozen in the ice east of the mouth of the Copperimine River. Capt. Bernard had arrived in from Nome, Alaska in the previous summer (1916) and was engaged in trading with the natives for furs and curios...

Topographical: ... The south shore of Melville sound is very high and rugged and barren, and the sound itself is strewn with islands. The south end of Bathurst inlet is altogether different from the maps in our possession, the shore line being a great deal more indented with bays and small inlets than what these maps show.... In the mouth of Bathurst inlet and in the inlet itself there are a great many more islands than are charted; these islands are mostly very high and nearly all have perpendicular cliffs, from 200 to 500 feet high....

Natives in police employ: ... The native woman was also of great assistance to us on the travel, mending our clothes at night and keeping them generally in repair. She was also of great assistance to us when we came in contact with the Killin-e-muits who were responsible for the murders of Messrs. Radford and Street, as she herself belongs to this tribe....

> I have the honour to be, sir,
> Your obedient servant,
> F. H. French, Inspector,
> O. C. Bathurst Inlet Patrol.

This extract is taken from R.N.W.M.P. *Report,* 1918, pp. 7–18. The party returned to Baker Lake the next winter, having travelled over 2,400 miles. Inspector French was subsequently awarded the Imperial Service Order; Sergeant-Major Caulkin was given the King's Police Medal.

Notes

NOTES TO THE INTRODUCTION

1. For a discussion of northern historiography, see K. S. Coates and W. R. Morrison, "Northern Visions: Recent Developments in the Writing of Northern Canadian History," *Manitoba History* (Autumn 1985).
2. Three useful studies along these lines are A. J. Ray and D. Freeman, *Give Us Good Measure* (Toronto, 1978); Charles Bishop, *The Northern Ojibway and the Fur Trade* (Toronto, 1974); and Shepherd Krech III, ed., *The Subarctic Fur Trade: Native Economic and Social Adaptations* (Vancouver, 1984).
3. This process has been described as it applied to the prairies in R. C. Macleod, "Canadianizing the West: The North-West Mounted Police as Agents of the National Policy, 1873–1905." In L. H. Thomas, ed., *Essays on Western History* (Edmonton, 1976).
4. See "Whalers and Missionaries at Herschel Island," *Ethnohistory* 28, no. 2 (1981); "Atomistic Order and Frontier Violence: Miners and Whalemen in the Nineteenth Century Yukon," *Ethnology* 22 (October 1983); "The Mounties as Vigilantes: Perceptions of Community and the Transformation of Law in the Yukon, 1885–1897," *Law and Society Review* 14, no. 1 (1979).
5. Keith Walden, *Visions of Order: The Canadian Mounties in Symbol and Myth* (Toronto, 1982), p. 213.
6. See Morris Zaslow, "Administering the Arctic Islands, 1880–1940: Policemen, Missionaries, Fur Traders." In M. Zaslow, ed., *A Century of Canada's Arctic Islands, 1880–1980 (Ottawa, 1981).*

NOTES TO CHAPTER ONE

1. The terms "police," "Mounted Police," "North-West Mounted Police" (N.W.M.P.), "Royal North-West Mounted Police" (R.N.W.M.P.), and "Royal Canadian Mounted Police" (R.C.M.P.) are all used here when speaking of this organization. The first two are used indiscriminately, the third is used for the pre-1904 period, the fourth for the years 1904–1919, and fifth for the post-1919 period.
2. K. S. Coates and I have made this distinction in "Northern Visions."
3. A discussion of the technical aspects of the question appears in W. R. Morrison, *Under the Flag: Canadian Sovereignty and the Native People in Northern Canada* (Ottawa, 1984).
4. On this point see Carl Betke, "Pioneers and Police on the Canadian Prairies, 1885–1914," *Canadian Historical Association Historical Papers, 1980* (Ottawa, 1981).
5. For example, R. C. Fetherstonhaugh, *The Royal Canadian Mounted Police* (New York, 1940), p. 3. R. C. Macleod, *Law Enforcement, 1873–1905* (Toronto, 1976) entitles one of his chapters "The Military Tradition in the NWMP," and remarks on the persistence of the force's "original semi-military attributes," p. 102.
6. For an account of the genesis of the force, see S. W. Horrall, "Sir John A. Macdonald and the Mounted Police Force for the Northwest Territories," *Canadian Historical Review* 53, no. 2 (June 1972). Macdonald in 1872 asked Sir John Rose for information on the Royal Irish Constabulary. In 1880 the Commissioner of the N.W.M.P. visited Ireland to study the force at first hand. See N.W.M.P. *Report,* 1880, p. 3.
7. R. C. Macleod, *Law Enforcement, 1873–1905,* chapter 7, deals at length with the political nature of the force.
8. Comptroller Frederick White to Commissioner A. B. Perry, 13 February 1905, R.C.M.P. Papers, Public Archives of Canada, Comptroller's Letterbooks, v. 92.
9. On the subject of patronage in late nineteenth century Canada, see two articles by Gordon T. Stewart: "Political Patronage under Macdonald and

Laurier, 1878–1911," *American Review of Canadian Studies* 10 (1980); and "John A. Macdonald's Greatest Triumph," *Canadian Historical Review* 63, no. 1 (March 1982).

10. The order of 15 May 1901 to the police, R.C.M.P. Papers, Public Archives of Canada, Comptroller's Correspondence, v. 347.

11. Ibid.

12. Sifton to Laurier, 5 February 1897, Compt. Corr., v. 347.

13. R. C. Fetherstonhaugh, *Mounted Police,* p. 7. For a recent account of the massacre, see Robert S. Allen, "A Witness to Murder: The Cypress Hills Massacre and the Canadian-American West during the 1870's," in I. A. L. Getty and A. S. Lussier, eds., *As Long as the Sun Shines and Water Flows* (Vancouver, 1983).

14. See G. Friesen, *The Canadian Prairies: A History* (Toronto, 1984), chapter 7, for a discussion of this point.

15. P. B. Waite, *Canada, 1874–1896: Arduous Destiny* (Toronto, 1971), p. 10.

16. R. C. Macleod, *Law Enforcement, 1873–1905,* p. 86. During the gold rush period 48 per cent of recruits were British born, 42 per cent Canadian.

17. R. C. Macleod, *Law Enforcement, 1873–1905,* pp. 85–86.

18. Originally the force fell under the secretary of state. By the 1880s it was under the minister of the interior.

19. The correspondence files from his office are much more useful for research purposes than those from the commissioner's.

20. "North-West" was the spelling used until 1905, when "Northwest" was adopted.

21. He also held the office of commissioner of the Northwest Territories, then largely a sinecure, from 1905–18. He was replaced as comptroller by Lawrence Fortescue, another man with decades of service in the force.

22. In particular those by J. P. Turner, S. B. Steele, and R. C. Fetherstonhaugh.

23. On this point, see R. C. Macleod, *Law Enforcement, 1873–1905* and John L. Tobias, "Canada's Subjugation of the Plains Cree, 1879–1885," *Canadian His-* *torical Review* 64, no. 4 (December 1983).

24. An account of the patrol is in R. C. Fetherstonhaugh, *Mounted Police,* pp. 94–95. Documentary evidence in the police files for the period 1877–95 was extensively destroyed by a fire in the comptroller's office in 1897.

NOTES TO CHAPTER TWO

1. For an assessment of the controversy over the antiquity of *homo sapiens* in the Yukon, see W. R. Morrison, *A Survey of the History and Claims of the Native Peoples of Northern Canada* (Ottawa, 1984).

2. For modern accounts of this period, see Lewis Green, *The Boundary Hunters* (Vancouver, 1982) and Allen A. Wright, *Prelude to Bonanza* (Sidney, B.C., 1976).

3. For the pre-gold rush period in the Yukon, see William Ogilvie, *Early Days on the Yukon* (London, 1913), and Allen A. Wright, *Prelude to Bonanza* (Sidney, B.C., 1976).

4. See Frederick Schwatka, *A Summer in Alaska* (St. Louis, 1894).

5. Ogilvie, *Early Days,* pp. 85–87. Ogilvie does not name the man, referring to him as "a young man of the city of Toronto." Apparently the letter was in Ogilvie's possession.

6. Ogilvie, ibid., pp. 34–36.

7. Morris Zaslow, *The Opening of the Canadian North 1870–1914* (Toronto, 1971), pp. 82–83.

8. Ogilvie, *Early Days,* p. 245.

9. Thomas Stone, "The Mounties as Vigilantes: Perceptions of Community and the Transformation of Law in the Yukon, 1885–1897," *Law and Society Review,* vol. 14, no. 1, 1979.

10. Quoted in F. W. Howay, W. N. Sage, and H. F. Angus, *British Columbia and the United States* (Toronto, 1942), p. 350.

11. Ogilvie, *Early Days,* p. 144.

12. William Carpenter Bompas, Bishop of Athabasca 1874–84, Bishop of Mackenzie River 1884–91, Bishop of Selkirk (Yukon) 1891–1906.

13. Bompas to T. M. Daly, Ottawa, ? May and 9 December 1893, Constantine Papers, v. 3.

14. Charles Constantine was born in England in 1849, emigrated to Canada in

1854, and served with the Red River Expedition of 1870. Appointed Chief of the Manitoba Provincial Police in 1880, he joined the N.W.M.P. in 1886 as an Inspector and served in the Yukon and Northwest Territories. He died while on leave in 1912.

15. N.W.M.P. *Report*, 1894, C, p. 76. The "Hoo-chin-oo" were a Tlingit tribe of the Admiralty Island, Alaska, region, who were known to make a distilled liquor. The name is more correctly spelled "hutsnuwu," meaning "grizzly bear fort," Our slang word "hooch," which thus means "grizzly bear," comes from the name of this tribe.

16. C. H. Hamilton to T. M. Daly, n.d., Constantine Papers, v. 3.

17. See Lewis Green, *The Boundary Hunters*, chapter 3, and C. C. Tansill, *Canadian-American Relations, 1875–1911* (Gloucester, Mass., 1964), chapter 5.

18. J. P. Turner, *The Northwest Mounted Police, 1873–1893*, 2 vols (Ottawa, 1950), pp. 518–22. Lawrence W. Herchmer was born in England in 1840. He was appointed commissariat officer for the Boundary Commission, 1872–74, Commissioner of Rebellion Losses in 1885, and Commissioner of the N.W.M.P. in 1886. He led the police contingent to the Boer War. He retired in 1900, and died in 1915.

19. Frederick White was born in England in 1847, and emigrated to Canada in 1862. He worked for a time for the Grand Trunk Railway, and entered the civil service in 1869 as a clerk in the Justice Department. He was transferred to the Department of the Secretary of State and made clerk in charge of the N.W.M.P. branch of the department in 1876. In 1880 he became Sir John A. Macdonald's private secretary, and the same year he was appointed Comptroller of the N.W.M.P., which he held until 1913. He was appointed Commissioner of the unorganized North-West Territories in 1905, and held this post until his death in 1918 ended an unbroken career of forty-nine years in the public service.

20. White to Minister of the Interior, 2 May 1894, Constantine Papers, v. 3.

21. Canada, House of Commons, *Debates*, 1894, pp. 4651–83. The phrase "living like lords" must have caused some rueful hilarity among the police as they earned their fifty cents per day.

22. Ford McLeod *Gazette*, 26 July 1895.

23. Calgary *Herald*, 14 February 1895. R. C. MacLeod, *The NWMP and Law Enforcement, 1873–1905*, chapter 5, concludes that a majority of the officers owed their commissions to politics, but since there were so many more applications than vacancies, the government could choose the best Liberal or the best Conservative applicants, and the standards of the force did not suffer.

24. Calgary *Herald*, 26 March 1895.

25. Fort Macleod *Gazette*, 5 April 1895.

26. A copy is in Constantine Papers, v. 3. This shows the influence on the government of appeals from men on the scene.

27. Ibid.

28. Ibid. In *Canada North* (Toronto, 1967), p. 33, Farley Mowat gives the following account of how the police came to the Yukon: "It was touch and go whether she would even bother to uphold her claims. In 1898 the great Klondike rush into the Yukon triggered a move by the United States to annex that rich territory. There were those in Ottawa even that far back who felt that any attempt to withstand the Americans would be "bad business" and might endanger commercial relations. Fortunately not all Canadians were so spineless, and so a small detachment of the North West Mounted Police was sent to the Yukon to display the Canadian flag." Stirring stuff indeed for the patriotic, but, alas, a complete fantasy.

29. Constantine Papers, v. 1.

30. N.W.M.P., *Report*, 1894, C, p. 70.

31. The following improvements were suggested: "Tramways on the portages between Lake Linderman and Bennet [sic] at the canon and White Horse would be a great help to small parties, as they are not able to portage their boats alone.... The cost would not be great. The miners are of the opinion that the rocks in the channel of the Five Fingers could be removed in the winter when the water is low. This would make navigation safe for a steamer coming down;

then there would be uninterrupted navigable water to the foot of the White Horse, a distance of about 2,300 miles." Ibid., pp. 73–75. A privately-owned tramway was later built around Miles Canyon and the Whitehorse rapids.

32. Ibid., p. 77. Few eyewitness reports seem to be as unreliable as those concerning liquor. One man's quiet drink is another's debauch, and all reports have to be treated with much skepticism.

33. Ibid., p. 75.

34. Ibid., p. 77.

35. Ibid., p. 78.

36. For a discussion of this point see K. S. Coates, "Best Left as Indians: Native-White Relations in the Yukon Territory, 1840–1950" (Ph.D. dissertation, University of British Columbia, 1984).

37. The question of Indian population statistics is discussed in the Department of Indian Affairs and Northern Development publication *Indians of the Yukon and Northwest Territories* (Ottawa, 1970).

38. N.W.M.P., *Report,* 1894, C, pp. 78–79. Presumably the Indians had encountered the company on journeys to Fort McPherson or Rampart House, had memories of Fort Yukon, or had heard of its benevolence by word of mouth. Or perhaps, like many Natives, they simply told the white man what he wanted to hear.

39. Department of Indian Affairs to Constantine, 22 May 1894, Constantine papers, v. 3.

40. N.W.M.P., *Report,* 1894, C, p. 81.

41. Ibid., p. 84.

42. White to G. E. Corbould (M.P. for New Westminster), 23 May 1895, Compt. Corr., v. 110. This letter was, by the way, in reference to one of the Canadian merchants who, directly after the news of the proposed expedition was made public, patriotically offered to supply the police with genuine Canadian goods and thus keep the trade out of Yankee hands.

43. White to Lt-Col. W. White, Deputy Postmaster-General, 10 May 1895, Compt. Corr., v. 133. No money was mentioned in the exchange of letters, so presumably the police did not expect to be paid for this service.

44. N.W.M.P., *Report,* 1895, p. 7. Constantine says the party consisted of "two officers, one assistant-surgeon, and sixteen non-commissioned officer and constables," presumably including himself, since the only other officer on the expedition was Inspector Strickland.

45. Ibid.

46. J. N. E. Brown, "The Evolution of Law and Government in the Yukon Territory," in S. M. Wickett, ed., *Municipal Government in Canada* (Toronto, 1907), p. 198. The same order-in-council established the Districts of Franklin, Ungava, and Mackenzie.

47. The incident is recounted in detail in Constantine's report to White, 13 July 1896, Compt. Corr., v. 123.

48. M. H. E. Haynes, *Pioneers of the Klondyke* (London, 1897), p. 124.

49. Constantine to White, 13 July 1896, Compt. Corr., v. 123.

50. Thomas Stone, "The Mounties as Vigilantes," p. 101.

51. Particularly since his 1887 visit to the Yukon and his later involvement in the Anglo-American marine boundary discussions in the Alaskan region.

52. The correspondence is in Compt. Corr., v. 119.

53. Ibid.

54. RG 18, B-2, vol. 2182.

NOTES TO CHAPTER THREE

1. Pierre Berton's *Klondike Fever* (New York, 1958) is a vivid and accurate account, and articles and monographs on the rush and the colourful characters who participated in it are constantly being published.

2. For a lively history of Dawson, see Hal J. Guest, "A History of the City of Dawson, Yukon Territory, 1896–1920," Parks Canada Microfiche Report Series #7, particularly chapter 4, "Law Enforcement and the NWMP." It is a pity that this report, commissioned by the federal government, is not more widely available.

3. S. B. Steele, *Forty Years in Canada* (Toronto, 1918), p. 23.

4. N.W.M.P., *Report,* 1896, pp. 235–36.

5. Ibid., p. 237.

6. Berton, *Fever*, p. 77.
7. Constantine Papers, v. 3. The prohibition, which also applied to mining claims, was further emphasized when an order-in-council of 29 March 1899 formally forbade the practice.
8. L. Fortescue to A. E. Blount, Clerk of the Privy Council, 4 April 1912, RG 18, B-7, v. 3439.
9. Constantine to Herchmer, 11 August 1897, RG 18, B-2, v. 2183.
10. Comptrollers Correspondence Series, 1874–1919, v. 168.
11. R.N.W.M.P. *Report*, 1905, III, p. 3.
12. The phrase is borrowed from M. Morgan, *One Man's Gold Rush* (Seattle, 1967), p. 162.
13. Constantine to Herchmer, 11 August 1897, RG 18, B-2, v. 2183.
14. White to Herchmer, 17 December 1897, Compt. Corr., v. 139. The estimate was not moderate; it was four times too high.
15. J. W. Dafoe, *Clifford Sifton in Relation to His Times* (Toronto, 1931), p. 151.
16. D. J. Hall, *Clifford Sifton, I: The Young Napoleon, 1861–1900* (Vancouver, 1981), p. 164. Chapter 7 of this book is an excellent account of Sifton's role in the gold rush.
17. James Morrow Walsh was born in Upper Canada in 1840. He joined the militia in 1866 and served with the Red River Expedition of 1870. He joined the N.W.M.P. on its formation in 1873. He retired in 1883 and went into business. He was appointed Commissioner of the Yukon in 1897 and resigned in 1898. He died in 1905.
18. During the "Yukon Scandals" of 1899, in which the Conservative opposition exposed irregularities in the granting of claims in the Yukon during Walsh's regime, and which Dafoe denounces as political character assassination of the worst kind, Sir Charles Hibbert Tupper obtained permission to interview Frederick White and to search the police papers for material concerning Walsh's career in the force. At the time of Walsh's retirement in 1883 there had been an investigation into the administration of his command, and in particular into the loss of some government property. The papers relating to the investigation had been destroyed in a fire at the East Block in February 1897. Tupper asserted that it was a common belief that Walsh had been forced to resign because of his mismanagement, but White denied this, and for lack of evidence to the contrary, Tupper was forced to let the matter drop. See White's memo of 22 March 1899, Compt. Corr., v. 172.
19. Another important factor in Sifton's decision to bypass Regina was the attempt of the Territorial government in that city to assert authority over the Yukon in the matter of granting liquor licenses.
20. Marginal note on letter drafted by White to Herchmer, 25 September 1897, Compt. Corr., v. 172.
21. Dafoe, *Clifford Sifton*, p. 177.
22. Ibid., p. 180.
23. *Reports from Commissioner Walsh*, Canada, Sessional Paper no. 38B, 1898, p. 29.
24. It was at this time that the two divisions were set up. Steele commanded "B"division, and was responsible for "H" division, though he did not command it directly.
25. For a modern, though uncritical biography, see Robert Stewart, *Sam Steele, Lion of the Frontier* (Toronto, 1979).
26. The police records give his birthdate as 1848; apparently he added two years to his age when he first enlisted in the militia in 1866.
27. N.W.M.P., *Report*, 1899, B, p. 53. See also A. L. Disher, "The Long March of the Yukon Field Force," *The Beaver* (Autumn 1962), pp. 4–15.
28. N.W.M.P., *Report*, 1898, III, p. 24.
29. S. B. Steele, *Forty Years*, p. 296.
30. S. B. Steele, in N.W.M.P., *Report*, 1898, p. 4.
31. Ibid.
32. Harwood Steele, *Policing the Arctic* (London, 1936), p. 22.
33. N.W.M.P., *Report*, 1898, III, p. 47. The previous customs post, opened in September 1897, was at Tagish, on the Yukon waterway.
34. Ibid. See also chapter 5, below, and Lewis Green, *The Boundary Hunters* (Vancouver, 1982), chapter 4.
35. Ibid., p. 93.
36. Ibid., p. 94.
37. The partner of the deceased was re-

quired to make the report. R.C.M.P. papers, Yukon Records, General Yukon Orders, Public Archives of Canada, RG 18, D-2, v. 12.

38. N.W.M.P. *Report*, 1897, p. 313.
39. S. B. Steele, *Forty Years*, p. 324.
40. Yukon Orders, 1898–1910, Yukon Records, v. 12.
41. Edmonton *Bulletin*, 5 August 1897.
42. D. J. Hall, *The Young Napoleon, 1861– 1900* has a good account of Sifton's role in this affair.
43. A full account of the patrol is in N.W.M.P., *Report*, 1898, II. J. D. Moodie was criticized in some quarters for having picked the wrong route, and for general incompetence. The report shows his obstacles to have been all but overwhelming.
44. Edmonton *Bulletin*, 30 August 1897.
45. J. G. MacGregor, *The Klondike Rush through Edmonton* (Toronto, 1970), p. 235.
46. Compt. Corr., v. 146. J. W. Dafoe and D. J. Hall both deal with this episode.
47. J. W. Dafoe, *Clifford Sifton*, p. 165. This casts light on Walsh's political orientation.
48. Quoted in Berton, *Fever*, p. 281.
49. This was not the first such order; a similar one had been issued early in 1898 by the Commissioner of the Yukon, requiring a year's provisions. N.W.M.P. *Report*, 1898, III, p. 21.
50. Compt. Corr., v. 159.
51. n.d., Constantine Papers, v. 3.
52. See K. S. Coates, "Best Left As Indians." Unpublished paper presented to the Canadian Historical Association, Vancouver (June 1983).
53. This occurred towards the end of 1897. N.W.M.P. *Report*, 1897, p. 307.
54. An original undated copy of this notice, signed by D. W. Davis, Collector of Customs, and T. Fawcett, Gold Commissioner, is in Constantine Papers, v. 3. Constantine did not sign the note, but his opinion of the situatiion was the same.
55. N.W.M.P., *Report*, 1897, p. 308. Rations were issued to the police in generous amounts. At Tagish in 1898 a single ration was made up of 2 oz. dried fruit, 2 oz. beans, 1¼ lbs. biscuits or flour, 1½

lbs. fresh beef or 1 lb. bacon or corned beef, ½ oz. coffee, ½ oz. tea, ½ oz. salt, 1 oz. oatmeal, 1 oz. onions, 2 oz. butter, 2 oz. potatoes, 1/36 oz. pepper, 1 oz. rice, 3 oz. sugar. Each man got 1½ rations per day, but was not permitted to sell any surplus. RG 18, D-2, v. 12.
56. The correspondence is in Constantine Papers, v. 3.
57. N.W.M.P., *Report*, 1897, p. 309.
58. "A considerable number of the people coming in from the Sound cities appear to be the sweepings of the slums and the result of a general jail delivery." Ibid.
59. N.W.M.P., *Report*, 1899, B, pp. 3–4.
60. A. N. C. Treadgold, *Report on the Gold Fields of the Klondike* (London, 1899), pp. 73–75.
61. N.W.M.P., *Report*, 1897, p. 309.
62. Z. T. Wood to Rev. John Pringle of Bonanza, 25 April 1902, R.C.M.P. Papers, Yukon Records, Dawson City Letterbooks, Public Archives of Canada, RG 18, D-1, v. 5. This was in reply to a complaint which is not extant.
63. The Territorial government in Regina successfully claimed the authority to issue licences for the Yukon and did so until the Yukon was made a separate territory. See John A. Bovey, "The Attitudes and Policies of the Federal Government towards Canada's Northern Territories, 1870–1930." M.A. thesis, University of British Columbia, 1967. See also C. E. S. Franks, "How the Sabbath Came to the Yukon," *Canadian Public Administration*, X, 1967.
64. Dawson Letterbooks, 1899–1905, Yukon Records, v. 5.
65. Zachary Taylor Wood, grandson of the American general and president and son of a Confederate naval veteran, was born in the United States in 1861. He attended Royal Military College, served in the 1885 rebellion, and joined the N.W.M.P. as an Inspector the same year. He served in the Yukon from 1897 to 1912. He was made Companion of the Order of St. Michael and St. George in 1913 and died on leave in 1915. His son, S. T. Wood, was later Commissioner of the R.C.M.P.
66. R.N.W.M.P., *Report*, 1905, III, A, p. 26.
67. Dawson Letterbooks, v. 4.

68. Letter of 27 June 1900, Department of the Interior, Northern Administration Branch Papers. Public Archives of Canada, RG 85, v. 658, f. 3418.
69. Sifton to Ogilvie, 6 January 1900, ibid.
70. Ogilvie to Sifton, 14 May 1900, ibid.
71. Sifton to Ogilvie, 14 August 1900, ibid.
72. Ogilvie to Sifton, 12 September 1900, ibid.
73. S. D. Clark, *The Developing Canadian Community* (Toronto, 1962), p. 94. See also chapter 5, below.
74. A. N. C. Treadgold, *Gold Fields of the Klondike*, p. 69. An example of the treatment given hard characters is Supt. P. C. H. Primrose's account of conditions in the Dawson jail: "some half dozen hard cases have marred an otherwise good record, but remembering the class of prisoners we have had to deal with, the scum and outlaws of the Coast cities [that phrase again!], stern discipline and heavy punishments, had the desired effect. In two cases of rank insubordination, I placed the offenders in irons ... and this degradation, coupled with five days' bread and water, regulated them to the required obedience, and had a good effect upon others." N.W.M.P., *Report*, 1899, II, B, p. 44.
75. RG 18, D-4, v. 1.
76. A. N. C. Treadgold, *Gold Fields of the Klondike*, p. 70.
77. N.W.M.P., *Report*, 1899, II, pp. 42–43.
78. Dawson Letterbooks, v. 5.

NOTES TO CHAPTER FOUR

1. N.W.M.P. *Report*, 1902, III, p. 5.
2. For an account of the growth of the Yukon bureaucracy, see David R. Morrison, *The Politics of the Yukon Territory, 1898–1909* (Toronto, 1968), chapters 2 and 3.
3. Department of the Interior to White, 28 July 1896, Comptrollers Correspondence Series 1874–1919, v. 119.
4. Letter of 13 March 1897, Compt. corr., v. 133.
5. Constantine to White, 22 June 1896, ibid.
6. White to Herchmer, 30 April 1897, ibid.

7. W. D. LeSueur of the Canadian Post Office Department to White, 11 June 1898, and Wood to Perry, 12 October 1898, Compt. Corr., v. 147.
8. White's memo of 22 November 1899, Compt. Corr., v. 158.
9. Ibid.
10. N.W.M.P., *Report*, 1899, II, A, p. 28.
11. Dawson Letterbooks, 1899–1905, Yukon Records, v. 4.
12. N.W.M.P., *Report*, 1902, III, p. 22.
13. This is well brought out in S. B. Steele, *Forty Years in Canada*, (Toronto, 1918), pp. 297–298.
14. For example, Inspector McIlree's letter to White, 27 May 1897, recommending a customs post at Lake Bennett. Compt. Corr., v. 137.
15. Steele to White, 27 April 1898, Compt. Corr., v. 145.
16. Steele to White, 30 June 1898 and 2 July 1898, ibid.
17. Z. T. Wood to White, 6 March 1899, Compt corr., v. 163.
18. Barwis to Laurier, 7 November 1899; Wood to White, 27 December 1899, Compt corr., v. 180.
19. Yukon Orders, 1898–1910, Yukon Records, v. 12.
20. Dawson Letterbooks, v. 4.
21. See D. J. Hall, *Clifford Sifton, I: The Young Napoleon* (Vancouver, 1981), pp. 164 ff. for a discussion of the government's policy on gold royalties.
22. Police estimates for 1904–05, Compt. Corr., v. 268. The figures agree with those published in the Auditor-General's reports.
23. *Report of the Auditor-General for 1898*, Canada, Sessional Paper no. 1, 1899, II, p. 2 and pp. 35–37.
24. D. R. Morrison, *Politics of the Yukon*, chapter 9. describes the later triumph of the anti-vice element in the Yukon.
25. N.W.M.P. *Report*, 1894, C, p. 70.
26. Steele to Walsh, 26 August 1898, Compt. Corr., v. 155.
27. Constantine to Herchmer, 6 December 1896, Compt. Corr., v. 140.

NOTES TO CHAPTER FIVE

1. As was mentioned earlier, the Council

of the North-West Territories had been eager to exercise its authority in the Yukon, especially in the matter of granting liquor licenses, which brought in considerable revenue.

2. See J. N. E. Brown, "The Evolution of Law and Government in the Yukon Territory," in S. M. Wickett, ed., *Municipal Government in Canada* (Toronto, 1907), p. 200, for a discussion of this question.

3. Z. T. Wood to J. H. Ross, 15 April 1901, requesting a bylaw to prevent the riding of bicycles on sidewalks. Dawson Letterbooks, 1899–1905, Yukon Records, v. 4.

4. Wood to officer commanding "B" Division, 16 November 1901, regarding prostitutes disguising their premises as cigar stores. Ibid.

5. Herchmer to White, 26 January 1898, Comptrollers Correspondence Series, 1874–1919, v. 152.

6. White to F. C. Wade, n.d. F. C. Wade Papers, Public Archives of Canada, MG 30, E-13, v. 1.

7. Perry to White, 8 January 1898, Compt. Corr., v. 145. See also Lewis Green, *The Boundary Hunters* (Vancouver, 1982), chapter 4.

8. White to Perry, 15 January 1898, ibid. A rather different interpretation is given by H. G. Classen in *Thrust and Counterthrust*, (Chicago, 1965), in which he has the initiative coming from Steele. The letters exist, however, to show that it came from Ottawa.

9. Ibid.

10. H. G. Classen, *Thrust and Counterthrust* (Chicago, 1965), describes the skirmishing, most of it having to do with the transit of goods across U.S. territory.

11. Wood to White, 15 October 1901, Dawson Letterbooks, v. 4.

12. Wood to White, 25 January 1902, ibid.

13. Wood to Perry, 4 February 1899, Compt. Corr., v. 162.

14. The relevant letters, from Woods' first report to White of 15 August 1899, to White's final instructions to Wood of 25 November 1899, are in Compt. Corr., v. 179.

15. N.W.M.P., *Report*, 1898, III, p. 48, and Compt. Corr., v. 146.

16. N.W.M.P., *Report*, 1897, LL, p. 307.

17. Morris Zaslow, "The Yukon: Northern Development in a Canadian-American Context." In Mason Wade, ed., *Regionalism in the Canadian Community, 1867–1967* (Toronto, 1969), p. 188.

18. Each issue was four pages long and cost fifty cents.

19. 30 August 1898.

20. 16, 20, and 23 July 1898.

21. Canada, House of Commons, *Debates*, 27 June 1899, p. 5962.

22. R. C. Macleod, "The North-West Mounted Police, 1873–1905: Law Enforcement and the Social Order in the Canadian North-West." Unpublished Ph.D. thesis, Duke University, 1971, p. 152. There are no figures for those who came directly from Britain to join the force; presumably many were already in Canada when they enlisted. This percentage dropped sharply on the outbreak of the Boer War; for 1900–1902 it was only sixteen percent.

23. Hal Guest, "A History of the City of Dawson," chapter 4.

24. Yukon Orders, 1898–1910, Yukon Records, v. 12.

25. General Yukon Order 2048, 30 May 1903, and Yukon Order 225, 22 April 1899. Copies kindly furnished by S. W. Horrall, R.C.M.P. Headquarters, Ottawa.

26. Dawson Letterbooks, v. 7.

27. See RG 18, D-2, v. 6, General Yukon Order 544 and 556 for examples. After several cases of this sort the chair used by the guards was removed from the corridor, forcing them to stand.

28. General Yukon Order 1228, ibid.

29. General Yukon Order 1234, ibid.

30. General Yukon Order 880, ibid.

31. General Yukon Order 3635, RG 18, D-2, v. 11.

32. General Yukon Order 963, RG 18, D-2, v. 6.

33. Ibid.

34. N.W.M.P., *Report*, 1902, III, B, p. 79.

35. N.W.M.P., *Report*, 1901, III, D, p. 62.

36. Pierre Berton, *Klondike Fever* (New York, 1958), p. 322.

37. The relevant papers are in Compt. Corr., v. 179. Hal Guest, "A History of the City of Dawson," cites other exam-

ples of Harper's misconduct.

38. R. Stewart, *Sam Steele: Lion of the Frontier* (Toronto, 1979), p. 233.
39. Hal Guest, "A History of the City of Dawson," concludes that "most of the policemen ... were upright and honest."
40. S. D. Clark, *The Developing Canadian Community* (Toronto, 1962), pp. 97–98.
41. Ibid., p. 82.
42. R.N.W.M.P., *Report,* 1905, III, p. 5.
43. In 1905 seven permanent posts were abandoned: Halfway, Selwyn, White Pass Summit, Pleasant Camp, Kynocks, Montague, and Yukon Crossing. Ibid., p. 8.
44. Ibid., pp. 9–10.
45. Ibid., p. 3.

NOTES TO CHAPTER SIX

1. V. K. Johnston, "Canada's Title to the Arctic Islands," *Canadian Historical Review* 14 (March 1933): 29–30.
2. Diamond Jenness, *Eskimo Administration: II, Canada* (Montreal, 1964), pp. 16–17.
3. Ibid., p. 16.
4. The best history of Herschel Island is Richard Stuart, "Herschel Island Resource Assessment," agenda paper for the Historic Sites and Monuments Board of Canada, n.d. It is unfortunately unpublished.
5. G. W. Porter, George B. Leavitt, J. A. Tilton, and J. A. Wing.
6. John R. Bockstoce, *Steam Whaling in the Western Arctic* (New Bedford, 1977), p. 40, quoted in Thomas Stone, "Whalers and Missionaries at Herschel Island," *Ethnohistory,* vol. 28, no. 2, 1981, pp. 102–103.
7. R.N.W.M.P., *Report,* 1908, K, p. 140.
8. Jenness, *Eskimo Administration,* p. 14.
9. T. C. B. Boon, *The Anglican Church from the Bay to the Rockies* (Toronto, 1962), p. 232.
10. Constantine to Herchmer, 4 September 1895, Comptrollers Correspondence Series, 1874–1919, v. 135. The man is not named.
11. R. C. MacLeod makes this point in *The NWMP and Law Enforcement, 1873–1905* (Toronto, 1976), chapter 5.

12. N.W.M.P., *Report,* 1896, p. 238.
13. Insp. D. M. Howard, ? August 1906, Compt. Corr., v. 309.
14. White to A. E. Forget, Lieutenant-Governor of the North-West Territories, 7 October 1903, Comptrollers Letterbooks, 1883–1919, p. 90.
15. 18 June 1896, Compt. Corr., v. 314.
16. Memo of 19 October 1896, ibid.
17. R. W. Scott to Bompas, 2 October 1896, ibid.
18. White to Supt. A. H. Griesbach, 8 May 1900, ibid.
19. Under the Treaty of Washington, 1871, Canada had transit rights to these two rivers.
20. White to Sifton, 23 January 1901, Compt. Corr., v. 314.
21. For the early history of the area, see Ethel G. Stewart, "Fort McPherson and the Peel River Area" (M.A. thesis, Queen's University, 1953).
22. White to Sifton, 23 January 1901, Compt. Corr., v. 314.
23. Ibid.
24. Only the police were concerned with the Mackenzie Delta expedition, but the two were planned at the same time. J. A. Smart, Deputy Minister of the Interior, to Sifton, 21 March 1903, Northwest Territories Correspondence, Department of the Interior Papers, Public Archives of Canada, RG 15, B-1a, v. 232.
25. J. A. Smart, memo, n.d. (probably summer 1903), Compt. Corr., v. 293.
26. Constantine's report of the expedition was printed in N.W.M.P. *Report,* 1903, I, D.
27. N.W.M.P., *Report,* 1903, C, p. 32.
28. Constantine Papers, v. 4.
29. See Gabriel Breynat, *Cinquante Ans au Pays des Neiges,* 3 vols. (Montreal, 1945–48), 2: 182–85. No date is given for the incident; it probably occurred around 1910. Breynat was certainly a conservative. Some years later, writing about the work of the police in the Northwest Territories, he expressed his view of the role they should play in controlling the Natives: "I completely agree with you about the good work done by the R.C.M. Police.... They should be empowered with the means to prevent,

among the native population, the teaching by the whites and [the] practice of gambling, brewing, birth control, bolchevism, etc." Letter of 27 January 1923 to Col. J. K. Cornwall, President of the Northern Trading Co., Edmonton. In J. D. Craig Papers, Public Archives of Canada, RG 85, v. 582, f. 567. One wonders who was preaching communism in the Mackenzie Valley in 1923.

30. White to Perry, 6 June 1904, Compt. Lbks., v. 91.
31. 6 August 1904, Compt. Corr., v. 293.
32. N.W.M.P., *Report*, 1903, I, D, p. 46.
33. White to J. J. Thomas, Guelph, Ont., 23 July 1903, Compt. Corr., v. 89.
34. Compt. Corr., v. 452.
35. Constantine to F. J. Fitzgerald, 18 June 1903, Constantine Papers, v. 3.
36. See N.W.M.P., *Report*, 1903, I, C, p. 32, and I, D, p. 53. The reports of Constantine and Fitzgerald differ in detail concerning Herschel Island, Fitzgerald's is the more reliable account, since Constantine got his information at second hand.
37. R.N.W.M.P., *Report*, 1905, I, L, p. 126.
38. In 1908 three deserters from the *Karluk* were brought back to their ship by the police. R.N.W.M.P., *Report*, 1908, L, p. 148.
39. R.N.W.M.P., *Report*, 1905, I, L, p. 129.
40. T. Stone, "Atomistic Order and Frontier Violence: Miners and Whalemen in the Nineteenth Century Yukon," *Ethnology*, vol. 22 (October 1983), p. 334.
41. Ibid. Fitzgerald himself later formed a liaison with an Inuit woman. See chapter 11.
42. N.W.M.P., *Report*, 1903, I, D, p. 49.
43. Ibid., p. 53.
44. Maurice Metayer, trans., *I, Nuligak* (Toronto, 1966), p. 29.
45. Ibid., pp. 31–33.
46. Ibid., p. 135.

NOTES TO CHAPTER SEVEN

1. See the *Dictionary of Canadian Biography*, 1: 374, for a short account of the early history of the bay.
2. D. Jenness, *Eskimo Administration: II.*

Canada (Montreal, 1964), pp. 11–12. A popular account of whaling in the area is R. A. Stackpole, *American Whaling in Hudson Bay, 1861–1919* (Mystic, Conn., 1969). A more scholarly treatment is W. Gillies Ross, *Whaling and Eskimos: Hudson Bay 1860–1915* (Ottawa, 1975).
3. Jenness, *Eskimo Administration*, p. 19.
4. A good account of the expedition from the government's point of view is A. P. Low, *Cruise of the Neptune* (Ottawa, 1906). There had been four previous expeditions to Hudson Bay, mainly exploratory, in 1884, 1885, 1886, and 1897.
5. J. A. Smart to White, 4 December 1902, Comptrollers Correspondence Series, 1874–1919, v. 314.
6. White to J. A. Smart, 16 July 1903, Compt. Corr., v. 293.
7. White to A. B. Perry, 23 July 1903, ibid.
8. White to Perry, 11 August 1903, ibid.
9. Ibid.
10. Ibid.
11. White to J. A. Smart, 16 July 1903, Compt. Corr., v. 293.
12. J. A. Smart, memo, n.d., ibid.
13. Ibid.
14. 31 October 1903.
15. Ibid.
16. Ottawa *Evening Journal*, 19 October 1903.
17. He must have had a good constitution, since he lived to be 99.
18. 5 October 1903.
19. Unsigned memo, 5 August 1903, Compt. Corr., v. 293.
20. Ibid.
21. A. P. Low, *Cruise*, p. 3.
22. Ibid., p. 7. Port Burwell would be to the eastern Arctic what Herschel Island was to the western. An R.C.M.P. detachment was established there, but not until 1920.
23. Moodie to White, 9 December 1903, Compt. Corr., v. 281. At one point the doctor set fire to his cabin in order to sterilize it.
24. Moodie to White, 6 September 1903, Compt. Corr., v. 293.
25. Moodie to White, 9 December 1903, Compt. Corr., v. 281.
26. Ibid.

27. R.N.W.M.P., *Report,* 1904, IV, p. 5.
28. White to Laurier, 8 August 1904, Compt. Corr., v. 293.
29. R.N.W.M.P., *Report,* 1904, IV, p. 5.
30. For a different aspect of Moodie's relations with the Inuit, see chapter 11.
31. Compt. Corr., v. 281.
32. R.N.W.M.P., *Report,* 1904, IV, p. 12.
33. Ibid.
34. Ibid. The *Era,* commanded by captain George Comer, was the only ship in Moodie's immediate vicinity. Comer, a man of considerable intellectual curiosity and an amateur ethnographer, kept a diary during this period, which has been published by W. G. Ross as *An Arctic Whaling Diary: The Journal of Captain George Comer in Hudson Bay, 1903–1905* (Toronto, 1984).
35. Ibid., p. 113.
36. Ibid.
37. Ibid., p. 11.
38. R.N.W.M.P., *Report,* 1904, IV, p. 5.
39. Ibid.
40. R.N.W.M.P., *Report,* 1904, IV, p. 8; also Compt. Corr., v. 281.
41. Toronto *Mail and Empire,* 27 August 1904. This was a Conservative newspaper, sniffing for scandal.
42. Moodie to White, 30 August 1904, Compt. Corr., v. 280.
43. White to Perry, 6 July 1904, Compt Corr., v. 293.
44. White to Perry, 18 June 1904, ibid.
45. J. E. Bernier, *Master Mariner and Arctic Explorer* (Ottawa, 1939), p. 305. This would refer to Captain Comer and the *Era,* and was, if true, only a small part of the object of the trip.
46. Montreal *Star,* 10 October 1905. Moodie, like Sam Steele, could be overbearing at times. Comer came to dislike Moodie so much that he became physically ill on two occasions when dealing with him. Comer told Dr. L. E. Borden that he bore "a fearful enmity for the Major" and would "get even if ever the opportunity offers itself." Quoted in W. G. Ross, *The Journal of Captain George Comer,* p. 106.
47. Ibid. The legality of Moodie's actions was doubtful.
48. Pelletier to Laurier, 27 January 1905, Compt. Corr., v. 298.
49. Laurier to White, 20 April 1905, ibid.
50. Moodie to White, 22 September 1905, ibid. But Moodie was a prickly man, and it is hard to know what he considered a "large scale."
51. White to Moodie, 2 May 1905, ibid.
52. White, memo, 1 August 1904, Compt. Corr., v. 293.
53. The convention of 1818 had barred Americans from the "inshore fisheries" of British North America. This prohibition had been withdrawn by the Reciprocity Treaty of 1854 and again by the Treaty of Washington in 1871. The United States terminated the fisheries clause of this latter treaty in 1885, so in 1904 it was open to the Canadian government to ban Americans from fishing in Hudson Bay, which it considered to be its territorial waters.
54. F. Gourdeau to Moodie, 18 September 1904, Compt. Corr., v. 293.
55. Moodie to White, 10 September 1904, ibid.
56. "Notice to all Masters of Whalers, Agents of Stations, and all whom it may concern," 19 July 1904, Compt. Corr., v. 408.
57. Moodie to White, 10 September 1904, Compt. Corr., v. 293.
58. F. Gourdeau to White, 18 July 1906, Compt. Corr., v. 408. The *Arctic* went north again in 1906, and cairns were set up in several places in the eastern Arctic, including Cape Herschel on Ellesmere Island, which had been the location of Sverdrup's base camp. In each cairn were deposited notices stating that the Mounted Police were stationed at Fullerton to enforce the law, especially the customs law. See J. E. Bernier, *Cruise of the "Arctic", 1906–7* (Ottawa, 1909), p. 14.
59. White, memo, 1 August 1904, Compt. Corr., v. 293.
60. Ibid.
61. Moodie to White, 25 January 1905, Compt. Corr., v. 319.
62. White to Moodie, 9 September 1904, Compt. Corr., v. 293.
63. Moodie, report for 17 September 1904 to 31 December 1904, Compt. Corr., v. 319.
64. R.N.W.M.P., *Report,* 1905, IV, p. 10.

65. Ibid.

66. White to Clifford Sifton, 11 August 1903, Compt. Corr., v. 314.

67. White to H. S. Blake, 23 July 1907, Comptrollers Letterbooks, 1883-1919, v. 138.

NOTES TO CHAPTER EIGHT

1. Fort McPherson and Herschel Island, the two detachments of the Fort McPherson Sub-district, were part of "N" Division (northern Alberta), with headquarters at Athabaska.

2. Information on the location and strength of all detachments was printed in the annual reports of the police.

3. Perry, R.N.W.M.P., *Report*, 1911, p. 25.

4. Insp. D. M. Howard's report, 30 August 1906, Comptrollers Correspondence Series, 1874–1919, v. 309.

5. Ibid.

6. S/Sgt. F. J. Fitzgerald's report, 30 November 1906, Compt. Corr., v. 353.

7. Insp. Howard's report, 17 May 1906, Compt. Corr., v. 309.

8. Compt. Corr., v. 353.

9. S/Sgt. Fitzgerald's report, 30 November 1906, ibid.

10. Fitzgerald reported on the situation in detail on 30 November 1906, Compt. Corr., v. 353.

11. Insp. D. M. Howard, ibid.

12. Insp. Howard's report, 18 January 1907, Compt. Corr., v. 353.

13. Insp. Howard's report, 28 August 1906, ibid.

14. For the best modern biography of this controversial man, see R. J. Diubaldo, *Stefansson and the Canadian Arctic* (Montreal, 1978).

15. D. M. Le Bourdais, *Stefansson, Ambassador of the North* (Montreal, 1963), p. 10.

16. Inuit starved on occasion before the arrival of whites. Stefansson says little about this.

17. V. Stefansson, *My Life with the Eskimo* (New York, 1913), pp. 40–41.

18. Ibid., p. 41.

19. Ibid.

20. Ibid., p. 42.

21. Ibid., p. 21.

22. A. M. Jarvis to Perry, 4 August 1907, Compt. Corr., v. 353.

23. S/Sgt. Fitzgerald's report, 4 December 1908, Compt. Corr., v. 372.

24. Perry to Jarvis, 7 May 1907, Compt. Corr., v. 353.

25. Ibid.

26. Constantine had recommended in 1903 that a stipendiary magistrate be sent to the region; he would have had the authority to try serious cases. This was not done.

27. The correspondence relating to the case is in Compt. Corr., v. 336.

28. *Discovery* (New York, 1964), p. 73.

29. The story is told in Stefansson, ibid.

30. Jarvis to Perry, 24 August 1907, Compt. Corr., v. 353. There is a copying error here; Jarvis must have meant 116.30 W., which would have put him off the Prince Albert peninsula of Victoria Island.

31. Perry to Jarvis, 28 January 1908, Compt. Corr., v. 353. Later in 1907 Klengenberg was tried in San Francisco (the *Olga* carried U.S. registry) and acquitted.

32. Insp. Howard's report, 16 July 1907, Compt. Corr., v. 353.

33. R.N.W.M.P., *Report*, 1907, K, p. 114.

34. Ibid.

35. P. G. Keyes, Secretary, Department of the Interior, to White, 30 June 1908, Compt. Corr., v. 372.

36. R.N.W.M.P., *Report*, 1907, K, p. 112.

37. Ibid., pp. 112–13.

38. Ibid.

39. Ibid.

40. Correspondence on the subject between Perry and C. C. Chipman, Commissioner of the Hudson's Bay Company, is in Compt. Corr., v. 372.

41. Compt. Corr., v. 353.

42. S/Sgt. Fitzgerald's report, 16 May 1909, Compt. Corr., v. 372.

43. Ibid.

44. R.N.W.M.P. *Report*, 1907, p. 11.

45. S/Sgt. Fitzgerald's report, 10 February 1909, Compt. Corr., v. 372.

46. Insp. G. L. Jennings' report, 16 February 1910, Compt. Corr., v. 383.

47. Insp. Jennings' report, 15 July 1910, ibid.

48. Insp. Jennings' report, 16 Feburary 1910, ibid.

49. Prescribed by the 1906 amendments to the Fisheries Act.

50. This was not the case in Hudson Bay, the whole of which Canada claimed as territorial waters; there, licences were required no matter how far from shore the fishing was done.
51. Correspondence on this matter between White and R. N. Venning, Superintendent of Fisheries, from 18 December 1909 to 1 February 1910, is in Compt. Corr., v. 384.
52. Insp. Jennings' report, 16 February 1910, Compt. Corr., v. 383.
53. R.N.W.M.P., *Report,* 1910, N, p. 170.
54. Ibid.
55. Sgt. E. A. Selig's report, 31 January 1909, Compt. Corr., v. 372.
56. R.N.W.M.P., *Report,* 1910, O, p. 184.
57. Ibid., p. 24.
58. Insp. Jennings' report, 16 February 1910, Compt. Corr., v. 383.
59. Reports of 16 February 1910 and 7 August 1909, Compt. Corr., v. 383; and R.N.W.M.P., *Report,* 1911, O, p. 165.
60. Insp. Jennings' report, 16 February 1910, Compt. Corr., v. 383.
61. Compt. Corr., v. 421.
62. Cpl. Somers' report, 7 July 1911, R.N.W.M.P. *Report,* 1911, O, p. 165.

NOTES TO CHAPTER NINE

1. A good short discussion of the issue is A. M. Pratt and J. H. Archer, *The Hudson's Bay Route* (Governments of Manitoba and Saskatchewan, 1953).
2. Ibid., p. 49.
3. Later the terminus was shifted to Port Nelson, and later still it was moved back to Churchill.
4. White to Oliver, 25 February 1907, Comptrollers Correspondence Series, 1874–1919, v. 330.
5. The specifications of the *Rouville* and reports on its trials are in ibid. This incident does not speak well for the administrative competence of the Laurier government. Patronage was doubtless involved in the ship's construction.
6. R.N.W.M.P. *Report,* 1907, p. 10.
7. Ibid. Mafeking is a town on the C.N.R. about fifty miles north of Swan River, Manitoba. In 1907 it was the closest point by rail to Churchill.
8. Supt. Moodie's report, 1 January 1907,

Compt. Corr., v. 334.
9. Ibid.
10. White to Moodie, 15 April 1907, ibid.
11. Perry to White, 19 May 1908, Compt. Corr., v. 357; and 23 March 1909, Compt. Corr., v. 371.
12. R.N.W.M.P., *Report,* 1909, pp. 22–23.
13. Ibid., pp. 22 ff. Compt. Corr., v. 364 contains the private correspondence pertaining to this patrol.
14. An excellent survey of all the fur trading posts in the area is T. Smythe, "Thematic Study of the Fur Trade in the Canadian West, 1670–1870," an unpublished Staff Report for the National Historic Sites Service (Ottawa, 1968).
15. It should be noted, however, that relations between the police and C. C. Chipman, commissioner of the company in Winnipeg during this period, were extremely cordial.
16. Moodie's report, 28 February 1908, Compt. Corr., v. 354. This was an unusual event. The clerk must have been uncommonly stupid or rude.
17. Perry to D. C. McTavish, 6 May 1908, Compt. Corr., v. 359.
18. In the summer of 1906, Moodie had on his own authority ordered five hundred tons of coal and lumber landed at Fullerton for the use of the detachment of Baker Lake which he advised the police administration year after year to open. It was not opened, and the detachment at Fullerton found itself with a huge oversupply of both items. Churchill needed both, but transportation was so chancy that there was no way to bring it from one post to the other. The coal and lumber stayed for years at Fullerton, unused. Such were the vicissitudes of supplying the Hudson Bay detachments. See Moodie's report, 31 December 1907, Compt. Corr., v. 354.
19. Perry to White, 23 March 1909, Compt. Corr., v. 371.
20. Moodie's report, 31 October 1909, Compt. Corr., v. 365.
21. Cpl. Joyce's report, 1 July 1909, ibid. Moodie wrote in the margin opposite this paragraph "Already reported more than once."
22. Moodie's report, 31 October 1909, R.N.W.M.P., *Report,* 1910, III, A, p. 7.

23. Cpl. Joyce's report, 9 July 1910, Compt. Corr., v. 385.
24. Ibid.
25. Cpl. Joyce's report, 1 July 1909, Compt. Corr., v. 365.
26. G. Comer to White, 25 April 1910, Compt. Corr., v. 390.
27. Comer to White, n.d., ibid.
28. The police in turn reciprocated by taking mail to Comer from his wife when he was wintering in the bay. White wrote Mrs. Comer on one occasion, "Please do not put any valuables— beyond love messages in the letters as I could not guarantee their delivery." In the papers relating to his thirty-seven years' service with the police, this was his sole attempt at humour. Compt. Corr., v. 411.
29. Cortlandt Starnes replaced Moodie in command of "M" Division in November 1909, and later succeeded Perry as Commissioner.
30. Comer to Starnes, 12 January 1912, Compt. Corr., v. 424.
31. D. C. McTavish, in charge of the store at Churchill, to Perry, 29 March 1908, Compt. Corr., v. 359.
32. Moodie to Perry, 29 July 1909, ibid.
33. White to H. S. Blake, K.C., 20 July 1907, Comptrollers Letterbooks, 1883 – 1919, v. 138.
34. Compt. Corr., v. 354.
35. Ibid.
36. Moodie's report, 31 October 1909, R.N.W.M.P. Report, 1910, A, p. 247.
37. R.N.W.M.P. Report, 1910, p. 23.
38. White, memo, 26 February 1910, Compt. Corr., v. 400.
39. White to Perry, 25 May 1910, Compt. Corr., v. 400.
40. The wreck occurred on 9 September 1910, and the crew reached civilization at Gimli on 15 January 1911. See R.N.W.M.P. Report, 1911, p. 27; also White to Bartlett, 16 January 1911, Compt. Corr., v. 400. Bartlett did not go north with his ship.
41. Sgt. A. F. Borden's report, 13 March 1911, Compt. Corr., v. 402. Note that the police were by this time using igloos while on patrol.
42. R. Ferries, Anglican missionary at York Factory, to Starnes, 1 February 1911, Compt. Corr., v. 410. It will be apparent by now that ideas as to what constituted "indiscriminate use of liquor" varied widely. Some missionaries saw debauchery in every drop.
43. Cpl. R. H. Walker's report, 15 February 1911, Compt. Corr., v. 402.
44. Sgt. C. N. C. Hayter's report, 31 August 1911, ibid. Presumably the seizure was made on White's authority as Commissioner of the Northwest Territories.
45. White to H. Hall, Fur Trade Commissioner at Winnipeg, 21 April 1911, Compt. Corr., v. 410.
46. Supt. F. J. A. Demers' report, 19 September 1913, Compt. Corr., v. 438.
47. The complement of police at Port Nelson in 1913 was originally two, increased to eleven in 1914.
48. Sgt. R. H. Walker's report, 29 December 1913, Compt. Corr., v. 462.
49. The police did not become involved in the strike itself. An account of the incident is in Compt. Corr., v. 470.
50. Sgt. Walker's report, 13 February 1914, Compt. Corr., v. 462.
51. Perry, in R.N.W.M.P., Report, 1913, p. 39.
52. Commissioners Files, 1897–1919, v. 60, and Compt. Corr., v. 464. The building at Baker Lake was in connection with the patrol to that region which will be dealt with in the next chapter.
53. Supt. D. M. Howard's report, 4 December 1914, Compt. Corr., v. 480.
54. Pratt and Archer, The Hudson's Bay Route, p. 56.
55. Comm. Files, v. 61.
56. Supt. Demers' report, 17 February 1913, Compt. Corr., v. 438.
57. Sgt. W. G. Edgenton's report, 31 October 1913, Compt. Corr., v. 462. In 1919 the Hudson's Bay Company bought this post and closed it.
58. R.N.W.M.P., Report, 1911, IV, C, p. 264.
59. Sgt. Edgenton's report, 31 October 1913, Compt. Corr., v. 462.
60. Compt. Corr., v. 547.
61. R.N.W.M.P., Report, 1918, p. 15.

NOTES TO CHAPTER TEN

1. An annual winter patrol was made, be-

ginning just before the turn of the century, from what is now northern Alberta into the Northwest Territories, to see that the law regarding the killing of buffalo was obeyed. The patrol for 1899 is described in N.W.M.P. *Report*, 1899, pp. 1–2.

2. See chapter 13.

3. See Dick North, *The Lost Patrol* (Anchorage, Alaska, 1978) for a recent account of the patrol.

4. The ex-constable's name was Carter; he had taken his discharge, married an Inuit woman, and settled at Fort McPherson. It was the first properly conducted white-Inuit marriage in the area. Inspector Fitzgerald also had a Native wife, "after the custom of the country," but despite the urgings of the local Anglican missionary, had not legally married her.

5. R.N.W.M.P., *Report*, 1911, V; also Comptrollers Correspondence Series, 1874–1919, v. 440.

6. A. B. Perry to White, 18 April 1911, Compt. Corr., v. 440.

7. Copy of a letter from C. E. Whittaker to Bishop I. O. Stringer at Dawson, 24 March 1911, ibid.

8. Edmonton *Bulletin*, 24 April 1911.

9. Supt. Cuthbert to Perry, 1 May 1911, Compt. Corr., v. 446.

10. Ibid.

11. R.N.W.M.P., *Report*, 1911, p. 26.

12. Ibid., V, p. 310.

13. R.N.W.M.P., *Report*, 1912, K, p. 1; also Compt. Corr., v. 447. These were similar to the huts put up north of Churchill along the coast of Hudson Bay.

14. See chapter 8.

15. Stefansson, *My Life With the Eskimo* (New York, 1913), p. 339.

16. Ibid., p. 340.

17. Ironically, the record sought by F. J. Fitzgerald was set by the rescue patrol, which under Cpl. W. J. D. Dempster went from Dawson to Fort McPherson and back in forty-two days, including a stopover. Perry to White, 18 April 1911, Compt. Corr., v. 440.

18. Some special patrols of the 1920s which were made for purposes of sovereignty are discussed in chapter 12.

19. There is a record from that year of him presenting his credentials to the police at Fort Chipewyan. Compt. Corr., v. 383.

20. Commissioners Files, 1897–1919, v. 60. On his first trip to the north, Radford had made himself so unpopular with the crew of the boat carrying him down the Athabasca that they played a practical joke on him. Radford, who was keen on collecting trophies, was called on deck to shoot a bear which had been discovered on shore. He fired numerous shots at it, only to discover that the "bear" was a log, dressed in an old fur coat. He took the joke badly. Ibid.

21. H. H. Hall to G. R. Ray, Hudson's Bay Company man in charge of the Nelson River District, 11 June 1913, Compt. Corr., v. 556; also Comm. Files, v. 60.

22. Edmonton *Journal* (Conservative), 15 December 1913.

23. Edmonton *Bulletin* (Liberal), 15 December 1913.

24. Perry, in R.N.W.M.P., *Report*, 1914, p. 23.

25. It was reported at great length in the annual reports of the police during the years it was being carried out.

26. Const. Kennedy's report, 1 August 1916, Comm. Files, v. 58.

27. This must refer to the party headed by J. W. Tyrrell, which explored the country between Great Slave Lake and Hudson Bay for the Topographical Surveys Branch of the Department of the Interior in 1900. Compt. Corr., v. 556.

28. Insp. French's report, 27 March 1918, Compt. Corr., v. 557.

29. Borden to Lawrence Fortescue, 5 May 1914, Compt. Corr., v. 557. Fortescue joined the N.W.M.P. on its formation in 1873, was commissioned in 1875, and tranferred to the "inside service" in 1879. He became chief clerk in 1892 and succeeded Fred White as comptroller in 1913. He retired in 1918.

30. Supt. D. M. Howard, commenting on a copy of a letter from Radford to S. A. Ford, Hudson's Bay Company officer at Chesterfield Inlet, n.d., in which Radford described his method of dealing with Inuit: "However, his [an Inuit's] 'butting in' aggravated me considerable [sic], and I was tempted to hand

him a little chastisement. Street and I, finding that his influence is being used against us decided to give him some mild punishment, and since then he has been excluded from our igloo." Compt. Corr., v. 556.

31. Perry to Fortescue, 28 November 1916, Compt. Corr., v. 550.

32. Compt. Corr., v. 579.

33. Statement of Sinnisiak, 17 May 1916, ibid. There is a long series of reports on the case in R.N.W.M.P., *Report*, 1916, appendices O to W. See also R. G. Moyles, *British Law and Arctic Men* (Saskatoon, 1979), for an account of the case.

34. Perry to La Nauze, 10 May 1915, Comm. Files, v. 58.

35. These figures are for the outward trip only; by the time the men reached Baker Lake again they had covered 5,153 miles. For a popular account of the patrol see I. S. Anderson, "Bathurst Inlet Patrol," *The Beaver* (Spring 1972).

36. On the return journey, early in January 1918, they experienced temperatures of −72 degrees F. south of Aberdeen Lake.

37. The reports from Insp. French's patrol were printed in R.N.W.M.P., *Report*, 1918, A. A shortened version of the main report, illustrating the points made in this chapter, appears in appendix A of this book.

NOTES TO CHAPTER ELEVEN

1. D. Jenness, *Eskimo Administration: II. Canada* (Montreal, 1964), p. 20.

2. The word "Natives" is used simply as a collective noun for Indians and Inuit when the two are considered together; it also allows, in some areas, for a certain admixture of white blood.

3. Jenness, *Eskimo Administration: II. Canada*, p. 21.

4. Ibid., p. 23.

5. See his book *The Desperate People* (Boston, 1959) for an angry but not unreasonable history of the Inuit of the central Barrens.

6. Ibid., p. 108.

7. R. A. Davies, *The Great Mackenzie* (To-ronto, 1947), p. 96. Davies writes from a Marxist point of view, and could not be expected to think well of the police. Exactly what "stimuli" were suppressed he does not say.

8. The Fort McPherson Indians were Hare, Kutchin, and Dogrib. Those at the Hudson Bay posts were mostly Cree, with some Chipewyan.

9. Cpl. Haylow's report, 31 December 1906, Comptrollers Correspondence Series, 1874–1919, v. 353.

10. Insp. Pelletier's report, 22 March 1907, Compt. Corr., v. 327.

11. Ibid.

12. R.N.W.M.P., *Report*, 1907, K, p. 115.

13. Supt. Moodie's report, 31 December 1907, Compt. Corr., v. 354. It is difficult to say why the company capitulated, since Moodie's threat was pure bluff; what he proposed was strictly against police regulations.

14. Insp. A. M. Jarvis' report, Fort McPherson, 12 February 1908, Compt. Corr., v. 353.

15. A. W. Patterson to Rev. R. Faries, 25 March 1915, Commissioners Files, 1897–1919, v. 58. Faries wrote a highly indignant reply, condemning the company for deserting the "people who have been the BACKBONE of a profitable business."

16. Supt. A. McDonnell's report, 1 October 1915, R.N.W.M.P., *Report*, 1915, G, p. 146.

17. Ibid.

18. Insp. G. L. Jennings' report, 1 August 1909, Compt. Corr., v. 383. A treaty was signed in 1921.

19. Supt. Starnes' report, 8 August 1911, R.N.W.M.P., *Report*, 1911, IV, A, pp. 251–52.

20. Supt. D. M. Howard's report, 8 December 1915, Compt. Corr., v. 506.

21. Acting Assistant Surgeon P. E. Doyle's report, 12 January 1915, Compt. Corr., v. 480.

22. Supt. Howard's report, 8 December 1915, Compt. Corr., v. 506.

23. Insp. W. J. Beyts' report, 2 January 1918, Compt. Corr., v. 527.

24. Chief Charles Dastercoot to the Deputy Minister of Indian Affairs, 29 December 1915, Comm. Files, v. 58.

25. Supt. Starnes' report, 4 December 1911, Compt. Corr., v. 402.
26. The name may have come from the fact that the police had a lock-up at Churchill. The government had sent up a steel cage, like a monkey cage in a zoo, for use as a cell.
27. Ibid.
28. Insp. Beyts' report, 2 January 1918, Compt. Corr., v. 527.
29. Supt. Howard's report, Port Nelson, 4 December 1914, Compt. Corr., v. 480.
30. Compt. Corr., v. 413; also R.N.W.M.P., Report, 1913, A, p. 315.
31. Correspondence relating to this case is in Compt. Corr., v. 455.
32. White to Laurier, 29 June 1906, Compt. Corr., v. 320.
33. Quoted in W. G. Ross, ed. An Arctic Whaling Diary: The Journal of Captain George Comer in Hudson Bay, 1903–1905 (Toronto, 1984), p. 152.
34. C. E. Whittaker, "Memoranda" (July 1907), Archives of the Ecclesiastical Province of Rupertsland, Public Archives of Manitoba, MG 7, A-1, box N, #4003. The daughter, Annie, did not come to the official attention of the police until 1926, when at the age of seventeen or eighteen she was a student at the Hay River Residential School. The principal, Rev. J. A. Vale, tried to get the government to assume responsibility for her. She was in a "pitiable" condition—a hunchback—but because she was over sixteen years of age special dispensation was required to enable her to continue at the school. The Commissioner of the R.C.M.P., while expressing concern (and surprise), declined to provide funding for her. Eventually the Northern Administration Branch provided an annual grant of $145 for three years to enable her to continue at school until she could get a job as a "helper in the home of some . . . Government official." PAC, RG 85, v. 772, f. 5450. Annie died soon after at the age of 18. See Dick North, The Lost Patrol (Anchorage, Alaska, 1978).
35. Cpl. J. Somers' report, Fort McPherson, 7 July 1911, Compt. Corr., v. 411.
36. Ibid. It might be mentioned here that Stefansson harshly condemned the missionaries for teaching cleanliness to the Mackenzie Inuit. Apparently the Inuit believed that washing one's face was an essential of Christianity; they therefore did so frequently, but never changed the water or the towel. The result was that disease spread faster than when they never washed at all. See My Life With the Eskimo (New York, 1913), p. 374.
37. Insp. Fitzgerald's report, 14 December 1910, Compt. Corr., v. 383.
38. Insp. Jennings' report, 16 February 1910, R.N.W.M.P., Report, 1910, K, p. 152.
39. Moodie to White, 8 December 1903, Compt. Corr., v. 281.
40. Insp. Jarvis' report, 12 February 1908, Compt. Corr., v. 353.
41. On the other hand, the Indians who carried goods over the Yukon passes were certainly shrewd businessmen, as were Pacific coast Indians generally.
42. R.N.W.M.P., Report, 1904, IV, p. 8.
43. W. G. Ross, The Journal of Captain George Comer, p. 76.
44. Ibid., p. 10.
45. Jenness, Eskimo Administration, p. 20.
46. Insp. Jennings' report, 8 October 1910, Compt. Corr., v. 383; also R.N.W.M.P., Report, 1910, O, p. 184.
47. Stefansson, My Life With the Eskimo, p. 430.
48. Ibid., p. 20.
49. Insp. Jennings' report, 16 February 1910, R.N.W.M.P., Report, 1910, K, p. 152.
50. Ibid.
51. Supt. Moodie's report, 30 December 1905, R.N.W.M.P., Report, 1905, IV, p. 14.
52. In The Desperate People, pp. 290–92, he quotes approvingly an article by R. A. J. Phillips of the Department of Northern Affairs to this effect.
53. Insp. Jennings' report, 1 August 1909, Compt. Corr., v. 383.
54. Cpl. W. V. Bruce's report, 23 June 1916, Comm. Files, v. 58.
55. S/Sgt. Fitzgerald's report, 19 May 1909, Compt. Corr., v. 372.
56. La Nauze to A. B. Perry, 18 August 1917, Compt. Corr., v. 580. A recent account of the case is R. G. Moyles, British

Law and Arctic Men (Saskatoon, 1979).
For a lawyer's comments on the case,
see Cornelia Schuh, "Justice on the
Northern Frontier: Early Murder
Trials of Native Accused," *Criminal Law
Quarterly,* vol. 22, no. 1 (December
1979).

57. Letter from Pere P. Fallaize to G.
Breynat, n.d., in Breynat, II, p. 327.
58. Comm. Files, v. 59.
59. R.C.M.P. *Report,* 1919, p. 15.
60. Insp. F. H. French to Perry, n.d. (probably 1919), Comm. Files, v. 60.
61. No fewer than five Inuit were tried at
Herschel Island in July 1923 for various
killings. See R.C.M.P., *Report,* 1923.
62. Solicitor for the Northwest Territories
office and son of the Deputy Minister of
the Department of the Interior.
63. T. L. Cory to O. S. Finnie, Director,
Northwest Territories Branch of the
Department of the Interior, 12 September 1922, Department of the Interior, Northern Administration
Branch Papers, Public Archives of
Canada, RG 85, v. 607, f. 2580.
64. Starnes to Finnie, 14 August 1922, ibid.
65. Guelph *Mercury,* 25 October 1923; London *Advertiser,* 26 October 1923.
66. Toronto *Globe,* 24 October 1923.
67. The trader shot by Alikomiak, one Otto
Binder of the Hudson's Bay Company,
had apparently appropriated the wife
of the man who killed him. It was also
reported, and denied by the government, that the other accused was only
sixteen years of age, and of subnormal
intelligence.
68. Hamilton *Herald,* 24 October 1923.
69. Ottawa *Citizen,* 22 October 1923.
70. 6 November 1923.
71. Toronto *Globe,* 1 March 1924.

NOTES TO CHAPTER TWELVE

1. 10 Geo. V, c. 28, s. 1.
2. This is true in the sense that the police
were becoming increasingly involved
with the regulation of narcotics, national security, and so forth. Actually,
the proportion of the force in the north
increased in the 1920s. In 1920 the
police numbered 1,532, of whom 27

were on service in the Northwest Territories and Hudson Bay; in 1926 the
figures were 69 out of 876. R.C.M.P.,
Report, 1926, p. 6.
3. *Statutes of Canada,* 1896, pp. xlvii–xlix.
4. J. E. Bernier, *Report on the Dominion of
Canada government expedition to the Arctic
islands and Hudson Strait on board the
D.G.S. "Arctic"* (Ottawa, 1910). The "sector theory" has never been formally
adopted by Canada; this would involve
passing a statute. See G. W. Smith,
"Sovereignty in the North: The Canadian Aspect of an International Problem," in R. St. J. MacDonald, ed., *The
Arctic Frontier* (Toronto, 1966), for a
good discussion of the question of Arctic sovereignty, and of the sector theory
in particular.
5. J. A. Bovey, "The Attitudes and Policies
of the Federal Government towards
Canada's Northern Territories, 1870–
1930" (M. A. thesis, University of
British Columbia, 1967), p. iv.
6. Ibid., p. 57.
7. V. Stefansson, *The Adventure of Wrangel
Island* (New York, 1925), p. 71.
8. 2 Ed. VII, c. 12, s. 2.
9. *Report of the Royal Commission to Investigate the Possibilities of the Reindeer and
Musk-ox Industries in the Arctic and sub-
Arctic Regions of Canada* (Ottawa, 1922).
10. P. D. Baird, *The Polar World* (London,
1964), p. 174.
11. Ibid.
12. The chronology of these events is given
in an undated memo of the Advisory
Technical Board in the J. B. Harkin
Papers, v. 1. Harkin was the Commissioner of Dominion Parks in the Department of the Interior, and was the
civil servant primarily concerned with
Arctic sovereignty in this period.
13. Cited in a copy of a letter from Rasmussen to Stefansson, 11 May 1920, Harkin
Papers, v. 1.
14. G. W. Smith, "Sovereignty in the North:
The Canadian Aspect of an International Problem." R. St. J. MacDonald,
ed., *The Arctic Frontier* (Toronto, 1966),
p. 208.
15. Governor-General to the Secretary of
State for the Colonies, 13 July 1920,
Harkin Papers, v. 1.

16. Memo, n.a., n.d., Harkin Papers, v. 1.
17. Minutes of a special meeting of the Advisory Technical Board, 1 October 1920, ibid.
18. Memo, n.a., n.d. (probably October 1920), "Title to Northern Islands," ibid. These memos were prepared for the Deputy Minister of the Interior.
19. Harkin to W. W. Cory, 14 June 1920, Harkin Papers, v. 1.
20. Ibid. Stefansson also wanted the R.C.M.P. to establish a post on the southeast corner of Wrangel Island, north of Siberia, another area of the Arctic he considered ripe for the assertion of Canadian sovereignty because of its occupation for a time by members of the Canadian Arctic Expedition. See R. J. Diubaldo, "Wrangling over Wrangel Island," *Canadian Historical Review* 48, no. 3 (September 1967).
21. He succeeded Frederick White as Commissioner of the Northwest Territories in 1919 and held that post until 1931.
22. "Title to Northern Islands." The first trading post on Ellesmere Island was not set up until 1953, when the government opened one at Craig Harbour. See P. J. Usher, *Fur Trade Posts of the Northwest Territories, 1870–1970* (Ottawa, 1971), p. 133.
23. R.C.M.P., *Report*, 1920, pp. 23–24.
24. Memo to Harkin from (illegible), 8 November 1920, Harkin Papers, v. 1.
25. Christie to Meighen, February 1921, ibid.
26. Memo, Advisory Technical Board, n.d., ibid.
27. Harkin to W. W. Cory, 6 December 1920, ibid.
28. 2 March 1921, Harkin Papers, v. 1.
29. Harkin to Cory, 15 March 1921, ibid.
30. Harkin to Cory 2 March 1921, ibid. This correspondence also appears in the Department of the Interior Papers, Northwest Territories and Yukon Branch, PAC, RG 15, A-2, v. 1.
31. R. J. Diubaldo, "Wrangling over Wrangel Island," p. 208.
32. Harkin Papers, v. 1.
33. Harkin to Cory, 26 May 1921, ibid.
34. His papers from this period are in PAC, MG 30, C-65.

35. Generally called "Pond's Inlet" in this period.
36. He wanted to put it at Fram Fiord (76 deg. 29' N., 81 deg. 15' W.), but found it unapproachable. He then chose a harbour nearby to which he gave his own name.
37. J. D. Craig to Wilcox, 27 August 1922; Wilcox to Craig, 28 August 1922, Department of the Interior, Northern Administration Branch Papers, Public Archives of Canada, RG 85, v. 582, f. 567.
38. Transcript in Department of the Interior, Northern Administration Branch Papers, v. 601, f. 2502 (1). The police did not always find it easy to take this advice, as the 1930 report from the Bache Peninsula detachment shows: "During the hunting last fall Cst. Fraser was forever grumbling about the way the natives were hunting, so knowing that this man had no idea of hunting in this country I told him to never mind the natives and pay attention to his own affairs, immediately he invited me to take off my hat and fight and he would show me whether he knew anything or not, but I refrained from this method as long as possible, but in December he carried it into personal affairs and it came to blows." Constable N. McLean's report, R.C.M.P. Papers, Division and Detchment Records, Bache Peninsula Detachment, 1926–32, Public Archives of Canada, RG 18, C-10, v. 1.
39. This involved a different area—the west coast of Ellesmere Island and the Sverdrup Islands.
40. P. J. Usher, *Fur Trade Posts*, p. 131.
41. Insp. C. E. Wilcox gave a full account of the Janes case in R.C.M.P. *Report*, 1923. Speaking of the sentences, he said they "will have a more beneficial effect than a sentence of death. Noo-kud-lah was led away immediately after sentence was passed, to the ship, through a gazing crowd of his own people ... hardly possible that a native with the prestige that Noo-kud-lah must have had with the other Eskimo at the times he killed Janes could have been subjected to greater humiliation." Ibid., pp 33–34. Peter Freuchen, on the other hand,

thought the sentence was "utterly fruit-less and meaningless." *Book of the Es-kimos,* (Fawcett Crest edition, 1961), p. 137.

42. Canada PC 2473, 15 January 1923.

43. At first it was called the "Inter-departmental Advisory Committee re. Canada's Arctic Islands." Copies of the minutes of its meetings are in the Har-kin Papers, v. 2.

44. They were not all present at each meet-ing. The board met intermittently for about two years.

45. See D. H. Dinwoodie, "Arctic Con-troversy," *Canadian Historical Review* 53, no. 1 (March 1972).

46. Canadian Hydrographic Service, *Pilot of Arctic Canada, I* (Ottawa, 1970), p. 76. Possibly it was an ice-island.

47. The most important documents are printed in Lovell C. Clark, ed., *Docu-ments on Canadian External Relations, 3.* 575–80.

48. Dinwoodie, "Arctic Controversy," p. 56. In subsequent expeditions, carried out in 1926, 1927, and 1928, MacMillan sought and obtained the requisite per-mission from the Canadian authorities. See G. W. Smith, "Sovereignty in the North," p. 210, also A. E. Millward, *Southern Baffin Island* (Ottawa, 1930), pp. 100–1.

49. Copy of a telegram from the Governor-General to the Canadian Charge d'Affaires in Washington, 26 May 1925, Harkin Papers, v. 2.

50. Meeting of the Northern Advisory Board, 11 June 1925, ibid.

51. G. P. Mackenzie's report to the North-ern Advisory Board, 19 October 1925, ibid.

52. The detachment, opened on August 6th 1926, was on the north side of Flagler Fiord. Wilcox called it "by far the most pleasant and attractive place in the eastern Arctic." R.C.M.P., *Report,* 1926, p. 43.

53. The modern detachment is at Alexan-dria Fiord, a bit to the south.

54. Dinwoodie, "Arctic Controversy," *pas-sim.*

55. The patrol is described in R.C.M.P., *Re-port,* 1927, pp. 55–60.

56. The patrol is described in R.C.M.P., *Re-port,* 1929, pp. 62–71.

57. The Bache Peninsula detachment was very hard to supply. In 1928, 1929, and 1930 the supply ship had to discharge cargo for the post some distance away on the ice. In 1932 the ship could not get near enough even for this expe-dient, and the cargo was put off at Craig Harbour. In 1933 Bache Peninsula was closed.

58. *Pilot of Arctic Canada, I,* p. 77.

59. R.C.M.P., *Report,* 1932 and 1934. Dr. Krueger and his party, including A. R. Bjare, a Dane, arrived at Bache Penin-sula in March 1930 with government permits to explore in the area of Axel Heiberg Island. Stallworthy found re-cords in 1932 indicating that the Krueger party had perished near Meighen Island in the winter of 1930–31.

60. V. K. Johnston, "Canada's Title to the Arctic Islands," *Canadian Historical Re-view,* 14, no. 1 (March 1933), p. 40.

61. Canada, *Statutes,* 14–15 Geo. V, c. 47. In 1928 responsibility for the Inuit was transferred to the Commissioner of the Northwest Territories. In 1936 it was transferred again, this time to the De-partment of Mines and Resources. See D. Jenness, *Eskimo Administration: II. Canada* (Montreal, 1964), p. 33.

62. *Report of the Superintendent General of In-dian Affairs for 1925,* pp. 10–12. Knud Rasmussen, a member of the Fifth Thule Expedition (which operated under government authorization), was profusely thanked for his "highly valu-able information" on the Inuit, which had given the government "a more complete and detailed census of the Es-kimos than has previously been availa-ble."

63. Ibid., p. 10.

64. R.C.M.P., *Report,* 1926, p. 46.

65. Ibid. The incident took place at Milne Inlet. The N.C.O. in charge of the Pangnirtung detachment in 1927 ob-served that "undoubtedly we often cure, or at least relieve, due ... more to 'faith' on the part of the patient, than to the very simple drugs to which the av-erage policeman confines himself." R.C.M.P., *Report,* 1928, p. 80.

66. R.C.M.P., *Report,* 1926, p. 46.

67. R.C.M.P., *Report,* 1928, p. 84. A consta-

ble was stationed at the Department of Marine and Fisheries base at Wakeham Bay and another at the base on Nottingham Island. Both were on loan from the Lake Harbour detachment.

68. Jenness, *Eskimo Administration*, p. 46, quotes cheerful reassurances from several years. The Inuit population at Coppermine was reported in 1931 to be free of contagious disease at a time when a doctor engaged by the government had discovered that one in five of the local Natives was tubercular. The government did open a medical post at Pangnirtung in 1924, and the resident doctor there accompanied the police on patrol. The Anglican hospital at Chesterfield (1929) received government support. Aklavik had two hospitals by 1927, one Anglican and one Roman Catholic. Ibid., pp. 44–45.

69. R.C.M.P., *Report*, 1928, p. 80.

70. R.C.M.P., *Report*, 1923, pp. 36–37.

71. R.C.M.P., *Report*, 1928, p. 77.

72. Ibid.

NOTES TO CHAPTER THIRTEEN

1. R.C.M.P., *Report*, 1921, p. 46. The plane was in the north in connection with the intense but short-lived boom which occurred when that company struck oil at Norman Wells in the summer of 1920.

2. R.C.M.P., *Report*, 1929, p. 39.

3. In 1928 there were transmitting stations at Port Burwell, Cape Hope's Advance, and Nottingham Island (Department of Marine and Fisheries); Fort Smith, Fort Simpson, Aklavik, Herschel Island, and Fort Resolution (Canadian Corps of Signals—the last two summer only); Hudson's Bay Company ships *Baymaud* and *Fort James* R.C.M.P. schooner *St. Roch* Port Nelson and Churchill (Department of Railways and Canals); Rankin Inlet (Dominion Explorers Ltd.); Baker Lake (Northern Aerial Mining Exploration Co.). R.C.M.P. *Report*, 1928, p. 61.

4. Ibid.

5. The affair received very wide publicity; it is summarized in Harwood Steele, *Policing the North*, chapter 38, and in R.C.M.P., *Report*, 1932, pp. 106–110. A good popular account is Dick North, *The Mad Trapper of Rat River* (Toronto, 1972).

6. The murder of Cpl. Doak (see chapter 11) is a partial exception.

7. Henry Larsen, *The Big Ship* (Toronto, 1967), is a good account of the work performed by the *St. Roch.*

8. By D. Jenness, *Eskimo Administration: II. Canada* (Montreal, 1964), p. 50. On the evolution of the economy in the region, see Peter J. Usher, "The Growth and Decay of the Trading and Trapping Frontiers in the Western Canadian Arctic," *Canadian Geographer* 19, no. 4 (1975).

9. R.C.M.P., *Report*, 1925, p. 47. The first patrol covered 1,000 miles, the second 1,500. Tree River is at 111 degrees 51' W.; Perry River is at 102 degrees 33' W.; and Adelaide Peninsula is at 97 degrees 30' W.

10. The Arctic Sub-district was a part of "G" Division, which then included detachments in northern Alberta and all those in the Northwest Territories west of the Barren Lands. Later it was enlarged to comprise all "northern" detachments, including those in Hudson Bay, and was directed from Ottawa.

11. R.C.M.P., *Report*, 1925, p. 27.

12. R.C.M.P., *Report*, 1947, p. 53. Some of this increase was due to the population increase attendant on defence projects. The number of civil cases increased also, but not to the same extent. In 1945, for instance, Criminal Code cases for the Yukon and Northwest Territories numbered 559, and cases concerning federal statutes, 530—an increase over 1925 of sixteen times in the first instance and eleven times in the second. R.C.M.P., *Report*, 1945, p. 27.

13. Son of the Z. T. Wood who had served in the Yukon.

14. R.C.M.P., *Report*, 1949, p. 65.

15. See chapter 5.

16. Then including all detachments in the Yukon and Northwest Territories, Hudson Bay, and northern Quebec. In 1949 it had forty-one detachments.

17. R.C.M.P., *Report*, 1950, p. 57. The distances are in miles. All but one of these patrols was listed as "routine." The total for the Yukon reflects the work done

patrolling the Alaska highway by automobile.

18. For the excesses and absurdities of this genre, see Pierre Berton, *Hollywood's Canada, The Americanization of our National Image* (Toronto, 1975).

19. L. and C. Brown discuss this period of police history in *An Unauthorized History of the R.C.M.P.* (Toronto, 1973), chapter 3. A more balanced account, which also deals with this transition period, is S. W. Horrall, "The Royal North-West Mounted Police and Labour Unrest in Western Canada, 1919," *Canadian Historical Review* 61, no. 2 (June 1980).

20. See chapter 12 for an account of these patrols.

21. On Canadians' choice of heroes, see Douglas Owram, "The Myth of Louis Riel," *Canadian Historical Review* 63, no. 3 (September 1982).

22. D. H. Breen, "The Turner Thesis and the Canadian West: A Closer Look at the Ranching Frontier," in L. H. Thomas, ed., *Essays on Western History* (Edmonton, 1976).

23. See above, chapter 7.

24. R. C. Macleod, *The NWMP and Law Enforcement, 1873–1905* (Toronto, 1976), chapter 2, "The Benevolent Despotism of the NWPM, 1874–85."

Bibliography

MANUSCRIPT COLLECTIONS IN THE PUBLIC ARCHIVES OF CANADA

Royal Canadian Mounted Police Papers
  Comptroller's Office, Official Correspondence Series, 1874–1919.
  Comptroller's Office, Letterbooks, 1883–1919.
  Comptroller's Office, Miscellaneous Subject Files, 1919–1921.
  Commissioner's Office, Official Correspondence Series, 1876–1920.
  Commissioner's Office, Subject Files, Correspondence, 1897–1919.
  Commissioner's Office, Letterbooks, 1873–1904.
  Commissioner's Office, Personal Records, 1873–1954.
  Commissioner's Office, Investigations re Members of the Force, 1892–1919.
  Commissioner's Office, Orders and Regulations, 1880–1954.
  Commissioner's Office, Crime Reports, 1880-1938.
  Division and Detachment Records, Chesterfield Inlet, Daily Diaries, 1925–1926.
  Division and Detachment Records, Bache Peninsula, Daily Diaries, 1926–1932.
  Division and Detachment Records, Lake Harbour, Daily Diaries, 1935–1960.
  Yukon Records, Dawson City Letterbooks, 1899–1905.
  Yukon Records, Yukon General Orders, 1898–1910.
  Yukon Records, Detachment Records, 1898–1920.
  Yukon Records, Miscellaneous, 1898–1951.
  Yukon Records, Police Gaol Records, Dawson, 1899–1903.
J. E Bernier Papers
Sir Robert L. Borden Papers
Charles Camsell Papers
Loring C. Christie Papers
Charles Constantine Papers
J. D. Craig Papers
J. B. Harkin Papers
A. H. Joy Papers
Henry Larsen Papers
Sir Wilfrid Laurier Papers
A. P. Low Papers
William Ogilvie Papers
Clifford Sifton Papers
Frank Oliver Papers
H. S. Stallworthy Papers
Otto Sverdrup Papers
Zachary Taylor Wood Papers

PUBLISHED GOVERNMENT DOCUMENTS

Canada, Parliament, House of Commons, *Debates,* 1895–1940.

Canada, Parliament, *Sessional Papers,* "Report of the Commissioner of the North-West Mounted Police," 1890–1903. Ottawa, 1891–1904.

Canada, Parliament, *Sessional Papers,* "Report of the Royal North-West Mounted Police," 1904–1919. Ottawa, 1905–1920.

Canada, Parliament, *Sessional Papers,* "Report of the Royal Canadian Mounted Police," 1920–1935. Ottawa, 1921–1936.

Canada, Parliament, *Sessional Papers,* "Report of the Auditor-General," 1896–1901. Ottawa, 1897–1902.

Canada, Parliament, *Sessional Papers,* "Report of the Department of Indian Affairs," 1894–1930. Ottawa, 1895–1931.

Canada, Parliament, *Sessional Papers,* "Report of the Department of the Interior," 1897–1901. Ottawa, 1898–1902.

Canada, *Statutes,* 1896.

Canada, *Revised Statutes,*1906.

Canadian Hydrographic Service, *Pilot of Arctic Canada, I.* Ottawa, 1970.

Department of Indian Affairs and Northern Development, *Indians of Yukon and Northwest Territories.* Ottawa, 1970.

Report of the Royal Commission to Investigate the Possibilities of the Reindeer and Musk-ox Industries in the Arctic and sub-Arctic Regions of Canada. Ottawa, 1922.

Royal Canadian Mounted Police, *Law and Order in Canadian Democracy.* Ottawa, 1952.

NEWSPAPERS AND PERIODICALS

The Beaver
Calgary *Herald*
Canadian Historical Review
Dawson *Daily News*
Edmonton *Bulletin*
Fort Macleod *Gazette*
Klondike *Nugget*
Ottawa *Citizen*
Ottawa *Evening Journal*
R.C.M.P. Quarterly
Scarlet and Gold
Toronto *Globe*
Yukon *Midnight Sun*

MONOGRAPHS

Adney, T. *The Klondike Stampede of 1897–98.* New York: Harper, 1900.

Amundsen, R. *The North West Passage.* 2 vols., London: Constable, 1908.

Baird, P. D. *The Polar World.* London: Longmans, 1964.

Bernier, J. E. *Report on the Dominion of Canada government expedition to the Arctic islands and Hudson strait on board the D.G.S. "Arctic".* Ottawa: Government Printing Office, 1910.

Berton, Pierre. *Klondike Fever.* New York: Knopf, 1958.

Black, Martha L. *My Ninety Years.* Anchorage, Alaska: Northwest Publishing, 1976.

Blanchet, G. H. *Keewatin and Northeastern Mackenzie.* Ottawa: Department of the Interior, 1930.

Bockstoce, John R. *Steam Whaling in the Western Arctic.* New Bedford: Old Dartmouth Historical Society, 1977.

Boon, T.C.B. *The Anglican Church from the Bay to the Rockies.* Toronto: Ryerson, 1962.

Breton, P. E. *Irish Hermit of the Arctic.* Edmonton: Editions de L'Ermitage, 1963.

Breynat, Msgr. G. *Cinquante Ans au Pays des Neiges.* 3 vols., Montreal: Fides, 1945–48.

Brown, Lorne and Brown, Caroline. *An Unauthorized History of the R.C.M.P.* Toronto: James Lorimer, 1973.

Campbell, William. *Arctic Patrols: Stories of the Royal Canadian Mounted Police.* Milwaukee: Bruce Publishing, 1936.

Camsell, C. *Son of the North.* Toronto: Ryerson, 1954.

Chambers, E. J. *The Unexploited West.* Ottawa: King's Printer, 1914.

Classen, H. G. *Thrust and Counterthrust.* Chicago: Rand McNally, 1965.

Clark, L. C., ed. *Documents on Canadian External Relations, III.* Ottawa: Department of External Affairs, 1970.

Clark, S. D. *The Developing Canadian Community.* Toronto: University of Toronto Press, 1962.

Cody, H. A. *An Apostle of the North: Memoirs of the Right Reverend William Carpenter Bompas, D.D.* Toronto: Musson, 1908.

Cramer, J. *The World's Police.* London: Cassell, 1964.

Dafoe, J. W. *Clifford Sifton in Relation to His Times.* Toronto: Macmillan, 1931.

Denny, C. E. *The Law Marches West.* Toronto: Dent, 1939.

De Windt, H. *Through the Gold Fields of Alaska to Bering Strait.* London, 1898.

Diubaldo, Richard. *Stefansson and the Canadian Arctic.* Montreal: McGill-Queen's University Press, 1978.

Fairley, T. C. *Sverdrup's Arctic Adventures.* London: Longmans, 1959.

Fetherstonhaugh, R. C. *The Royal Canadian Mounted Police.* New York: Carrick and Evans, 1938.

Finnie, O. S. *Canada Moves North.* Toronto: Macmillan, 1942.

Fisher, Robin. *Contact and Conflict: Indian-European Relations in British Columbia, 1774–1890.* Vancouver: University of British Columbia Press, 1977.

Friesen, G. *The Canadian Prairies: A History.* Toronto: University of Toronto Press, 1984.

Freuchen, P. *Book of the Eskimos.* Greenwich, Conn.: Fawcett Crest, 1961.

Green, L. *The Boundary Hunters*. Vancouver: University of British Columbia Press, 1982.

Godsell, P. H. *They Got Their Man: On Patrol with the North West Mounted*. Toronto: Ryerson, 1939.

Hall, D. . *Clifford Sifton, I: The Young Napoleon*. Vancouver: University of British Columbia Press, 1982.

Harrison, Dick. *Best Mounted Police Stories*. Edmonton: University of Alberta Press, 1978.

Hayne, M. H. E. and Taylor, H. W. *The Pioneers of the Klondyke*. London: Sampson Low, Marston, 1897.

Hoare, W. B. *Conserving Canada's Musk-Oxen: Being an Account of an Investigation of the Thelon Game Sanctuary, 1928–29*. Ottawa: King's Printer, 1930.

Horrall, S. W. *The Pictorial History of the Royal Canadian Mounted Police*. Toronto: McGraw-Hill Ryerson, 1973.

Howay, F. W., Sage, W. N. and Angus, H F. *British Columbia and the United States*. Toronto: Ryerson, 1942.

Innis, H. A. *Settlement and the Mining Frontier*. Toronto: Macmillan, 1936.

Jenness, D. *Eskimo Administration: II. Canada*. Montreal: Arctic Institute of North America, 1964.

Jefferies, Sir Charles. *The Colonial Police*. London: Max Parrish, 1952.

Kelly, Nora and Kelly, William. *The Royal Canadian Mounted Police: A Century of History*. Edmonton: Hurtig, 1973.

Kemp, V. A. M. *Without Fear, Favour or Affection*. Toronto: Longmans, 1958.

King. W. F. *Report upon the Title of Canada to the Islands North of the Mainland of Canada*. Ottawa: King's Printer, 1905.

Larsen, H. *The Big Ship*. Toronto: McClelland and Stewart, 1967.

Lee, H. P. *Policing the Top of the World*. London: John Lane, 1928.

Longstreth, T. M. *The Silent Force*. Toronto: Macmillan, 1954.

Macbeth, R. G. *Policing the Plains*. London: Hodder and Stoughton, 1922.

McCourt, E. *The Yukon and Northwest Territories*. Toronto: Macmillan, 1969.

MacGregor, J. G. *The Klondike Rush Through Edmonton 1897–1898*. Toronto: McClelland and Stewart, 1970.

————.*The Land of Twelve Foot Davis: A History of the Peace River Country*. Edmonton: Applied Arts Ltd., 1952.

Macleod, R. C. *The NWMP and Law Enforcement 1873–1905*. Toronto: University of Toronto Press, 1976.

Millward, A. E. *Southern Baffin Island*. Ottawa: Department of the Interior, 1930.

Morgan, M. *One Man's Gold Rush*. Seattle: University of Washington, 1967.

Morrell, W. P. *The Gold Rushes*. London: Macmillan, 1940.

Morrison, D. R. *The Politics of the Yukon Territory, 1898–1909*. Toronto: University of Toronto Press, 1968.

Morrison, William R. *A Survey of the History and Claims of the Native Peoples of Northern Canada*. Ottawa: Indian Affairs Canada, 1983.

————. *Under the Flag: Canadian Sovereignty and the Native People in Northern Canada*. Ottawa: Indian Affairs Canada, 1984.

Mowat, F. *Canada North.* Toronto: McClelland and Stewart, 1967.

———. *The Desperate People.* Boston and Toronto: Little, Brown, 1959.

Moyles, R. G. *British Law and Arctic Men.* Saskatoon: Western Producer Prairie Books, 1979.

Munday, L. *A Mounty's Wife.* Toronto: Macmillan, 1930.

Munn, H. T. *Prairie Trails and Arctic Byways.* London: Hurst, 1932.

North, D. *The Lost Patrol.* Anchorage, Alaska: Northwest Publishing, 1978.

———. *The Mad Trapper of Rat River.* Toronto: Macmillan, 1972.

Ogilvie, W. *Early Days on the Yukon.* London: John Lane, 1913.

Peake, F. A. *The Bishop Who Ate His Boots: A Biography of Isaac O. Stringer.* Don Mills: T. H. Best, 1966.

Phillips, R. A. J. *Canada's North.* Toronto: Macmillan, 1967.

Pratt, A. M. and Archer, J. H. *The Hudson's Bay Route.* Governments of Manitoba and Saskatchewan, 1953.

Rea, K. J. *The Political Economy of the Canadian North.* Toronto: Univeristy of Toronto Press, 1968.

Reith, C. *A New Study of Police History.* Edinburgh: Oliver and Boyd, 1956.

Rivett-Carnac, C. *Pursuit in the Wilderness.* London: Jarrolds, 1967.

Ross, W. G., ed. *An Arctic Whaling Diary: The Journal of Captain George Comer in Hudson Bay, 1903–1905.* Toronto: University of Toronto Press, 1984.

Schwatka, F. *A Summer in Alaska.* Philadelphia: J. Y. Huber, 1891.

Secretan, J. H. E. *To Klondyke and Back.* London: Hurst and Blackett, 1898.

Service, R. W. *Collected Verse of Robert Service.* Toronto: Ryerson Press, 1932.

Sissons, J. *Judge of the Far North.* Toronto: McClelland and Stewart, 1968.

Stackpole, R. A. *American Whaling in Hudson Bay 1861–1919.* Mystic, Conn.: The Marine Historical Association, 1969.

Steele, H. *Policing the Arctic.* London: Jarrolds, 1936.

Steele, Sir S. B. *Forty Years in Canada.* Toronto, 1918. (London: Jenkins, 1915).

Stefansson, V. *The Adventure of Wrangel Island.* New York: Macmillan, 1925.

———. *Discovery.* New York: McGraw-Hill, 1964.

———. *The Friendly Arctic.* New York: Macmillan, 1921.

———. *My Life with the Eskimo.* New York: Macmillan, 1913.

———. *The Northward Course of Empire.* London: Macmillan, 1922.

Stewart, R. *Sam Steele: Lion of the Frontier.* Toronto: Doubleday, 1979.

Sverdrup, O. *New Land: Four Years in the Arctic Regions.* 2 vols., London: Longmans Green, 1904.

Tansill, C. C. *Canadian-American Relations, 1875–1911.* Gloucester, Mass.: P. Smith, 1964.

Thomas, L. H., ed. *Essays on Western History.* Edmonton: University of Alberta Press, 1976.

Treadgold, A. N. C. *Report on the Gold Fields of the Klondike.* London, 1899.

Turner, J. P. *The Northwest Mounted Police, 1873–1893.* 2 vols., Ottawa: King's Printer, 1950.

Usher, P. J. *Fur Trade Posts of the Northwest Territories 1870–1910.* Ottawa: Department of Indian Affairs and Northern Development, 1971.

Walden, K. *Visions of Order: the Canadian Mounties in Symbol and Myth.* Toronto: Butterworths, 1892.

Waite, P. B. *Canada, 1874–1896: Arduous Destiny.* Toronto: McClelland and Stewart, 1971.

Wright, A. A. *Prelude to Bonanza.* Sidney, B.C.: Gray's Publishing, 1976.

Zaslow, M. ed. *A Century of Canada's Arctic Islands 1880–1980.* Ottawa: The Royal Society of Canada, 1981.

————. *The Opening of the Canadian North 1870–1914.* Toronto: McClelland and Stewart, 1971.

ARTICLES

Anderson, I. S. "Bathurst Inlet Patrol." *The Beaver,* Spring 1972.

Betke, C. "Pioneers and Police on the Canadian Prairies, 1885–1914." *Canadian Historical Association Historical Papers 1980.*

Brown, J. N. E. "The Evolution of Law and Government in the Yukon Territory." S. M. Wickett, ed., *Municipal Government in Canada,* (University of Toronto Studies, vol. II, no. 4), Toronto, 1907.

Coates, K. S. and W. R. Morrison. "Northern Visions: Recent Developments in the Writing of Northern Canadian History." *Manitoba History,* Fall 1985.

Dinwoodie, D. H. "Arctic Controversy." *Canadian Historical Review,* vol. LIII, no. 1, March 1972.

Disher, A. L. "The Long March of the Yukon Field Force." *The Beaver,* Autumn 1962.

Diubaldo, R. J. "Wrangling over Wrangel Island." *Canadian Historical Review,* vol. XLVIII, no. 3, September 1967.

Ellis, F. H. "Arctic Airfield Survey." *The Beaver,* September 1945.

————. "First Flight Over Hudson Strait." *The Beaver,* March 1944.

Head, I. L. "Canadian Claims to Territorial Sovereignty in the Arctic Regions." *McGill Law Journal,* IX, 1963.

Horrall, S. W. "Sir John A. Macdonald and the Mounted Police Force for the Northwest Territories." *Canadian Historical Review,* vol. LIII, no. 2, June 1972.

————. "The Royal North-West Mounted Police and Labour Unrest in Western Canada, 1919." *Canadian Historical Review,* vol. LXI, no. 2, June 1980.

Johnston, V. K. "Canada's Title to the Arctic islands." *Canadian Historical Review,* vol. XIV, no. 1, March, 1933.

Joss, W. F. "Eskimo Sleds." *The Beaver,* March 1951.

Macleod, R. C. "Canadianizing the West: the N.W.M.P. as Agents of the National Policy." L. H. Thomas, ed., *Essays on Western History,* Edmonton, 1976.

Morrow, W. G. "Arctic Circuit." *The Beaver,* Winter 1966.

Nicholson, L. H. "The Problem of the People." *The Beaver,* Spring 1959.

Robinson, J. "Among the Caribou-Eaters." *The Beaver,* December 1944.

Schuh, Cornelia. "Justice on the Northern Frontier: Early Murder Trials of Native Accused." *Criminal Law Quarterly,* vol. 22, no. 1, December 1979.

Scott, J. B. "Arctic Exploration and International Law." *American Journal of International Law,* vol. III, October 1909.

Stewart, G. T. "John A. Macdonald's Greatest Triumph." *Canadian Historical Review,* vol. LXIII, no. 1, March 1982.

———. "Political Patronage under Macdonald and Laurier, 1878-1911." *American Review of Canadian Studies,* vol. X, 1980.

Stone, T. "Atomistic Order and Frontier Violence: Miners and Whalemen in the Nineteenth Century Yukon." *Ethnology,* vol. 22, October 1983.

———. "The Mounties as Vigilantes: Perceptions of Community and the Transformation of Law in the Yukon, 1885–1897." *Law and Society Review,* vol. 14, no. 1, 1979.

———. "Whalers and Missionaries at Herschel island." *Ethnohistory,* vol. 28, no. 2, 1981.

Smith, G. W. "Sovereignty in the North: The Canadian Aspect of an International Problem." R. St. J. MacDonald, ed., *The Arctic Frontier,* Toronto, 1966.

Tobias, J. L. "Canada's Subjugation of the Plains Cree, 1879–1885." *Canadian Historical Review,* vol. LXIV, no 4, December 1983.

Usher, P. J. "The Canadian Western Arctic: A Century of Change." *Anthropologica,* vol. 13, 1971.

———. "The Growth and Decay of the Trading and Trapping Frontiers in the Western Canadian Arctic." *Canadian Geographer,* vol. 19, no. 34, 1975.

Wilkinson, D. "A Vanishing Canadian." *The Beaver,* Spring 1959.

Zaslow, M. "Administering the Arctic Islands 1880–1940: Policemen, Missionaries, Fur Traders." M. Zaslow, ed., *A Century of Canada's Arctic Islands 1880–1980,* Ottawa, 1981.

———. "The Yukon: Northern Development in a Canadian-American Context." Mason Wade, ed., *Regionalism in the Canadian Community, 1867–1967,* Toronto, 1969.

UNPUBLISHED WORKS

Bovey, J. A. "The Attitudes and Policies of the Federal Government Towards Canada's Northern Territories, 1870–1930." Unpublished M.A. dissertation, University of British Columbia, 1967.

Coates, K. S. "Best Left as Indians: Native-White Relations in the Yukon Territory, 1840–1950." Unpublished Ph.D. dissertation, University of British Columbia, 1984.

Diubaldo, R. J. "The Canadian Career of Vilhjalmur Stefansson." Unpublished Ph.D. dissertation, University of Western Ontario, 1972.

Guest, Hal J. "A History of the City of Dawson, Yukon Territory, 1896–1920." Parks Canada Microfiche Report Series #7.

Macleod, R. C. "The North-West Mounted Police 1873–1905: Law Enforcement and Social Order in the Canadian North-West." Unpublished Ph.D. dissertation, Duke University, 1971.

Maier, C. R. "Responsible Government and Federal Administration in Yukon, 1898– 1913." Paper presented to the Canadian Historical Association, Vancouver, June 1983.

Morrison, W. R. "The Mounted Police on Canada's Northern Frontier, 1895– 1940." Unpublished Ph.D. dissertation, University of Western Ontario, 1973.

Mulhall, D. "The Missionary Career of A.TG. Morice, O.M.I." Unpublished Ph.D dissertation, McGill University, 1979.

Murray, J. G. E. "Organization, Functions, and Jurisdiction of the Royal Canadian Mounted Police." Unpublished M.A. dissertation, Carleton University, 1970.

Stewart, E. G. "Fort McPherson and the Peel River Area." Unpublished M.A. dissertation, Queen's University, 1953.

Stuart, R. "Herschel Island, Resource Assessment." Unpublished agenda paper for the Historic Sites and Monuments Board of Canada, n.d.

Index